GUERRILLA ADVERTISING

Cost-Effective Techniques for Small-Business Success

Jay Conrad Levinson

Houghton Mifflin Company

Boston   New York   1994

Copyright © 1994 by Jay Conrad Levinson

Library of Congress Cataloguing-in-Publication Data
Levinson, Jay Conrad.
  Guerrilla advertising : cost-effective techniques for small-
business success / Jay Conrad Levinson.
     p.   cm.
  ISBN 0-395-68718-7
  1. Advertising — Cost effectiveness. 2. Small business —
Management. I. Title.
  HF5823.L52 1994
  659.1 — dc20   94-3957
                    CIP

Printed in the United States of America

MP 10 9 8 7 6 5 4 3 2 1

I dedicate this book to
the incredibly tiny number of
people who can create advertising
that generates profits — and to
the goal of you joining them.

Contents

I

Focusing on Your Goals

I DON'T KNOW WHY you bought this book. Maybe you invest your money in advertising. Perhaps you actually create advertising for yourself or for someone else. It could be that you're just plain fascinated with advertising.

You'll get the most out of this book if you're an investor or a creator. Advertising observers may learn many inside truths, but probably won't be able to convert their knowledge into the heady profits that result from the insights of the guerrilla advertising practitioner. Those insights enable guerrillas to obtain more profits with less advertising investment. The idea isn't to spend less, although you unquestionably do spend less, but to *get more*.

The guerrilla isn't funded for making mistakes with advertising, even though he or she knows that the media abound with advertising mistakes every day of the year. In business, mistakes are far more common than successes, especially in the haze and maze of the advertising world.

Guerrilla advertising avoids these mistakes, guiding the conscientious practitioner through the labyrinth all the way to a bright and shining bottom line. A characteristic of guerrilla advertising, differentiating it from standard advertising, is that it is based upon reality: your real audience, their real needs, the real competition, the real world at the time you are advertising, the real results you can expect from your leap of faith into the murky arena of ads, commercials, signs, brochures, and publicity.

Unlike the traditional advertising scene, guerrilla advertising is not very glamourous. The only stars are the products and services being advertised. When the spotlight moves from these stars, the process ceases to be guerrilla advertising. If the advertising investment isn't clearly cost-effective, the process probably never was guerrilla advertising. The insights and secrets revealed in these pages can help you faithfully follow the guerrilla's path.

The fact that you're reading this book is a good indication that you're aware of the importance of advertising. But at the outset, I want you to know of the *unimportance of advertising*. In 1983, 70 percent of retailer marketing budgets was invested in advertising. In 1993, 25 percent of the budget went into advertising. The rest? It went into promotions such as couponing and other weapons of guerrilla marketing.

This is a healthy trend, because advertising has tended to be overemphasized in the marketing spectrum. Advertising is something that most otherwise bright business owners do at the outset. But if their minds were honed to guerrilla awareness, they would know that *advertising is what you do last*. There are many other areas to put into order before any advertising should be done.

Advertising is a potent weapon, indeed. But it is not the only weapon. To a guerrilla, it is part of a marketing arsenal. *It makes almost all of the other weapons work more effectively.* Advertising fits most comfortably into a company's quest for profits when it is balanced with other marketing efforts.

The necessary balance for the future is advertising that builds a share of mind — blended with promotions that build a share of market. The necessity for this balance is the *economy*, as if you didn't know. Ralph Waldo Emerson once said, "Can anybody remember when the times were not hard and money not scarce?" That's guerrilla reality.

Guerrillas know that people are now more price-sensitive

than ever before in the modern age, according to the president of Quaker Oats and according to my local grocer.

This means that advertisers and ad makers themselves must know exactly what they want to gain from their advertising, how to get what they want, and where to direct their message. If you don't focus on clear targets, you can't score bull's-eyes.

1

The Guerrilla Advertising Strategy

Advertising strategy is a fancy term that means *what you want and how you'll get it*. If you don't have one, you have no business advertising.

A guerrilla advertising strategy forces you to focus upon the people to whom your advertising is targeted — *always start with the people, then work backward to the offering*. It zeros in on the results you want your advertising to achieve, the way you'll obtain those results, and the specific action you want your target audience to take. It also provides you with a guide for judging all advertising efforts for the next ten years, or one hundred years if you go about it right.

Expressed in a mere six sentences, the strategy guides you or the people who create your advertising — without hampering anyone's creativity. It must be expressed in writing, and it should not contain headlines, theme lines, or copy. The strategy is devoid of specific advertising because it must be solid, yet flexible. Specific words and phrases pin you down. A guerrilla advertising strategy should be developed to serve as a guide, not a master.

A mere six sentences

Your strategy should be deceptively simple when you first read it, but not when you write it. After reading it a couple of times, put it away for twenty-four hours. It's too important to be accepted — or rejected — with a snap decision. Look at it in a new frame of consciousness on a different day.

Don't forget, it's supposed to generate handsome returns on your advertising investment for the next century. All future ads, commercials, signs, brochures, and many business decisions will be measured against it.

When is the best time to change an advertising strategy? The week that you first see it, before any advertising has been created according to its dictates, before any money has been spent bringing it to life. After that, the strategy should be reviewed annually, keeping your fingers crossed that you don't have to change one word of it. Ideally, you got it right the first time.

That approved strategy should be pinned up on the bulletin boards and fixed in the brains of everyone who creates advertising for you: ad makers (that rare combination of writer and designer), writers, art directors, and producers. Keep it handy in a drawer or file so that you can reach for it the moment anyone presents even a tiny shred of advertising to you or when you come up with a killer idea yourself.

When to toss your advertising away

What if you love the advertising, but it does not fulfill the strategy? Toss it away this very moment.

Suppose you hate the advertising, but it does fulfill the strategy. Give it a second thought. At least it's 50 percent of the way home. Still, you have every right to love the advertising *and* for the advertising to fulfill the strategy. Truth is, you have a sacred obligation to settle for nothing less.

If you're enthusiastic about the advertising and it is created according to the guerrilla principles coming up in future chapters, that enthusiasm will be for your store, product, or service — rather than for the advertising itself. The enthusiasm will spread to your employees, then to your customers, and because you do the customer follow-up of a seasoned guerrilla, it will spread to your customers' friends and associates.

I've intentionally put off listing the six sentences of a guerrilla advertising strategy because I want you to be aware of the wide array of options available to you through advertising. Your strategy will clearly list what you want to accomplish with your advertising.

Fifty reasons to advertise

You can choose any or many of the following fifty things to accomplish, reasons that you ought to be advertising in the first place:

1. You want your advertising to *produce leads* for you, people who respond to your offer of more information. That's a clear goal and might be the heart of the first sentence of your advertising strategy. But maybe you should focus on one of the forty-nine other potential goals.
2. Your advertising is designed to *educate prospects about the benefits you offer*, perhaps even the special features that make those benefits possible.
3. You're advertising to *expand into new markets*, either demographically or geographically. A worthy goal.
4. You're out to *influence the people who influence others*, and that's why you're advertising — to reach the trend-setters — and start a trend toward buying what you sell. Sometimes that's the essence of a strategy.
5. You want to *make your name known to some people who have never heard of you*, even though other people know you well.
6. You advertise to set the stage for your other marketing, to *pre-sell your offering* before your salespeople do the actual selling. Your pre-selling makes their selling job a whole lot easier. Many firms advertise for this reason. They've learned that pre-selling is a survival technique in today's economy.
7. Your goal in advertising is to *expand upon a public relations story* that appeared about you, to let the whole world — or at least your audience in the world — know of the positive things said about you by the media or by an expert.
8. You want to *tell the story of your company*, your product or service, and the reasons folks should buy from you. Although a free publicity story can be very helpful, only with advertising do you have total control over the content.
9. Your message is being told by salespeople and you want to *add authority* to it by putting it in print or on TV. People equate advertising with success; they figure that unsuccessful companies don't advertise.
10. You advertise to establish and *build your corporate*

identity, to let your company personality come shining through. Big companies do this more than little ones.

11. You need to *build confidence in your product or services.* Maybe a negative publicity story undermined this confidence and it needs shoring up — for your customers, your prospects, your employees, and your suppliers. Advertising can help.

12. You are advertising to *dispel an ugly rumor,* to explain or even apologize for an unfavorable incident. The sabotaged Tylenol, tainted Perrier, and impure Jack in the Box incidents come to mind.

13. You advertise to *keep your name in the forefront of your customers' minds.* "Out of mind, out of money" sounds like a guerrilla adage, even if it's a newly minted one.

14. *Competitors are coming in from all sides and you want to head them off at the pass* and anywhere else you can thwart them, so you advertise to accomplish this goal.

15. The tables are turned and *you're going after the business that your competitors now have,* so you mount a guerrilla advertising attack aimed at their customers.

16. You advertise to *prove your quality with success stories,* case histories of delighted customers who have patronized your business, and other specific data that will win profits and influence prospects.

17. You want to *make your stockholders happy,* so you advertise to reassure them that you're still a player and that they can count on you. Your ads don't actually say this, but they do the job in other ways.

18. You may be about to talk to venture capitalists, bankers, or other holders of important purse strings, so you advertise to *impress the financial community.*

19. You know that life is easier for everyone if you are perceived as the leader, so you advertise to *assert your leadership* and prestige. Your ad even has the look of a leader.

20. You advertise with an institutional message to *maintain a constant public presence* and build confidence in your company. This is advertising in slow motion, but tortoises are known to win races. It helps if they're rich tor-

toises because institutional ads do not produce instant results.

21. The reason you are advertising is to *help your direct mail pay off,* because you know that if people haven't heard of you, they may not buy from your mailing, but if they've seen your advertisements, they have a more positive feeling about you and will respond more favorably to your direct mail offer. To the world, it appears as if you expect to profit from your ads, but *you* know you'll reap the profits from the direct mail and that the ads merely opened the door to the sale.

22. If it works in the mail, it may work on the phone. You're advertising *so that your telemarketing campaign will be successful* and your telemarketers will be representing a known company, not a stranger. You can be sure they'll appreciate you for having greased the skids for them. They can even open the conversation by saying, "Maybe you've seen our commercials on prime-time television." (The cost for prime-time TV, in case you're new to the guerrilla game, is about twenty bucks in most major markets; read all about it in *Guerrilla Marketing.*)

23. Go into a store and see how shoppers gravitate toward your product because *they see a point-of-purchase sign and remember your recent advertisement,* recalling the reasons to buy it. This is "push-pull" advertising: The ad does the pushing toward the sale; the sign does the pulling into the sale. Pushing always helps pulling.

24. You're advertising because you want to *gain distribution,* and you know that retailers are more likely to stock advertised than unadvertised brands. Because you're a guerrilla, you may have even mentioned the name of the store in your ad or commercial, nailing down an even larger order from the retailer.

25. You're advertising simply to *announce the existence of your product.* Today I asked a friend where he learned of a marvelous new book he had recommended to me. "I saw an ad for it yesterday," he said. Frankly, I was floored. Most advertising doesn't work instantly.

26. Your product or service is new, and you advertise to *gain the credibility* you so urgently need at this point — at every point, as you'll learn.

27. You know how people trust brand names, so you are advertising in the noble quest to *become a brand name*. Don't think that you've got to be a national brand name. Having a local brand name will do very nicely. In my part of the world, Yet Wah is a Chinese restaurant with a very well-known brand name — locally. If you live in Florida, you've probably never heard of Yet Wah. But the Yet Wah folks don't care. The local populace all know of Yet Wah, and that's all that really matters. After all, Yet Wah is more interested in fortune than in fame. I hope the same is true of you.

28. You're *advertising a major promotion* that your company is engaged in at the moment. The promotion is a knockout, but unless you advertise, many people won't know about it.

29. You want your target audience to know exactly what you stand for. That's why advertising makes sense to *establish your niche*, your position in the marketplace, especially with regard to your competition.

30. Knowing that the American public accepts much advertising with that proverbial grain of salt, you advertise to *highlight testimonials from satisfied customers* or even from the media. Perhaps your ads will center on a single testimonial or on a series of quotes from several testimonials. As a guerrilla, you're aware of the power, believability, and economy of testimonials.

31. You're advertising to *test something*: a headline, an offer, a price, a graphic device, almost anything, including the pulling power of the medium in which you are advertising. Just be sure you're not testing more than one thing at a time or you'll end up confused, maybe even broke.

32. You advertise with the sole purpose of *creating a desire to buy* in the minds of your prospects and customers. This is one of the most common reasons that companies ad-

vertise at all. This is also quite different from selling; creating a desire requires a different artfulness.

33. You know you must *establish a presence in your community*, in your industry, on your planet for that matter; advertising does a dandy job of achieving that goal.

34. You are advertising to *attract foot traffic into your store*, knowing that your salespeople can convert that traffic into completed sales.

35. You advertise to *make sales*, whether those sales arise from foot traffic, phone calls, or completed coupons.

36. As a practicing guerrilla, you advertise to *obtain names for your prospect or customer mailing list*, confident that your intense follow-up will transform prospects into customers and customers into repeat customers.

37. You are advertising to *inform many people at the same time* about the glories of your offering. It's not as warm a contact as a one-on-one meeting, but it's the way many smart companies play the numbers game.

38. You advertise to *motivate people to call your toll-free number* (or even non-toll-free number) and either order or request more information.

39. You use advertising to persuade as many prospects as possible to *complete and mail your coupon*, which will result in an order or a request for further details.

40. You are advertising to *engage in research* by studying the consumer profiles of respondents to your offer. Older males might have been your prime customers, but more young females are actually taking you up on your offer. Advertising can accomplish a dual purpose if you combine it with research. The research can tell you who is buying, where they live, where they heard of you, and what they like most from your selection. When Oysterbed Home Environments, a San Francisco furniture retailer, ran a newspaper campaign on Sundays and Wednesdays throughout the San Francisco Bay Area, it learned these four important things by merely writing up the sales invoices: Most of the buyers were females (a fact

Things you can learn when advertising

that is reflected in current Oysterbed offerings); a dispro-
portionate number of them came from Marin County,
north of San Francisco (which is why Oysterbed now
runs a very successful campaign in the Marin County
newspapers); buyers heard of Oysterbed by seeing its ads
in the Sunday paper (explaining why 75 percent of the
newspaper budget is now spent on Sundays, rather than
the 50 percent on Sundays and 50 percent on Wednesdays as originally planned); and many people purchased
large entertainment units (which weren't even in the advertisements but certainly appear there these days), leading Oysterbed to expand its selection of them. Oysterbed
also learned that nearly 33 percent of buyers purchase
the most expensive model, in oak, while only 10 percent
want the least expensive pine unit. As with many advertisers, Oysterbed profited from the newspaper ads, but
learned even more profitable information by analyzing
the customers who responded to the ads.

41. You advertise to *emphasize exactly how the competition
measures up to you,* possibly even a single competitor.
The purpose of the measurement is to annihilate the
beast.

42. Because you have before-and-after photos, diagrams, or
research findings to communicate, you advertise to *prove
your superiority,* using hard data rather than mere copy.

43. You are advertising simply to *buy new customers* by attracting them with an exceptional offer at a very small, if
any, profit to your business, but knowing exactly how to
follow up to assure that your investment will be rewarded
with their repeat and referral business. The name of the
game to guerrillas is to do almost anything to get a customer to buy from you that first time, then cashing in big
with conscientious and caring follow-up.

44. You advertise to *demonstrate publicly your own confidence* in your product or service. If you're confident in
it, perhaps others will be, too. But if you display no confidence, it will be tough for others to gain any.

45. You wish to welcome yourself to the universe and advertise to *become part of the community,* part of your industry, part of the consciousness of your prospects. If you're trying to save money by not buying advertising, recognize that such an attitude is akin to trying to save time by not buying a wristwatch.

46. You are advertising because *it's the politically savvy thing to do,* putting you on the same level as other respected advertisers, making friends with the media, and showing that you are responsible and here to stay.

47. You advertise because *you are planning to use reprints of your ad* in other marketing: direct mailings, brochures, window signs; flip charts, posters, and a burgeoning arsenal of other weaponry.

48. You know that *firms are known by the company they keep,* and so you advertise because other firms, companies with which you wish to be associated, are also advertising in the same media. You figure, and rightly so, that you will gain from the respectability they have built up during the years. I mean there you are, right between Rolls-Royce and American Express. How bad can you be?

49. You invest in advertising because *you want to show your sales reps, distributors, and employees that you are squarely behind them.* You use your radio and TV commercials plus blowups of your print ads to enthuse your employees at company meetings.

50. *You advertise to earn a profit* — the underlying motivation for the other forty-nine reasons to advertise. Although this straightforward, beautifully capitalistic idea is your reason for existing — unless you are a nonprofit group — it need not be stated in your advertising strategy because it is already part of your DNA.

※　※　※

I've merely scratched the surface with this list of fifty reasons to advertise. There are more than fifty, you know. You may also advertise to announce your grand opening, your going-out-of-business sale, your new location, your expanded service, your new lines, or possibly even a community event to prove to your prospects how civic-minded you are.

Now that you are aware of the many goals you can attain through advertising, select those that are appropriate for your company. Perhaps you have only one goal: to obtain phone calls requesting further information. Even so, you'll be accomplishing many other goals at the same time. The important thing for a guerrilla is to single out the main goal and make that part of the six-sentence advertising strategy.

Now that we've scoured the potentials of advertising, let's look into the six statements that will make up your strategy. Let's say you run a tour company. It's two years old, has three other employees, and grossed $750,000 last year. You've used direct mailings to travel agents in the past, but you feel that now is the time to advertise and tell the public about your touring services. Because the destinations you visit on your tours are so visually exciting, you know that only a video brochure can really do them justice, that the places you tour transcend any mere print advertising, and that they are too drop-dead gorgeous to cram into a thirty-second TV spot. So your advertising has a clear purpose, and your strategy can be clearly stated.

A guerrilla advertising strategy

1. *The first sentence tells the prime purpose of your advertising.* "The purpose of Galactic Tours advertising is to motivate people to call or write requesting a free video brochure."
2. *The second sentence spells out the prime benefit you will offer in order to accomplish your purpose.* "The main benefit stressed will be the unique and exciting destinations that Galactic Tours' customers can visit."
3. *The third sentence lays out the secondary benefits that will entice your prospects.* "Emphasis will also be placed upon the convenience and economy of any Galactic Tours holiday, along with the highly trained tour guides."
4. *The fourth sentence states the target audience at which your advertising is directed.* "Our target audience is ad-

venturous males and females, both singles and couples, aged twenty-one to thirty-four, who have the financial resources to afford a Galactic Tours trip."

5. *The fifth sentence says exactly what you want your target audience to do.* "The action to be taken by our audience is to make a phone call or send a card or note requesting our video brochure."

6. *The sixth sentence describes the personality of your company, as it will be expressed in your advertising.* "The personality of Galactic Tours advertising will reflect innovation, excitement, conscientiousness, and a warm, caring attitude toward all customers."

Galactic Tours did a good job of focusing. But now it's *your* turn. Focus upon what you want advertising to do for your company. Focus upon the main reason prospects will want to become customers. Focus upon the secondary benefits that will attract a high response rate to your offer. Focus upon the people who are most likely to enjoy, afford, and take you up on your offer. Focus upon the specific action you want those people to take. Focus upon the true identity of your company as it will be reflected in your advertising.

There. You have focused on your goals, then translated your clear focus into a clear advertising strategy that can guide you to success for many years to come. It will do this by providing a road map that will be followed by all your future advertising.

You didn't have to spend an inordinate amount of time creating the strategy, but without it, your advertising has no landmarks to follow, no ways of measuring its success or failure, no guidelines for those who will create brilliant advertising for you in the coming years. Guerrillas know that the path to advertising success is seen only when they focus on their goals.

2

Targeting Your Audience

Every advertiser, except for pioneers in new industries, begins with three target audiences: people who *already buy* the kind of things they sell, people who *ought to buy* those things, and people who *are about to buy* what they sell.

Guerrilla advertising hits all three targets by giving those about to buy a reason to buy *right now*, by giving those who already buy such offerings a reason to buy *soon*, and by educating those who ought to buy why they ought to buy *eventually*. The advertising thrust may be to only one of these targets, but *never* to the exclusion of the other two. When one dollar can do the work of three, let it.

Crucial to your accomplishments with advertising will be your ability to aim your advertising at the hottest of your hot prospects and get through to them with every attempt. That means *learning about them*. The key to hitting where you aim comes from information about your hot prospects.

The key to hitting where you aim

Hot prospects are those who have an inclination to buy right now or who offer a glowing future potential. How do you reach them? What do they read? Watch? Listen to? Do? Picasso said that the only trouble with computers is that all they can do is come up with the right answers.

You've got to come up with the questions that can lead right to your prospects' pocketbooks or purchase orders. You've got to find out how to get to where your prospects are influenced. There are places to look.

The first place to look is within your own industry. Learn

where your competitors aim their advertising and marketing. Get a fix on how much they spend and where they spend it. This information is easily obtainable through trade publications, at trade shows, through computer databases, and by talking to others in your industry, especially competitors who do not compete directly with you.

Because guerrillas rarely do what they can delegate, they tap the resources of a large state-of-the-moment media management firm to help them aim at the right targets and select the truest arrows. Living up to my original recommendation of them in *Guerrilla Marketing* back in 1984 is CPM Media Management at 312-527-2100. Ask for their free brochure to get a solid footing for selecting your best target audience or audiences.

Resources to tap

Fortunately for guerrillas who need not capture gigantic shares of gigantic markets, it is possible to home in on a small segment of a small market and still make a fortune — if you're a guerrilla company and not a behemoth.

The global marketplace is the most complex and inviting it has ever been. Guerrillas feast on fragments of markets that they can target geographically, demographically, by economics, by lifestyle, even by sexual preference. By assiduously studying their own customers, their competitors' customers, and customers of their entire industry, guerrillas are able to identify specific groups, then match them with specific media and hit their targets with uncanny accuracy.

When targeting your audience, open your mind to addressing audiences you may have been neglecting. For instance, the size and purchasing power of ethnic groups, especially Asians and Hispanics, is growing rapidly in America. It's happening on both coasts, in cities and in suburbs, and is one reason, along with our climbing fertility rate, for the projection of our population from 260 million today to 383 million in 2050.

Neglect me not

The increasing number of older people is illustrated by the fact that *Modern Maturity* is now America's number-one magazine in circulation. New subgroups are springing up, groups that could be lucrative markets for you. New markets have sprung up around areas such as fitness, nutrition, the environment, religion, rehab, parenting, child care, the list goes on. Often these markets will have their own publications just ripe for advertising, with readers who are surprisingly quick to respond to advertisers that patronize their very own publication.

Engaging in micro-marketing

The idea for you is to engage in as much *micro-marketing* as possible — to convey your message to selected small groups and eliminate the mass-market consciousness. This is a financially sound tactic because it eliminates *waste circulation*, people who are exposed to your advertising but haven't the slightest chance of ever being your customer, even though you paid through the nose for their readership. It enables your creative team to tailor its message to readers of the publication in which you are advertising.

For instance, if you happen to run an ad in a baseball publication — in the world of micro-marketing there are such publications — your headline can say, IF YOU'RE A BASEBALL FAN, YOU WON'T WANT TO MISS GETTING THIS FREE GIFT! Such a specific headline would hit a home run with readers of that publication, while it would probably strike out in *Time* magazine.

The case for narrowcasting

This guerrilla segmentation is also known as *narrowcasting* — saying something to somebody instead of saying nothing to everybody. The narrower your target audience, the better attuned you can become to them as individuals, not only improving your media selection capabilities but also your customer rapport and service. And let's not forget the economy of small numbers.

This is not to say that you must select your target audience with a teaspoon, but to remind you that you don't need a steam shovel. To target the right people, you must:

- *Investigate the potential of your product.* It may be of value to more audiences than you are aiming at. A large copying company realized several years after it had been in business that the legal market churned out the most copies. When it targeted that audience in legal media, profits shot up 30 percent.

- *Know the problems of your prospects.* It is far easier to sell the solution to a problem than to sell a positive benefit. Target the people who have the kinds of problems you can solve. Because law firms often need copies by yesterday, the copy firm I just mentioned offered to set up on-site copying services for law firms, and later, because emergencies are not limited to law firms, to other large companies as well. This service solved a major problem for law firms and many other big companies and made a mighty contribution to the profits of the copying firm.
- *Know who makes the purchase decision you want.* Women select most of the beds in America, but men write most of the checks for beds. In many firms the company president makes all purchase decisions, but in some the department heads sign the purchase orders. Who wields the influence in your target market? It's the guerrilla's job to find out, then hit them where they read and watch and listen.
- *Know your competition.* If you run the copying firm we've been discussing, determine who the most successful copying firms have targeted. Then either join in the fray or bypass that market, going after groups your competitors ignore. Although the big money comes from big companies, your copying firm could target small businesses. Most of your competitors pay little attention to them because they represent little money. But you know that loads of new small businesses are being founded in America — 1.5 million in 1993 — and that by targeting them you can get a little money from a lot of businesses. Here we've got a guerrilla's dream: a fast-growing market that is being overlooked by your competitors. Shhhh! Don't say a word. Just advertise to a virgin market.
- *Know the current business climate.* When the going gets tough, there's a lot less delegating going on, and decisions are made at the top.
- *Know your own limitations.* Don't overpromise, over-

advertise, or target an audience too large for you to service in a first-rate manner. The goal is profitability, not volume.

- *Know your customers' hot buttons.* Targeting is a whole lot easier if you know what's on the mind of your prospect. Your information-seeking efforts will reveal this.

Prospects are human beings first

When targeting your audience, it is paramount to remember that a prospect is a human being first and a consumer next. Perhaps you can reach that purchasing agent while she reads her travel magazine instead of her business magazine. Possibly you should target Denver business owners as Denverites instead of business owners.

The size of errors in targeting markets is enormous. So take nothing for granted. Learn from the past, but recognize that it is no longer the key to the future.

Information that you can hang your hat on is out there. Your job is to look, find, use what you find to define your ideal consumer, then act on that knowledge with your media selection, creative message, and advertising mission.

3

Selecting Your Advertising Media

Now that you've got a fix on your target audience, you're able to take the next big step and reach them. Naturally, that means knowing the most effective ways of finding them. Sometimes it's newspapers. It could be magazines, either consumer or trade publications. Maybe it's the radio. Perhaps it's television. Might it be brochures? The yellow pages? Possibly it's signs. *Guerrillas know that, most likely, it's a combination of these.*

The power of combinations

The direct marketing media such as direct mail, postcard decks, telemarketing, newsletters, catalogues, infomercials, home shopping shows, interactive commerce, canvassing, trade shows, and networking functions *all work better when combined with advertising, and advertising works better when combined with direct marketing.*

So don't go off and advertise as soon as you've completed this book. First, decide which of the direct marketing weapons you will employ to load your advertising guns with live ammo instead of blanks. Advertising without direct marketing makes a lot of noise, but noise doesn't generate profits — or hurt enemies.

In the early days of advertising, media selection was pretty much confined to newspapers. Magazines came next, offering exposure at first on a national scale only. Newspaper supplements followed, offering depth of local circulation along with the content and leisurely reading pace of magazines. The automobile turned out to be not only ideal transportation but also an ideal environment for listening to the radio. Already, radio had earned a large following in the nation's living rooms. Network television came onto the scene, changing everything and improving the effectiveness of advertising — at least for advertisers who could afford it. Cable TV is turning the world of network TV topsy-turvy because so many small advertisers who could not afford TV advertising can now get on the tube and advertise like crazy.

Turning the world topsy-turvy

Although network TV will have diminished significance on the media scene, it will remain the unquestioned leading provider of mass-audience broadcasting in an ocean of narrowcasting. With "video-on-demand" — phoning in for any movie or TV show you want — coming up like a freight train, the network prime-time schedule will probably fade into oblivion. Video stores have had their prospects dimmed by this up-and-coming technology. Video cassette recorders have already created the consumer momentum to change programming around to suit the tastes and time availability of viewers, not programmers.

In not too long a time, advertisers will be able to target commercials to individual homes. Some will receive a commercial for an expensive convertible while others will see a spot for an economy sedan. The precision of cable television and the cable company subscriber lists makes this possible.

While you're sitting there reading, other people are watching the Interactive Network, a guerrilla type of television because it functions unlike traditional television. Subscribers intentionally tune in to offers of brochures, participation in a survey, or, in the case of Chrysler Corporation, special incentives on cars and trucks. Arnold Liebler, Chrysler's vice president of marketing and communications, said, "We are always looking for ways to break through the clutter to get our message heard, and interactive programming appears to be an exciting, promising medium to hold viewers' attention." Spoken like a true guerrilla, Arnold.

Anyone for interactivity?

What do you suppose Interactive Network does that's so different? It broadcasts entertainment programs that allow viewers to play along with televised sporting events and game shows, making decisions that can earn prizes. Got that? Okay, now get this: *Chrysler's offers are inserted into the programs.* Everyone's feeling highly interactive and here comes Chrysler inviting more interactivity.

Change in advertising has been going on as long as advertising's been going on, and advertising media will continue to change with developments such as interactive TV, home shopping shows, and electronic catalogues. The moral is to keep your eye on the media so that you are keeping up. I do not advise you to run to the head of the media pack and commit your budget to the new media, but I heartily encourage experimentation. Media testing is a guerrilla must.

When selecting the media that will hit your target audience right where they live — or work — consider the *environment* in which your advertising will appear. Pick media that reaches your target audience and will provide the proper environment for the advertising you will create, advertising that fits the mood of the readers, listeners, or viewers. It's easier than ever to do this with the highly specialized media now available.

Consider the environment

Those same specialized media, both print and electronic, now make it mandatory for a right-thinking guerrilla to realize that media selection is not a do-it-yourself process. Instead, it's a do-yourself-in process if you attempt to make such important investments without the guidance of experts. You can call a media-buying service such as the one I suggested in chapter 2, or you can look under "media-buying services" in your own yellow pages and select one for yourself. Whichever you choose must be adept at buying media locally or nationally *for your specific target audience.*

A long, long time ago, media-buying services were for the big spenders only. Good news, guerrilla. They are now for any business owner with any common sense. Small business owners avoid expensive mistakes by tapping into this talent. The days of risking your marketing investment without investing a tiny portion of it with a media-buying service are gone — for the sane small business in our society.

With their expertise, media-buying services also offer economy, being able to negotiate lower prices for radio and

TV than you or I can. The better services also can assist you in launching weapons of marketing that serve as invaluable teammates to the advertising itself. Do they help you put place mats in local diners, circulars on community bulletin boards, brochures in strategic locations, signs at the point of purchase? Not yet they don't. But they should and they will and guerrillas ask them to. I hope you will.

True guerrilla media

True guerrilla media services, not usually handled by media-buying services but which you should search for — even demand — include:

- Circulars and circular distribution
- Signs on community bulletin boards
- Brochures where target audiences may be found
- Informational business cards and their distribution (A savvy media-buying service might place them in barbershops, auto service waiting rooms, medical waiting rooms, the imagination is the only limitation.)
- Tie-in opportunities with other businesses and groups
- Toll-free telephone consultation, maybe even services
- Catalogue consultation and services
- Yellow pages services (Never let the yellow pages people design your ad; turn that over to a design pro or your ad will look like most of the other ads in the yellow pages.)
- Newsletter preparation and distribution
- Classified ad services locally and internationally (These are the people who can help you go global.)
- On-line marketing to computer special-interest groups
- Direct mail letters and postcards along with postcard deck participation (These decks are also called marriage mail and let you share marketing and mailing costs with a bunch of noncompetitors. Call 1-800-323-2751 to learn more, or better still, ask the media-buying service you select.)
- Promotion coordination and development with the media, requesting the media to generate promotion ideas
- Public relations (*Public relations?* Yes, anything it takes to help guerrillas achieve their goals.)

Alas, no such services exist at this moment, but it's up to you to help *create* one from an existing service by telling them exactly what you expect from a state-of-the-moment media-buying service.

Help create the service you need

For now, the important contribution a pro buying service can make to your success and well-being is its *consulting* ability. And that's why you should meet with such a service before you invest one penny in any kind of advertising. A media-buying service makes its money by both consulting and *buying media at a discount*. What you want and need, at first, is their *consulting service only*. Perhaps you'll also want them to purchase the media for you. That's usually a good idea because of the mountains of paperwork you'll avoid. But for now, forget the buying of media and concentrate on the media that will be bought. Here are the kinds of questions you should be prepared to ask:

- If it's to be trade publications, which ones?
- What does a full page cost? A half page? Color? Black and white?
- If it's going to be consumer magazines, which regional editions?
- If it's newspapers, which ones and in which sections? What days are best for my business? Even media-buying services cannot control the placement of the ad unless you sign a long-term contract. Think about it. If you're going to select a flagship newspaper, you may as well travel in the first-class section.
- If it's to be TV, on which channels? Soon there will be over a thousand to choose from.
- If radio, which stations? How often? When?

The decisions have never been more complicated, the options more plentiful, or the mistakes more expensive. Fortunately, media-buying services have more information than ever before, thanks to computerization, so they can help you make the right decisions and avoid the wrong ones. Then, if you prefer, you can do the buying yourself. But whatever you do,

Complicated decisions, expensive mistakes

if you're going to use the media, regardless of your size or budget, talk to a media-buying pro first, okay?

You can use a local service or a national service. You can even use a network of regional media-buying services to help you with media planning and buying, along with local promotions.

It has always been known that you can learn a lot about media from newspaper, magazine, radio, and TV media representatives. They can tell you about the competition, the industry climate, the trends, and the distributor attitudes, along with a raft of information about their own medium. An uninitiated advertiser, exposed to a bright newspaper rep, will probably buy that medium for his or her company because the advertiser is dazzled by the facts relayed by the rep. Big mistake. It's not a mistake if you currently buy the media for Coca-Cola, Gallo wine, and IBM. But if you're an entrepreneur, however brave, you are putty in the hands of a bright magazine rep.

Cost per prospect
Be sure that you do not fall into the trap of selecting a medium based upon the old measurement of "cost per thousand," but instead base your selection on the criterion of "cost per prospect." Do not fall prey to the statistics quoted by reps of a specific advertising medium. While the statistics are usually true, they are often misleading. To see how misleading, talk to a rep from a competing medium. And remember that there are three types of lies: dirty, white, and statistics.

Working with a media-buying service is like working with an all-star lineup of the best media reps, with none of them championing for their own media and all of them on your side, thinking only of your profits. This is not true of even the best reps of an individual medium. I say this even though some of my best friends are media reps.

These days, even many gigantic advertising agencies, not to mention *Fortune* 500 firms, obtain their media information from media-buying services, who also do the buying. Because they buy so much media, they have enormous clout, which they can pass on to you.

Tiny firms, hoping to make the *Fortune* 500, also use media-buying services. The investment of a few hours of their time can prevent several years of media investing from going down the wrong track.

Once you've consulted for a couple of hours with a media-buying service and they make their recommendations, you might ask them to prepare a media plan based upon their recommendations. What might it look like?

If you ran a firm called Spa City and you had an annual revenue of $600,000, an annual marketing budget of $60,000, which is an aggressive 10 percent investment (good going!), and an annual advertising budget of $30,000, half your marketing budget, the media plan your service might submit could look like this:

Spa City's annual ad budget

Medium	Length/ Size	Reach	Frequency	Monthly Cost
WXCR-TV	30-second	10,000	20 per week	$ 800
WTVV-TV	30-second	6,000	20 per week	500
Daily Bugle	1/4 page	8,000	1 per week	1,200

Advertising budget for three media: $2,500

That investment of $30,000 per year is tiny, but if another $30,000 is invested in the other weapons of marketing, it might be enough for a local business. The media-buying service may have helped you aim your media at your target audience, negotiated a rate that is 75 percent of what you would have paid, suggested the ideal frequency for your goals, and checked that all TV spots and newspaper ads ran as scheduled. Now it's up to you to measure which of those media are doing the best job for the money and to raise your gross annual revenues to a point where that same $60,000 marketing investment represents only 5 percent of that gross. You've paid dearly for your media. Now see what you can do to increase the effectiveness while reducing the cost — by learning where people first found out about you.

Two crucial factors

Advertising legend John Caples said that the two most important factors in advertising are what you say in your ads and where you say it. What you say will be covered later. Where you say it means putting your message where it will get into the minds of the largest number of prospects — not people, but prospects — at the lowest cost.

The uninitiated may produce great ads that get lost with poor placement. Media-buying services can't really dictate where the ad will run in the print media they've recommended, but they can counsel you and maybe even abet your efforts to do everything possible to get the first right-hand page position in the publication in which you run your ad. Because of a strict adherence by the media of no crossover between the editorial department and the advertising department (observed by the majority of the media), even the largest media-buying services cannot guarantee you will get the ad position of commercial placement you want. But they can alert you to inside info such as if you're going onto the radio, invest in drive time, when most listeners have their car radios on during their commute. If you're going onto TV, avoid clutter by having your commercial appear at the start or end of a cluster of spots, not in the middle. There are tons of tips.

How I've changed

When I wrote my first book on marketing, I counseled advertisers to study media directories published by Standard Rate and Data Service, found in many libraries. Although it's still good advice, just to learn how much there *is* to learn about media, I no longer recommend it any more than I'd recommend an art course for an advertiser interested in designing an advertising campaign. The frontier has changed too much for guerrillas ready to take the next step with their advertising.

Selecting media is just too important and expensive to do it all by yourself, no matter how much you want to. Yes, I know, you want to save money. But guerrillas accomplish that by investing their advertising dollars wisely. Remember that your advertising is an investment and you want to do all you can to make that investment pay off, to remove the risk. That means staying the heck away from it yourself and enlisting the aid of true experts.

Selecting your advertising media is a foray into dangerous territory. Don't do it without an experienced guide. More media options than ever mean more chances to do it wrong than ever. The last thing you want is a terrific advertising campaign run to the wrong people in the wrong media.

4

Planning Your Campaign and Promotions

If you run one lousy ad, meaning, nobody responds, the world does not come to an end. But if you plan poorly, or not at all, you have cause to worry about your business coming to a halt.

Once you've determined where you should advertise, studied your target audience, and picked the media you'll use, the planning of what you'll say and when you'll say it is essential to your success. You've got to plan with your goals in mind as well as your budget, your competition, your plans for the future, and the realities of the moment.

Might your short- or long-range planning include promotions with other companies? Guerrillas are constantly on the lookout for fusion advertising opportunities — chances to **More ad** tie in with other advertisers so that the advertising gets more **exposure,** exposure but at a lower price, since the cost is shared with **lower price** others.

If three local stores, all compatible, such as a drapery store, a carpet showroom, and a wallpaper shop, combine to run a full-page ad in a regional edition of a national magazine, they all gain the credibility (and the limitless reprints) of the ad, but the cost will be only 33 percent of what it normally would be. That's one of the benefits of fusion advertising, and that's why you should consider the concept before planning your campaign. Just be sure that you never lose your own identity in fusion ventures.

Plan your advertising campaign with an eye toward what **What if** you'll do in case you are copied. If you come up with a dyna- **you're copied?** mite plan and it is highly successful, you can count on being copied. So be certain that your name, your look, your logo, the whole works, are synonymous with your name and identity. You may be copied, but your consumers won't confuse you with the others. Be certain that your plan takes into consideration five important variables:

1. Advertising
2. Promotions
3. Other marketing weapons
4. Coordination
5. Timing

Think of these as a basketball team with five players. No matter how good it is, if it lost only one player and had to play with a four-player team, it would lose most of its games to complete teams that excel at teamwork. A good plan includes all the players and is the essence of teamwork. Alone, each of these players just can't do the job. They need each other. Every guerrilla plays with his or her full team.

The guerrilla knows that an advertising campaign must have *continuity* to do the persuading job well. In advertising, intermittent communication is no communication at all. Your plan must have consistency built right into it. The idea is not to flirt with your public but to *convince* them. There is a huge difference between the two. Any true advertising expert will tell you that *frequency and persistence* are the secrets of success in advertising. A major commitment to one or a few of the media will work better in most cases than an across-the-board plan with a variety of media but a short insertion schedule.

You should plan your campaign so that you are consistent, but never boring, committed, but never predictable. You've got to build special promotions into your plan to keep your staff on their feet and your competitors off balance. The only part of the plan engraved in stone is your identity. Flexibility and an ability to make alterations in your advertising is crucial.

Never be predictable

The planning that goes into an advertising campaign, although more important than any of the individual ads or commercials, is also easier than actually launching the campaign and maintaining it. Planning takes *research and deep thinking*. But launching requires *action*, and maintaining requires *patience*. Most Americans who engage in advertising are long on thinking, but short on action and patience. A written advertising and promotion plan has action and patience at its core.

The reason much advertising goes awry is that it is created in a hurry, under emergency conditions, and with extra cost for overtime caused by the rush. A proper plan eliminates emergencies, avoids the need for a rush, and saves the advertiser overtime charges. The newspaper calls and tells you an ad is due to them by Friday. No problem. You send them the ad; it was created a month ago and doesn't have to be crafted in a few days, one of small businesses' most common emergencies.

Three factors to consider
All guerrillas know that when it comes to creating advertising, there are three factors to consider: speed, quality, and economy. They also know that they get to select *any two* of these factors. You can bet they opt for quality and economy. Their careful planning eliminates the need for speed.

When you plan your campaign, you plan for potential changes you might make, based on response, the tactics you will employ, and the times these efforts will take place. Everyone concerned is ready to move at a moment's notice because of all the intelligent planning you've done. You can even plan to repeat certain promotions, knowing they will be successful because you've done them before. For instance, a local florist regularly advertises a free delivery service at Valentine's Day and Mother's Day. Guess who gets the repeat business?

At the end of a year, which, by the way, is the length of a short-term plan, evaluate your promotions and get rid of those that didn't work. Double up on those that did. It takes about three years to make a perfect plan, but a perfect plan is worth far more than its weight in gold.

Remember: A winning plan is also one that looks ahead

and assumes the role of leadership, utilizing technology that makes it easier for you to learn about your prospects and for your prospects to buy from you. If you're technophobic, find an employee or consultant who can help keep your operation up-to-date. Fear of new gizmos can be fatal to a business.

The idea of coordinating an advertising campaign is complex, but it is simple to absorb and control with a marketing plan. The plan itself is coordination in writing, addressing the crucial issue of timing, based upon your goals, your competitors, and current events.

The guerrilla crystal ball

Look into your plan as you would a crystal ball. Envision the future and time your direct marketing to coordinate with your advertising. Direct mail efforts that might have otherwise failed take wing and fly when teamed up with an advertising push. The success will be due to the plan. Without it, both the direct mail and the advertising would be weak.

The cost to create an advertising plan is zero, but the cost to operate without one is in the thousands, the millions. Before you run one ad, mail to one person, or even print your business cards and stationery, have in your possession and your brain a guerrilla advertising plan that covers every week of the year.

A year at a glance

What might such a plan look like? Well, if you happen to be a florist and your name is Petal Pushers, it might look somewhat like this one:

Month	Advertising	Promotion	Cost	Result
January	Bugle/Sun	Subscribe to flowers	$ 500	B
February	Bugle/Sun/Journal WGMA-TV, WOO radio	Valentine's Day	1,000	A
March	Bugle/Sun	Emphasize delivery	500	B
April	Bugle/Sun	Community flower show	500	A

Month	Advertising	Promotion	Cost	Result
May	Bugle/Sun/Journal WGMA-TV, WOO radio	Mother's Day	1,000	A
June	Bugle/Sun/Journal WGMA-TV, WOO radio	Wedding flowers	1,000	B
July	Bugle/Sun	Flower workshop	500	C
August	Bugle/Sun	Rose competition	500	B
September	Bugle/Sun	Subscribe to flowers	500	A
October	Bugle/Sun	Subscribe to flowers	500	A
November	Bugle/Sun	Thanksgiving baskets	500	B
December	Bugle/Sun/Journal WGMA-TV, WOO radio	Holiday specials	1,000	A

The total cost for the constantly active florist to maintain this calendar is $8,000 for the year. And with so many offers and promotions scoring high grades, you can be sure the florist considers the eight grand a worthwhile investment. The "Subscribe to flowers" offer is one that results in repeat business for bouquets delivered on Fridays to homes and on Mondays to offices. The grades given to each promotion indicate that this isn't the first year Petal Pushers has been in business. Most first-time calendars have a few less dazzling grades mixed in. That's why it's so important to keep track.

Just like Petal Pushers', your own calendar will be a blend of advertising and promotions. It will empower advertising and the other weapons of marketing because they will be timed to abet one another. It will be simple to implement because of its clarity and sensibleness. Although it will leave little to spontaneity, it will have room for adaptation to an opportunity presented by the events of the times: the economy, your community, the competition, fusion options. The moment you have committed your plan to writing, know that you have in your possession one of your most valuable business assets. Even more than fine wine, it will improve with age.

Improves with age better than wine

5

Learning What Your Audience Really Wants

First of all, recognize that your target audience, if you've selected it right, really wants to buy your product or service if it
offers enough quality. In other words, your audience, like
yourself, wants a good value. Guerrillas know that a good
value is *whatever the prospective customer thinks it is.* If you've
convinced them that your offering is worth the ridiculously
high price you've attached to it, it's a good value. If you
haven't convinced them that it's worth the ridiculously low
price you've attached to it, it's obviously a poor value. A *great
value exists only in the mind of the consumer.* Do you think a
baseball card at $50,000 is a good value? I don't, but some
folks do. Do you think a 360-degree TV sound system at
$4,000 in your bedroom is a good value? I do, but some
people don't.

If people reading or hearing your advertising are reading
it because of a zinger of a headline or a gorgeous graphic,
either they're the wrong people or you've written poor advertising. They should be paying attention because you're offering them *a benefit that they need or want.* If so, you've picked
the right people and you've created good advertising.

**People buy
what they want,
not what they
need**

In order to do this, realize that people tend to buy what
they *want* instead of what they *need.* You can persuade them
from here to Saturday that they need what you are offering,
but there is absolutely no way in the world to get them to
buy it if they don't want it. Their screenless house is infested
with mosquitoes and flies. You sell and install screens. They
need screens. But they'll use their money to go take a cruise

instead because they want to take a cruise. Do they need a cruise?

The best way to determine what people want is also the most obvious, though it's often overlooked by most advertisers. The way to learn exactly what customers want is to *ask them*. You go to members of your target market — in person, by phone, with researchers, or with questionnaires — and you find out what they want by asking them. Ask them to describe an ideal version of what you are offering. Ask them what is wrong with existing versions. See what's right and what's wrong with what is already on the market.

If you are pioneering, let people try your product or service for a trial period, if possible, then ask what's right, what's wrong, and whether they would want the product or service. If they wouldn't, either you've gone to the wrong people or you've got to do more work on your offering. No matter how good you make it, it's only worth something to you if it's worth something to other people.

Go to school on your competition. Learn why the leaders are leading. Learn why those who buy the leaders do so. See what those people want by studying what they buy, then, with a bit more poking about, learn about those people so you will be able to reach them and inform them that you have what they want.

Go to school on your competition

You can be certain that consumers are always interested in a better value, and, hopefully, more convenience than they've been getting. They want to feel confident that you'll back whatever they buy from you and that the mere fact of you selling it attests to its quality. At the beginning, during the transaction, and after the purchase, they want to know that you recognize them as unique individuals. Your advertising must convey this.

At all times, your audience wants like crazy *not* to make a purchase error. They've made at least one in the past and they don't want to make another. That means they want credibility and they'll get it from your reputation, your other marketing, and the physical manifestations of your product or service — features they can see.

Perhaps your audience wants selection, the bigger the better, and for every one who wants the most inexpensive version, there will be at least one customer who wants the most expensive. They also want freedom from any risk whatsoever. Your reputation will help reassure them that there is little risk; your written warranty or guarantee accomplishes the same thing in a tangible manner.

Be aware that your audience most assuredly wants to know that others in the community have purchased what you want them to purchase. The more previous purchasers — meaning satisfied customers to your prospects — the better for both of you. Tell the world about them.

What everybody wants One thing you can be sure all audiences want is *convenience*. They want it to be easy to buy from you, easy to find you, easy to park, easy to find what they want, easy to pay. They want to be able to pay by any credit card, by check, or even with pennies from a piggy bank. They want a service contract, free delivery, installation. They want to know for sure what they are buying, and it better be guaranteed. Either the package, a sign, a sales aid, or a salesperson will provide this clarity for them. *Don't waste a penny advertising* until you know you can offer the convenience that comes with the territory in these time-saving days.

If your premises are messy or your sales reps are surly, know with certainty that your prospects *do not* want that. They want just the opposite. And your advertising must suggest the kind of convenience and service that separate the successes from the failures. Advertising is only great if it truly delivers the goods down to the purchase and use of your offering.

It is a complicated task, finding out what people want, then catering to that want. Remember: You cater to it first by the design of your product or service, then by your advertising.

People don't care about advertising People generally don't really care much for or about advertising. They don't really think about it. The down-home truth is that advertising is an intrusion — into the magazine, the newspaper, the radio show, the TV show, the consciousness of the member of the target audience. Being aware that people do not care about advertising, you've got to break through their apathy and surmount their barriers to it. You've got to get them to trust you — *in spite of your advertising and because of your advertising.*

Once you have a line on what your audience wants, you will have a relatively simple job of *involving* them. If they're involved with your message, there's a good chance they'll become a paying customer. If you've found out what your target audience really wants, you can more easily achieve the goal of reader or viewer involvement.

Most advertising fails because it neglects to involve the reader, listener, or viewer. A four-question test should be applied to all your advertising materials: **Why most advertising fails**

1. Who is my audience and do they really want what I am offering?
2. Why should my audience believe what I am saying here?
3. Does my product or service offer what my audience will perceive as an excellent value?
4. Is there any cleverness in my ad that distracts my audience from my primary offer?

Advertising that is honest is not enough. Advertising that is informative is not enough. Always keep in the forefront of your mind that it costs just as much to run an ad for something that people do not want as it does to run an ad for something that people want and want right now. Do the homework and legwork to find out what that is and you're off to a dandy start.

6

Being Specific to Yourself and Your Audience

The less you deal in generality, the more you will deal in profitability. The word "puffery" was created to describe what most of advertising is, but shouldn't be. I understand that you feel you must use adjectives to put across your points and accentuate your enthusiasm. But don't overdo it. As much as possible, try to keep your ad copy an adjective-free zone.

Give your advertising the benefit of believability by being as specific as you can. Use real names, real numbers, real facts, even real opinions if they're expressed by real customers and not by your advertising copywriter or yourself.

Naturally, you start on the road to specificity by being specific *to yourself* with your ultra-focused advertising plan. Your research enables you to be very specific to yourself because you know what the facts are. By talking to your prospects, you know specifically what they want. By assiduously studying your own product or service, you know specifically what it offers. This prospect insight combined with product insight gives you *guerrilla advertising power* — the power to win customers and influence profits with specific data.

Guerrilla advertising power

I've devoted an entire chapter to the importance of being specific to yourself with an advertising strategy. But I didn't even mention the importance of being specific to yourself with real goals, expressed as specifically as you can. That should not be part of a strategy as much as part of your very essence.

Don't say that you'll steadily increase your profits each month. Say that you'll steadily increase your profits by 2 percent each month. Don't say that you'll aim for a sales increase each month. Say that your sales will increase $3,000 each month — or $30,000 — or even $300 each month. The more clearly you state your goal, the more clearly you can see it, aim for it, and achieve it, or see by how much you missed it so you can do better next month. Hazy goals make hazy targets, and even Robin Hood couldn't hit bull's-eyes when Sherwood Forest was blanketed with fog.

Hazy goals make hazy targets

When you say, "ABC Consulting Services can help companies just like yours," you are putty in the hands of the advertiser who says, "XYZ Consulting Services enabled the Joel Coopersmith Company to triple its profits in four months."

A name is mentioned. Two numbers are mentioned. That's being specific in a way that makes prospects respond. Any merit of your offering that might be communicated with descriptive phrases should be communicated with names and numbers. They need not be big names or big numbers. Just be sure they are real names and honest numbers.

Give examples. They're specific. Quote case histories. They're very specific. Show testimonial letters. They, too, are specific. And what could be more specific than a before-and-after photograph of a renovated deck, a landscaped yard, a remodeled kitchen, a now slender but once fat guy? With computer graphics, you can add visual excitement to tedious numbers and be as specific as you would ever want to be and as specific as your prospects need you to be. We all want convincing reassurance whether we're buying a home computer or purchasing a system for an entire office.

Give examples

Believe me, prospects do not like taking purchase risks, most likely having been stung in the past. Specifics remove the sting from the purchase because they remove the risk. Prospects get to make their decisions based on hard data rather than advertising puffery. Even a child can tell puffery from facts in spite of most advertising being puffery.

As names, numbers, photos, testimonials, examples, case histories, and computer data provide your prospects with the comfort of specifics, so do diagrams, publicity stories, demonstrations, samples, and any past success stories you can relate. Satisfied customers are about the most specific proof of your quality that exists anywhere. How many of them are there? The answer to that is another specific that can impress prospects so much that they become customers. I've heard of a home builder who provides prospective buyers with a list of home owners he has built homes for. What could be a better ad or vote of confidence for his work than this list of folks willing to provide references and recommendations?

Get down to the nitty-gritty

A catalogue or brochure that gets down to the nitty-gritty and gives details is the essence of specificity — as long as there aren't too many adjectives in it. An annual report is a marvelous forum for being specific. Don't dismiss the idea of an annual report just because you don't run a public company. Annual reports are being used by increasing numbers of small businesses because they provide a way for a business to communicate with prospects and because prospects *expect them to be specific.*

Research studies, accomplished by you or by almost anyone, provide the fodder for specifics in advertising. If you quote from these studies, your advertising will be more believable because you are able to dazzle your prospects with fancy facts instead of fancy phrases.

Fancy phrase: Our bookstore offers the best selection of books in the entire community.

Fancy fact: Our bookstore has over 50,000 books in stock and can get you any of 500,000 more books within a week.

Which bookstore would most appeal to you?

Guerrillas know deep in their hearts that the American public has a built-in B.S. detector. When they sense that an ad is bragging, exaggerating, or telling elastic truths, red lights flash on in their brains and bells begin to clang. A clear inner voice rings out: "Baloney!" it says. They listen. And they respond by *not responding* to your ad.

"Baloney!" says that inner voice

Specific information does not set any lights to flashing or bells to ringing. What it does do is set prospects into motion. It starts the momentum that begins with questions and curiosity, then leads to sales and profits. It motivates and convinces. It persuades many prospects through the brute force of irrefutable facts.

Being specific in your offers is the difference between "Let's do lunch" and "Let's have lunch this Friday at one o'clock at Vanessi's on Nob Hill."

One of the most difficult tasks in advertising is saying things that people will believe. Tools to help you succeed at the task include the language you use and the specific information you state. If you haven't got the specifics right now, set about getting them:

- Talk to past customers and clients, obtaining real figures that you can use as testimony in your advertising.
- Research your prospects' buying habits: where they shop, how they spend, who and what they listen to, where they get their information. Find out how many times they frequent the mall, the service station, the church.
- Ask for testimonial letters written on the letterhead of the satisfied customer.
- Retain the services of an independent firm that will undertake a study in which you believe you will come out the clear winner. Good luck!
- Use before-and-after photographs to prove your abilities if you can communicate your benefits visually.

Specifics will help you in virtually all of your advertising, not to mention your other marketing efforts — and specifics are available to the imaginative advertiser.

Now that you know the importance of specific information, let me temper that insight with the caveat that *many people don't give a hoot about specifics* because they are known as right-brained. They make up about 45 percent of the population; 45 percent more are left-brained; 10 percent are balanced-brained.

Right-brained people are motivated by emotional, aesthetic appeals. Often they make purchase decisions with their intuition, but that intuition does feed upon both intangible and tangible data. So specifics, while having some influence, don't have as much influence with right-brained people as with left-brained people.

Right- and left-brained people

Left-brained folks are transformed to names on customer lists by logical, sequential appeals. Their purchase decisions are based upon solid, specific information. Appeals to their emotions presented with exquisite graphics don't carry much weight, not nearly as much as that list of twenty-five reasons why they should make the purchase.

Whether you are advertising computers, piano lessons, remodeling, or a new line of women's clothing, your audience will always be 45 percent left-brained and 45 percent right-brained.

The guerrilla's job is to create advertising that will woo the right-brained and the left-brained at the same time. Although specifics are not as crucial to one group as the other, they will always prove to be an invaluable key to the lock on the believability barrier.

The advertising for Apple's PowerBook did a superb job of giving specifics, aiming at both left- and right-brained people and selling a whale of a lot of PowerBooks. Their print ads showed a wide variety of users, proving anyone can use a PowerBook, and one ad emphasized the convenience of the PowerBook by showing former basketball great Kareem Abdul-Jabbar, all seven feet of him, sitting in an airline seat using his PowerBook. That ad appealed to the left-brained logic hunters who were pleased at the specificity of a tall athlete using a PowerBook easily, even while flying, and to the right-brained folks who had to grin when they saw the photo; there's no question that it evoked an emotional response in them as well as a positive feeling about Apple's offering. And there's no denying that the campaign moved merchandise, as attested to by PowerBook's grabbing 20 percent of the portable computer business.

Pepper it with specifics That's why you'll do everything you can to collect, generate, mine for, and pepper your advertising with specific information.

II

The Fountain of Creativity

THERE ARE MANY people in our world who believe they are not creative — when the truth is that they haven't yet learned to tap their inherent creativity. If you've got a brain, you've got the goods to be creative. All you've got to do is learn how. The time you spend reading this part of this book will help jump-start your creative engine if it's been dormant or prime your engine if it's raring to go.

Let's just be sure before the experience begins that we agree upon the meaning of *creative*. When guerrillas use the term *creativity*, it is relative to and measured by *profitability*. They know it has nothing to do with awards or compliments or pats on the back. If it's not profitable, it's not creative. Maybe it's pretty or funny, but creative it isn't if it doesn't pull.

The meaning of *creative*, then, in the context of your economic pursuits at this moment, is "advertising that generates profits."

In order to be creative, all you've got to do is dream up ways to generate profits through advertising. That does not take artistic ability. That does not happen strictly as a result of writing ability. It's not even the happy consequence of a monster advertising budget. But it certainly is a talent — *talent* assuredly is the right word — that almost anyone can develop.

Toss that "I'm not creative" attitude out the window and realize that you can, should, and will be creative — *if* you understand that creativity is connected to profitability. Ernest

Hemingway said he felt that writing creative advertising was considerably more difficult than writing novels. The measurements of creative advertising are more strict. The evidence of its excellence is able to be quantified, scrutinized, and analyzed.

Don't think for a moment that creative advertising *isn't* supposed to look attractive, sound appealing, and read enticingly. It is allowed, even encouraged, to do these things — *and also produce profits*. But these attributes are prohibited in guerrilla advertising if their appeal will in any way detract from the profits.

We are now as one in our view of advertising creativity. That view enables us to drink at the fountain of creativity, for there is a fountain, many of them in fact, and they do flow with potential profits for your company. You devote your time and energy to that company because, ideally, you enjoy the work, and naturally you want to earn high, honest profits. You surely don't run it for the purpose of running gorgeous, purposeless advertising.

Now we're ready to examine the source of this wonderful creativity.

7

Where Creativity Comes From

Once the Nestlé Corporation invited me to address its corporate marketing executives in the company's impressive building on the shores of Lake Geneva, Switzerland — if I could answer the question of where creativity comes from.

I set out to find out exactly where it does come from. I spoke to artists. I talked with writers. I gabbed with musicians, dancers, actors, photographers, directors. I struck up conversations with advertising people.

Everyone I asked came up with the same answer!

"Knowledge," they told me. Knowledge is where creativity comes from. The more knowledge you have, the more creative you can be.

Creativity comes from knowledge

Knowledge is easier to come by these days than ever before. Computer databases give us scads of information about our competitors, customers, prospects, industry, community, economic trends, almost anything else we wish to learn, and much that we don't. More knowledge is on the way. Knowledge is in greater supply than ever and also in more demand. Knowledge is more valuable than ever, and to the successful business owners of the twenty-first century, it will be more valuable than money, exceeded in value only by time.

Ten areas from which the guerrilla seeks knowledge are:

Ten sources of knowledge

1. Customers
2. Prospects
3. Competitors
4. The industry

5. The community
6. Current events
7. Economic trends
8. Equivalent businesses in other areas
9. His own product or service
10. Advertising that is succeeding

It isn't very hard to see the clear cause and effect between your access to knowledge and your ability to be a creative genius. Does this mean that if you have a computer, first-rate software, and a modem you can actually be more creative? Do you think Leonardo da Vinci might have used these gizmos if they were around when he was around? I think so, too.

Creativity comes from *combining seemingly unrelated facets of your knowledge.* When you combine personal data about a customer with fascinating data about how your service contributes to the well-being of that customer, you're well on your way toward being creative. Beef up your creativity with data about your competitors and the latest economic goings-on in town, and you can be even more creative. Knowing about highly successful advertising for a product or service similar to yours in such diverse communities as Santa Fe, New Mexico, and Sydney, Australia, is going to pump up your creative juices to the point that you have a darned good chance of coming up with creative advertising.

Knowing where to look, and where not to look, for creativity is the beginning of being creative. All creative ideas must be focused upon the benefits offered by the product or service, communicated in human terms, centered upon simplicity. Take the simple step of spending time inside your competitor's place of business. Read the trade magazines and catalogues. Don't be caught unaware.

When you sift through information in your quest for profit-producing advertising, view it first through your own eyes, as the creator of the advertising, then through the eyes **The eyes of** of your prospects, as the targets of it. In assessing this knowl-**your prospects** edge, always know what you want your prospects to do.

"Plan the sale when you plan the ad," said advertising

legend Leo Burnett, founder and guiding spirit of perhaps the solar system's finest advertising agency — as judged in the bright light of its clients' profitability. Much of what I learned about advertising came directly from him, and now it's going directly to you. We all could do worse in our choice of advertising idols.

The most creative people in advertising always seem to be the most curious. They always seem to be poking about the planet learning about people, things, attitudes, anything. Sometimes they dress in the stereotypical creative duds, but most often you can't tell them from the average citizen. They probably spend a lot of time among average citizenry, since that's most likely to whom they are directing their message. It takes one to know one, as you've heard.

Creative people entrusted with the advertising for consumer items tend to be keen observers of shoppers in stores. They ask a lot of questions. They're good at listening. The best of them have a well-developed sense of wonder, and even though they know a lot, they rarely act like know-it-alls. They will read any magazine, watch any TV program, listen to any radio station, shop at any outlet — just because they want to get a good bead upon their public's taste. Guerrillas are knowledgeable by staying *in touch* with the world around them. The more in touch you are, the more creative you'll become.

Staying in touch

*   *   *

A seagull flies in endless circles in a constant quest for food. After soaring circular sojourns too numerous to count, the seagull finds food, heads down to it, lands, and eats its fill. When the seagull has had a bellyful, it takes off again, only to fly once again in endless circles in a quest for even more food. The seagull has just been sated with food, yet continues to search for more because it has *an inner instinct that commands it forever to seek food.*

Human beings have a similarly strong instinct that remains forever with us, rivaled only by the need to survive as the most powerful human instinct. Do you know what it is?

A powerful human instinct

You can be sure that those who generate the most creative

advertising know exactly what it is. *It is the need to learn, to obtain knowledge forever.* The more you take heed of this instinct, which you already possess, the more you will be able to develop consistently creative advertising. Just think — the source of creativity is one to which you are already attracted.

Follow your natural instinct to learn, then use your knowledge to be creative. Now that you know the source of creativity, you will discover what empowers guerrilla advertising.

8

The Power of an Idea

The starting point for guerrilla advertising is not a headline, a graphic, a special effect, a music track, or a spokesperson, as in most humdrum advertising. Instead, it's an *idea* — something that is often missing from run-of-the-mill advertising.

When advertising is powered by a strong idea, these subsequent elements of advertising become simpler to create. The copy writes itself; the right visual becomes apparent. Decisions concerning the important details of print and electronic advertising become obvious.

Look at current advertising in all the media around you, especially television, and see if you can spot the ideas. You'll be surprised at their absence. That void represents an open door through which guerrillas rush with their clearly communicated ideas.

What's the big idea?

High-profile, big-budget companies such as McDonald's and Coca-Cola spend so much money advertising that they drop great ad campaigns in a short time because they are able to saturate the market with their ideas. McDonald's "You deserve a break today" communicated a clear idea and presented it appetizingly. Coca-Cola's "It's the real thing" communicated its relationship to other colas and distinguished itself as a classic. The idea behind the Energizer battery is easily recognizable because the ever-moving bunny symbolizes the very durability that Energizer is trying to communicate. The idea behind the Pillsbury Doughboy, now entering his middle age, though he doesn't look it, is freshness, softness, and fun. Nike commercials stress action, "Just do it," starring big-name professional athletes, and Reebok utilizes different superstar athletes, also conveying a strong sense of identity. Trouble is, both shoemakers have the same identity. Both lean on the action and the big names rather than the features, benefits, and styles of the shoes. There is much to be said for the comfort and support of today's sneakers, but nary a word is heard because the soul of the shoes is more important than the sole.

Blue jeans are presented in much the same manner, reflecting the ethos of the nineties, devoid of reasons to purchase the jeans, actually making TV viewers wait to see whose jeans are being hawked this time. Some teenagers may be able to recognize the jeans simply by seeing them, but then again, some others may not. The proper use of TV would dictate that the name of the maker be on the screen at all times, given the intensely visual nature of TV, but it is flashed on for only a moment at the tail end of many of today's jeans commercials. By the time you read this book, will shoes and jeans be advertised in a different way? Count on it. As one commercial **Image isn't** falsely reports, "Image is everything." It's a lot of things, to be **everything** sure. But it isn't everything.

In each of these cases, and in the not so many others that I could point out, the idea comes shining through brightly, whether stated or unstated, and the advertising doesn't require the viewers to spend much time ferreting it out. Viewers have far more important things to do.

The Gap has run fascinating advertising for over a decade and it undoubtedly built their business. But Gap advertising is flopping these days because so many competitors have come down the pike. The Gap's advertising shows that the company is struggling to position itself. Should it be a fashion company? The Gap once thought it should, but now has canceled much advertising slated to appear in fashion magazines. They uncorked a new slogan on us: "For every generation, there's a Gap." Good line? It flopped with a resounding thud. For a decade, The Gap positioned itself as not trendy or jaded. But the gears seem to have been changed and current Gap ads show it as both trendy *and* jaded. Gap advertising people say that's because The Gap never was a fervent believer in research and operated by the seat of its Levi's most of the time.

It wasn't until late in 1993 that Gap executives enlisted the aid of market research to evaluate its consumers. The Gap officials intentionally tried to be leaner, meaner, and looser, and they've been bright, no question about it. But bright is not what advertising is about. It's about being right.

Advertising is about being right, not bright

Adweek ad critic Barbara Lippert recently came down hard on the advertising run by Levi's, one of the nation's most successful advertisers. The campaign for Women's Dockers, modeled slightly after the enormously successful campaign for Men's Dockers, was described by Barbara thusly: "The cinematography is beautiful, and the music is interesting, but the women seem strangely blitzed out, as if they came from some robotic planet. It's as if the campaign is an ode to motherhood, apple pie and Prozac."

Motherhood, apple pie, and Prozac

Bill Backer, the creative force for Coca-Cola for a decade, was speaking of the jeans–sneakers–advertising boutique school of advertising of the nineties — especially the TV spots for Coca-Cola created by non-advertising-agency Creative Artists, a Hollywood talent management firm — when he said, "I have no problem with leaner, meaner, and looser, but . . . I regard it as making more out of less. I think most of the executions are not idea-driven, but technique-driven. Some of what they did may be interesting for film buffs, but if an agency had presented those same ideas to former Coke marketing chief Peter Sealey, I'd bet he would have kicked them out of the room."

The Effie Awards are the only advertising awards based upon the sales of the products being advertised rather than the glitz and exciting visual effects of the ads themselves. To give you a glimpse into cause and effect, I'll list the first-prize award winners for 1993 and you can see for which ones you recall the advertising. Even if you can't remember the ads, you can be sure each one was powered by an idea:

Award-winning advertisers

Alcoholic beverages: Coors Brewing
Apparel and accessories: Giorgio Armani

Associations:	Beef Industry Council
Automotive:	Saturn
Automotive products:	Castrol Syntec
Beauty aids:	Quintessence's Caliente
Beverages:	Campbell's V-8
Bottled waters and soft drinks:	Diet Dr Pepper
Breakfast food:	Total Raisin Bran
Business products:	Canon NP copiers
Business services:	Mobile Communications
Business-to-business:	Beacon Blankets
Computers:	Apple's PowerBook
Consumer communication:	AT & T's Calling Card
Corporate institutional:	Anderson Consulting
Credit and debit cards:	Discover Card
Diet/health/lite food:	Sugar-Free Jell-O
Entertainment:	*Beauty and the Beast*
Fast food:	Little Caesars
Financial services:	Aetna Life and Casualty
Government/political:	Senator Russ Feingold
Health aids:	Milk of Magnesia
Household furnishings:	RCA Home Theatre
Household supplies:	Ivory dishwashing liquid
Leisure products:	Flowers Direct
Main/side dish:	Gerber baby formula
Medical services:	HealthAmerica/Pittsburgh
Packaged food:	Lawry's seasoned salt
Pet food:	Kal Kan's Whiskas
Print/electronic media:	NBC's 1992 *Olympics*
Public service:	Partnership for a Drug-Free America
Real estate:	The Peninsula
Retail:	JCPenney
Snacks/confections:	Wrigley's spearmint gum
Transportation:	Midwest Express Airlines
Travel/tourism:	Australian Tourist Board
Trucks and vans:	Isuzu Rodeo
Utilities:	Consumers Power

Inducted into the newly created Marketing Hall of Fame, also on the basis of effectiveness and creativity in advertising, were Coca-Cola, Absolut, and Nike.

How many commercials for these advertisers do you remember? How many persuaded you to end up buying the product? Although I haven't seen the advertising for all of these products, and you didn't either, we both should pay homage to the companies because they created advertising that worked. Loving the ads and commercials had little to do with it. Pats on the back for high-level special effects also did not influence the judges. Their primary influence was a healthy sales curve and a stunningly beautiful bottom line.

A stunningly beautiful bottom line

It is enlightening to go back into advertising history and come up with ten examples of advertising that not only were propelled by the stunning power of an idea but are still zinging along, fueled by *the very same idea!* Consider:

Maytag's lonely repairman
Starkist's Charlie the Tuna
Pillsbury's Doughboy
Allstate's good hands
United's friendly skies
Green Giant's ho ho ho
Merrill Lynch's bull
The Dreyfus Fund's lion
Marlboro's cowboy
Energizer's bunny

If any of the 1993 award winners I listed have ideas as powerful and durable as these ten, both of us should be surprised. Classic advertising is hard to come by because the patience to create it then stay with it is rare. Still, I have the feeling that some of the advertisers that took Effie awards home have that patience.

Patience is hard to come by in advertising. One reason is that technology changes so fast that many companies adapt their advertising to the *product*, not the company. Procter & Gamble, one of the largest advertisers on earth, hardly ever

mentions its name in its advertising, attempting — and usually succeeding — in directing all the consumer awareness to
its products, from Tide to Folgers, from Pepto-Bismol to Prell.

AT & T advertises its technologies much more than its
name, and that job is becoming tougher and tougher as the
technologies multiply. IBM, Apple, even Microsoft, face the
same challenge. Their tasks: to sell the individual break-
throughs they've developed while selling their name at the
same time. Will one power-laden idea do the job?

Will one idea do the job?

It will for products. It won't for companies. While the
company, be it Sony, Panasonic, Budweiser, or Chrysler, stays
relatively the same from year to year, the models and line extensions put out by these companies vary in many crucial
ways. In technical fields, where innovation reigns supreme,
advertising changes because it has to. But even there, beneath
the surface of the advertising should be an idea that elevates
the company and pre-sells anything it offers. The world is not
abounding with examples.

Many of the companies I've listed in this chapter are national firms with bottomless bank accounts. Don't think for
one second that I'm directing my remarks to them. Instead,
I'm directing them to *you* — with your local company and
your limited financial resources. Your job is to find the right
idea and promotion to make advertising work at the local
level, advertising like the kind the Food Mart, Marelli Brothers' Shoe Repair, Kamikaze Restaurant, Superfine Cleaners,
the Cottage Bookshop, India Palace, Art and Larry's Deli, and
the Regency Cinema used to motivate me.

Each of these businesses communicated ideas, not necessarily award winners, that wooed and won my hard-earned
royalties. What were the ideas? The Food Mart said in my
local newspaper that it would open a house charge for me.
Bingo! Marelli Brothers' Shoe Repair advertised its many decades in business in the yellow pages. Home run! Kamikaze
merely advertised its menu in a teensy local paper. Got me!
Superfine said in a local magazine that it does twenty-four-
hour cleaning. Bull's-eye! The Cottage advertised on the radio
and in the zone edition of a large metropolitan newspaper that

it giftwraps and ships books. Perfect! India Palace played In- dian music in the background of its radio spots describing its special curries and that seemed to be enough to entice me. Victory! Art and Larry's used cable TV and merely advertised its nearby location. Ideal! And the Regency Cinema simply advertised its hours — morning till night. Just the ticket!

These are not fancy ideas, certainly not the kind that you would have seen on the tube or even in a magazine. But they hit home with me and gave me exactly what I wanted.

That's the whole concept of creativity in guerrilla advertising — find out exactly what people want, then give it to them. It would be great to have the endorsements of Shaquille O'Neal, Michael Jordan, Michael Jackson, Madonna, and Robert Redford, but guerrillas are able to substitute big ideas for big names. They know, and now you do, too, that all great advertising starts with an idea and that it isn't great advertising if it doesn't generate profits. Right, Mr. Marelli?

9

Guerrilla Brainstorming

Advertising ideas that can contribute giant increases to your profits are in great abundance all around you. Many are in the minds of your employees, but never get communicated because the troops are too wrapped up in the details of day-to-day business. The same is probably true of you. That's why you owe it to yourself before you spend a dime on advertising to conduct *the guerrilla brainstorming session.*

When I was working at one of America's largest advertising agencies, four or five of us would spend three days at a beautiful resort. We would do this twice a year. At the resort would be four or five representatives of our client, one of America's largest companies.

Get away to neutral turf The idea was to get away to *a neutral territory*, completely protected from the realities of daily business. The group of us would meet the evening of arrival, have dinner, and informally discuss the agenda for the coming days. It would be *a blend of play and work.*

Play included our choice of golf, tennis, skeet shooting, horseback riding, or loafing. We'd spend about half the daylight hours in these not unpleasant activities. I remember my feelings of good fortune at being paid to do these kinds of things.

Work consisted of the group gathering in a comfortable suite with everybody relaxed and one person taking copious notes. Just in case, we audiotaped the three-hour sessions. Our job: to brainstorm, to come up with new and good ideas. Our modus operandi: *suggestions.*

We brainstormed about one particular brand made by the company. Our marketing and advertising conversations, free-form as they were, were designed *to improve the profits of the brand*. Our suggestions could — and did — include anything about the brand: price, package, size, line extensions, TV, radio, magazines, enlarging the market for the brand, finding new audiences, headlines, theme lines, *anything*.

There was only one rule: *You can't say no to a suggestion.* **You can't say no**
Without that rule, the sessions would have been utter failures. But without fear of getting pelted with rotten tomatoes for a truly terrible idea, we were able to operate free of inhibitions and embarrassment. Fear of rejection is one of the greatest obstacles to creative advertising.

We had such a grand time playing during our leisure time that we were highly motivated, probably by guilt, to dive in with vigor to the work portions of the two days. We came up with a lengthy list of suggestions. Everybody felt free to make them, and because of our rule, nobody felt ashamed to make even the most off-the-wall suggestions. And some of the ideas were beyond off-the-wall.

Within a week of our return to our offices, each person who attended the brainstorming session — and no one else, thank heavens — received a typewritten list of the suggestions. This time, we were told to put stars by the suggestions we liked and X's by those we considered horrible.

We all were generous with our stars, even more so with our X's. We sent our marked lists to the brainstorming coordinator. Later that week, we received a list limited only to those suggestions that received stars by everyone.

During the three brainstorming sessions that I attended, at least five of the ideas *at each session* were turned into action — a minimum of fifteen ideas in all.

The profits from each one of the ideas paid many times over for the brainstormers at the luxury resort. The investment in brainstorming sessions was repaid at least fifteen times. **A 1,500 percent return on investment**

Brainstorming is often the last thing you think you have time for. Usually, employees are so involved in daily operations that they can't see clearly enough to give wing to their best ideas or encourage one another. But brainstorming is still highly recommended. A truly creative advertising idea doesn't care one bit where it comes from. Guerrillas provide their employees with creative freedom and encourage ideas, both in the form of suggestions made during a standard work week and in brainstorming sessions.

Company honchos, often too involved with putting out fires to spark new ideas in their firms, should make a point of calling brainstorming sessions together even if it's at the local pizza joint.

Naturally, you don't have to go to a fancy resort to have fancy ideas. But a neutral territory is the ideal stage for such sessions. They are important business functions because they have power to re-energize the troops, improve day-to-day operations, and spawn ideas based on collective knowledge.

Mix pleasure with profits

To get the most from brainstorming sessions, don't forget about the pleasure aspect, whether it's a pizza or a resort for your employees. Great ideas don't spring from tired brains. Getting out of the rut is the first step to fresh ideas, especially advertising ideas.

You'll be shocked at both the amount and the excellence of the fruits of a first-rate brainstorming session. It should take you nearly a year to activate the ideas you'll spawn. But guerrillas aren't in a hurry when it comes to advertising creativity.

You might be delighted to hear that you don't have to have many brainstorming sessions over the course of a year. One or two should easily be enough. But whatever you do, don't overlook this precious resource — your mind and the minds of your key employees.

Small-business expert Peter Orthmann suggests that everyone from the janitor to the president has ideas that can improve your business. Not only do they have them, but they want to share them. Get your share in regular, annual brainstorming sessions.

Brainstorming adds an element of fun to your business. It adds verve and freshness to your overall creativity — meaning your profitability. It gives all employees a special feeling of *involvement* in the company direction. Just having contributed a line of copy to an ad or seeing a suggestion put into effect can be worth more to many employees than a raise. Emotional income is never to be ignored.

Brainstorming gives you the synergy of multiple brains all working toward a common purpose. You won't really know the efficacy of brainstorming until you try it, and when you try it, you won't develop a full appreciation of it until the second or third session, when people really start to let their hair way down and come up with suggestions based on the suggestions of others.

It was during such a brainstorming session that a colleague read his idea for an ad for Crest toothpaste. I forget the headline, even the copy. But after the ad was read, someone chimed in with the simple question "Why doesn't everyone buy Crest?" He answered himself: "Must be the flavor. Why not offer a choice of flavors for Crest?" Added to the copy, to the TV spots, and to the Crest product line was a new flavor. Now all Crest advertising ended with the spoken or written words: "Regular or mint flavor." Creative? Doesn't look it. Doesn't sound creative. But it is.

That brainstorming session produced an idea that nearly doubled the sales of an already successful product. I predict that the same will happen for you if you follow the guerrilla's rules of brainstorming:

The guerrilla's rules of brainstorming

1. Conduct it at a neutral territory; provide some entertainment.
2. Welcome, in fact, encourage all notion of ideas.
3. No one is allowed to criticize or reject an idea.
4. Go for quantity; quality will come.
5. Record all ideas and suggestions on paper.
6. Don't fall in love with your own ideas. Listen.
7. Stay loose during sessions. Don't overthink things.
8. Circulate the list of ideas to all participants and ask them to rate the ideas.

9. Tally the ideas and develop a strategy or incorporate them into your existing strategy.
10. Hold sessions at regular intervals. And don't forget to have fun!

You know where creativity comes from. You're aware of the power of an idea. You know how to develop ideas. It's time now to learn the actual steps you can take to be creative.

10

The Five Steps
to Being Creative

You already know that without knowledge it's tough to be creative, and you know that *creative* pertains to profits more than art. So you're not going to be scouting about in your mind for a word, tune, or picture. It takes more than that to succeed in a society where millions of new businesses are launched each year. Instead, you'll be on the alert for ideas, and you even know how to enlist the minds of others in mining for good advertising ideas.

Guerrillas also use a remarkably potent technique for generating good advertising ideas *in their own minds*. They use this technique *after* the process of taking the five steps to being creative. But I want you to know of it *before* you learn the five steps so you can prime your mind to be creative. If your mind knows what is expected of it once it is creative, it will respond more brilliantly.

To tap into the enormous power of your unconscious mind in the quest for profit-producing advertising ideas, simply do three things:

Tapping into your unconscious mind

- *First*, spend five to fifteen minutes studying and thinking about the knowledge you have gained about your market — their wants, needs, and personal characteristics. Deeply concentrate on this task as you do it.
- *Second*, spend five to fifteen minutes studying and thinking about what you have to offer your market — your benefits, competitive advantages, and biggest appeal to

your specific audience. Again, give 100 percent of yourself during this time.
- *Third*, forget the whole project completely. Take your
mind off good advertising ideas and do anything but try
to come up with them. *Your unconscious mind will process your data and the idea will spring into your mind.*

Does this technique always work? You have my word on it.
Even though it is simple, it works, enabling you to utilize
your greatest store of brainpower — your unconscious. After
you have taken the matter out of your conscious mind and
turned it over to your unconscious, marvelous ideas spring
into your head at any time — from half a day later to three
days later. They explode into being while you're falling asleep,
taking a shower, reading in the john, driving, or watching TV.
Must you keep a pen and paper handy to write down these
gems? Nope. They'll be so good, so powerful, that you'll have
no trouble remembering them. Don't expect quantity. But you
can expect quality.

You should take five steps before using this technique.
These will provide ammunition to your unconscious, so that
you can select the cream of the information you have gathered
and use your own insights into human nature. Without these
steps to creativity you will be operating in a vacuum.

If you take these five steps to creativity every time you
must come up with an advertising idea, an advertising campaign, or an ad, you'll find your advertising investment pays
off far more handsomely than most do, even big ones. Take
four of the steps, and you'll be a hand without a thumb. You
need five steps.

**Five steps to
being creative**

Step One: Find Your Inner Amazement

Something about your product or service is amazing, fascinating, maybe even extraordinary. You may take that thing for

granted because it is part of your everyday life, but if your prospects knew about it, many of them would buy what you are selling immediately. The quest for guerrilla creativity begins at this specific point, a real-life fact about your product or service that is amazing. Find it by studying all facts of your offering, because it really is your *inner* amazement.

Step Two: Select Your Competitive Edge

Once you have found your inner amazement, see how it translates itself into benefits, because guerrillas know that people do not buy features as much as they buy benefits. Your inner amazement is there because it offers a benefit, possibly several benefits. Your job is to pick the one that gives you the sharpest competitive edge. Your finished ads and commercials may focus on several benefits, but if your competition offers the same ones, only your competitive advantage will stand out.

Step Three: Break the Advertising Barrier with Believability

Even if you're laden with scruples regarding your advertising copy and stretch the truth not one micron, chances are, it won't be believed. After all, people recognize advertising for what it is. So you've got to craft it for what it isn't: reeking with credibility, facts, and sincerity. Of course you've got to tell the truth, but you've got to tell it in the context of advertising, which is very akin to untruth. What to do? Be painstaking in your selection of words, using plain, short ones that are easy to believe. Pretend that an evil elf sits on your left shoulder peering down at your copy. Every time he sees a sentence that strains his belief, he screeches in your ear, "I don't believe that!" Write so as not to offend the sensibilities of that elf.

Step Four: Get Your Audience to Sit Up and Take Notice

There's no sense being creative in advertising that nobody will see, so you've got to recognize that people don't pay attention to advertising. They only pay attention to what catches their interest — and *sometimes* it's advertising. Your assignment: Get them to take notice, and *be sure it is your competitive advantage that they are noticing!* Capture their interest with a headline, a photo, or a combination of the two. They'll also probably be interested in a unique offer, a special benefit, a startling visual presentation.

Step Five: Tell Them Exactly What to Do Next

A lot of advertising focuses on the inner amazement, stresses a competitive edge, is presented believably, even commands the attention of the reader or viewer. Then what? Then it just sits there and dies. The readers and viewers move on with their lives. Guerrilla advertising always specifies exactly what people must do next: Make a phone call, visit a store, clip a coupon, look for a package at their supermarket, *something* that advances the sale. Most people just won't take the time to figure out what they're supposed to do next, and if given the chance not to buy, they won't. So don't give them this chance. Lead them by the hand — or the mind — to the next step in purchasing.

*   *   *

Measure all advertising that is scheduled to be produced against these five steps. Does it feature the inner amazement? Is a clear competitive advantage communicated, one that promises a meaningful benefit? Would the world's harshest skeptic believe what you are saying? Will newspaper and magazine browsers, along with their brethren, TV muters and channel surfers, pay any attention to your ad or commercial? If they do pay attention, will they know just what step they must take next?

Will channel surfers pay attention?

These are tough questions to answer affirmatively, obviously far too tough for most advertisers to do so. That's why they're different from guerrillas. That's why over half of them will fail in business within five years. But guerrillas will not only survive, they will prosper.

The reason will be because they took the time, expended the energy, and taxed their imaginations enough to give the right answers to all those hard questions. They knew what it took to be creative — five steps — and they took all five. Most likely, winning advertising ideas popped into their heads not long after the fifth step. They may have solicited aid from their ultra-powerful ally — their unconscious, using the technique I described earlier.

Creative advertising is the result of proper homework up front, five steps in the middle, and unconscious stimulation at the end. It assigns the proper role to creativity in the advertising process and provides five steps to being creative. If it takes any inspiration, that's because *inspiration* is the word people use when the entire process is completed and truly creative advertising is the result. They may think that it's inspiration. You and the guerrillas of the world know better.

It takes inspiration — NOT

11

Knowing and Outthinking Your Competitors

All too many advertisers are so wrapped up in the development of their advertising that they create ads and commercials in their own private worlds, concentrating only on the glorious creation of their identity in the media sun, oblivious to all competitors. They must realize that other businesses are vying for the same audience. Vying very hard.

What's your competition up to? What is the competition saying? Where are they saying it? How often do they put out the word? How much are they spending? Is their advertising working? What is their advertising strategy? What other weapons of marketing are they using? These are questions the guerrilla must ask and answer in order to advertise and succeed in the real world, where all the buying decisions take place.

The guerrilla strives to be proactive by taking charge, defining and enlarging the market, making powerful offers, and causing the competition to react. This attitude is tempered by a sensitivity that enables the advertising to change in order to react to a competitive thrust. Often the change is simply a matter of timing — running extra advertising in a particular market — rather than a creative overhaul. Your own advertising strategy will empower you to exercise the proactive stance you will require. Your knowledge of all competitive marketing will allow you to make the correct adjustments as the need may arise — and you should be prepared for it to arise.

If you go about things in the right way with your advertising, *you can expect to be copied.* This going-in information will allow you to react with intelligence, or even use the competitive advertising to bolster yours. In the sixties, when all the American automakers were spending a fortune boasting about the large size of their cars, the famous Volkswagen bug burst upon the scene, its ads asking Americans to "Think small." The advertising ignited both an advertising and an automotive revolution. Everyone who copied Volkswagen tacitly agreed that VW had the right idea.

The process of outthinking your competitors takes place at the beginning of the creative process, and is incorporated into your creative act. In order for you to outthink the competition, be intimate with their marketing strategies. You can't go against the grain if you don't know the grain. **Be intimate**

Now the meaning becomes clear. Into the river of data supplying the fountain of creativity flows a feeder stream comprised solely of competitive intelligence. It contains their plans, their goals, their budgets, their media, their identities, their strengths, their weaknesses, their position in the spectrum of marketing firepower.

Such information was once reserved for the big ad agencies and the big spenders. But the rules have changed and now the tiny and new businesses can employ the advanced weaponry that formerly was found only in the arsenals of the juggernauts. The feeder stream is now open to all.

Guerrillas tap into this spring by means of computer databases, media-buying services (most are wizards at this task), and advertising directories found at business libraries. Most of what you need to know has already been committed to disk or print and is readily available if you know where to look.

I'd start with a media-buying service, as you already know. **Where to start** They know exactly where to look and have a host of current directories in their existing libraries. So as to perform the advertising function as effectively as possible, the guerrilla taps the technologies and talents of others rather than risking an entire advertising investment in the quest to save a few bucks by doing all research in-house.

Once you know what your competitors are up to you can craft your plans to win their prospects, not to mention their existing customers. If they offer free delivery, you offer pickup and delivery. If they offer free gift wrapping, you offer a variety of free gift-wrapping papers along with a handsome gift card. If they have an early bird special from 4:00 P.M. to 6:00 P.M., extend your early bird hours from 4:00 P.M. to 7:00 P.M.

Outthinking your competitors requires an ability to see into the future, especially when it concerns your industry. What will your prospects need? What can you do now to position yourself for the sale later? You've got to keep abreast of the present if you want to glide smoothly into the future. To a guerrilla advertiser, that means studying your industry publications like crazy, being on the alert for new trends, while monitoring the media that reach your prospects, looking for signs of competitors, hoping that none are guerrillas and know the true secret of creativity.

A tactic guerrillas practice in their penchant for out-advertising their competition — not with financial power, but with idea power — is to study an ad, commercial, or letter created by the competition and draft an advertising strategy for it. This gives them a clear view of the competitive strategy and allows them to adjust their own to take advantage of this new-found intelligence.

Thwarting copycats   When your competitors copy you, as they should if your campaign is any good, you have three courses of action:

1. Ignore them completely, taking heart in the realization that many of their prospects *know* they are copying you and will therefore gain respect for you.
2. React with a small alteration in your ads. If a competitor heralds a price that beats yours, place more stress on your value and show how it is more important than price.
3. Take on the competitors head-to-head, obliterating them with comparisons, specific facts, testimonials, and advertising that highlights the competition publicly.

It is best to pursue course of action number one because few competitors will remain with a copycat strategy — unless it works like gangbusters. If that is the case, take course number two so as not to demean yourself by talking about your competition. Only if you are being demolished on the bottom line should you revert to course number three. Spending your money to advertise your competition's name is rarely a wise investment. Even if you are whipping them in the benefits department, you are generating awareness of them as a company. Better to let them do that with their money, not yours.

Outthinking your competitors is often merely an act of patience, as is true of so much of advertising. Let them prove their inconsistency, changing around their message and look, while you maintain your creative direction and earn the confidence of your prospects.

The entire creative process must be subjected to the penetrating illumination of a competitive marketplace, one that does not allow for shortsightedness, narcissism, or smugness. That marketplace is peopled by businessmen and women who want your prospects to buy from them, your customers to switch over to them, and everybody to believe that you are inferior to them.

Guerrilla advertisers, armed with this knowledge at the start, are able to be relatively competition-proof by:

How to be competition-proof

- Being difficult to copy
- Promoting value over price
- Consistently maintaining their identity
- Allowing for flexibility
- Knowing what to change if copied

Because your competitors weren't born last night, they're going to feel the pain of competing with you, and they're going to make changes when the going gets tough. They'll attack you and try like the dickens to woo your prospects.

This is why you must be constantly aware of them. This book will help you in the long run, as you make long-term plans, but for next month, reading the latest edition of your industry's main publication or the most popular magazine among your prospects may prove more helpful. They will clue you in on what is happening in your industry and in the lives of your prospects *right now.* The job of this book is to get you to read those publications and to keep up with the competition at all times. Only in that way can you keep ahead.

In every battle there are winners and losers. In advertising, you get to select at the beginning which group you wish to join.

12

Keeping Your Eye
on the Cutting Edge

Guerrillas must be aware of the moment as well as the past and the future. Not easy, to be sure, but necessary. It is estimated that the average college graduate is better informed than the average fifty-year-old. This is because the fifty-year-old ceased his or her education twenty-five or thirty years ago, keeping up with new knowledge only by reading selected books and periodicals.

The cream of this knowledge is funneled into the education system and continually spoonfed to students until they graduate and must work like mad to prevent themselves from falling behind in the knowledge department.

If you wanted information about the latest computer technology, MTV programming, fashions, or movies, would you ask a fifteen-year-old or a fifty-year-old? Marketers and advertisers know that youth is the market of tomorrow. This is the group that is setting trends, disseminating information, that is mobile and computer literate. Does this mean you forget the over-fifty crowd? You dare not do so because they are growing even faster than the youth market and they have a whale of a lot more money than the youngsters. They also have more experience buying and responding to advertising. But they are not as well-informed about goings-on in today's world. This is especially true of the new cultural scene and new technologies.

The market of tomorrow

While 92 percent of teenagers are comfortable using a variety of technical devices, only 74 percent of adults say they are, too. A whopping 32 percent of adults say they are intimidated by computers and worried they might damage one if they used it. Of that group, 22 percent were unable to set a digital alarm clock.

The minimum daily requirements for a guerrilla to keep up with current trends, not to mention trends for the future, are seven in number:

1. Watch a TV news show or listen to a radio news show every day; a TV magazine show doesn't hurt either.
2. Read at least one daily newspaper from your own metropolitan area. Maybe you can read a national newspaper, too. *The Wall Street Journal* comes to mind, but *USA Today* also qualifies.
3. Read at least one community newspaper so that you can keep your finger on the pulse of your own community, business or personal.
4. Read at least one weekly news magazine. I'm thinking of *Time, Newsweek,* or *U.S. News and World Report.* They present the highlights of the week's news, all distilled for you.
5. Read at least one, and preferably two or three, publications in your industry. Keep up with what others are doing, wherever they are. Don't let any brilliant innovations pass you by.
6. Read at least one advertising publication. Although *Advertising Age* has been around for ages and continues to be valuable, I prefer *Adweek* for its news and its service directories. Subscribe by calling 1-800-722-6658.
7. Read the publications, watch the TV shows, or listen to the radio stations that your prospects read, watch, or hear. Ideally, you will be advertising in these media and this makes you aware of the advertising environment.

It's also a good idea to read the best of the nonfiction books that deal with the future. Each year, there are new ones. Most seem to be right on target — ten years ahead of time. *Future Shock, Megatrends,* and *The Popcorn Report* come to mind. More will come to your bookstore.

Unless you keep an eagle eye on the cutting edge, you will be left in the dust by a hungry individual who uses her new-found knowledge to create more cogent advertising than you, utilize more targeted media than you, employ better special effects than you, obtain a higher response rate to ads than you, and who does it all while spending considerably less advertising money than you.

As I write this, the cost to run a thirty-second *prime-time* TV commercial in virtually any major market in the United States is around $20. Five years ago that cost was closer to $200 and perhaps even $2,000. Last week, when I gave a talk to a chamber of commerce attended by about 600 people (I'm withholding the name of the chamber so as to prevent any embarrassment), I asked for a show of hands of the people who knew TV costs have dropped to around twenty bucks. Six hands went up! Six hands out of 600 bright, informed, eager-to-learn people. Obviously, 594 of those people were unaware of the cutting edge. Obviously, many guerrillas are able to make substantial profits when they utilize important information that their competition has neglected to even learn.

The $20 cost for a prime-time commercial is actually *higher* than the average cost. This is because of the impact of cable television, which lets small advertisers run their spots to cable subscribers in selected *neighborhoods*, eliminating the cost of waste viewership, those viewers who live outside your marketing area. That $20 cost is also the reason that the TV networks lost over $600 million in 1992. That money wasn't really *lost*. Instead, it was *found* by cable companies.

Staying on top of the information flow allows you to use new media, new psychology findings, new economic realities, and new advertising techniques. By knowing what is happening at the forefront, you can maintain a position of leadership with a head start over your competitors that I'd reckon to be about one or two *years*.

I do not endorse using all cutting-edge technologies and findings. I well realize that pioneers lead precarious lives and that most of your prospects are scared to death of anything that

Left in the dust by a guerrilla

A two-year head start

smacks of the avant-garde. But I know it is crucial for you to be aware of all your options and, yes, even to be a pioneer in using some of them. Just don't get carried away.

Attending trade shows in your industry — and in the advertising industry — makes you privy to what is new, what is different, and what is coming up on the horizon. These forums are also ideal for cutting-edge workshops. Often, all it takes is one breakthrough thought to make a company's profits shoot up.

An urgent-care center in California did its own survey and learned that of all medical considerations connected with an urgent-care center, the most important — by far — was *waiting or not waiting* to see a doctor. This little insight, gleaned from an inexpensive customer survey, enabled the urgent-care center to advertise, "If you wait more than 20 minutes to see a doctor, your office visit will be free." Patient count skyrocketed as a result.

The data superhighway

As you read this, new advancements are taking place weekly in the media, in consumer understanding, in interactive technology, in the data superhighway that is already groaning under the load of new rush-hour traffic. The guerrilla considers it part of the job to know about these advancements — not necessarily to use them, but to be on the lookout for their efficacy, to ascertain whether or not the competition is using them, and to dig deeper and learn more about them.

Many articles in *Psychology Today* and shows on the Public Broadcasting System contain information about people and technologies that can lead to increased sales when analyzed by a guerrilla advertiser.

The whole idea is to remain committed to a position of leadership. If consistent profits may be attained or maintained by using the brand-new media and technologies, then the media or technology may be embraced. But don't use them unless they can propel you squarely in the direction of your primary goal — profitability.

Some advertisers rush to use new things in their advertising just for the sake of the novelty, for the feeling of power that comes with pushing buttons on a $500,000 TV special-effects doohickey. These are not valid reasons to wander out onto the cutting edge.

Your attitude should be characterized by a readiness to use new advertising weaponry, an awareness of all your options, and a desire to achieve your goals in the most effective manner possible. The most efficient does not always mean the most effective. Efficiency deals with speed and convenience; effectiveness pertains to profits.

Remember — and you read it here first — that every week you're in business something dynamite will come down the pike that can boost your profits, something that has escaped the notice of your competition. Only if you are aware that this happens will you be motivated to keep up with the speed of change and improvement in advertising.

Something dynamite's coming down the pike

I used to select the areas at which I ski because of the ads they ran in the skiing magazines and, naturally, by word of mouth. But I learned about Big Sky, Montana, in a different way. Sure, I saw their ad in the skiing magazines. Then I learned more about them by attending a special ski event they staged near where I live, by studying their video brochure, by reading their full-color printed brochure, by poring over the lift and trail maps they sent me, by receiving direct mail letters and postcards from them, and by hearing from them by phone — offering me a special deal because I'm a past customer. I've put the Big Sky, Montana, poster up in my house because it's great looking and because they sent it to me as a gift. Has it convinced several of my friends to plan ski holidays at Big Sky? It has. Does it help that I see Big Sky, Montana, featured in films and in TV specials? You bet it does.

I've done extensive advertising work for *Fortune* 500 companies, but I'm still mightily impressed by the Big Sky marketing department. Members of that department go out to speak to groups, use multiple audio-visual aids, and engage in a great deal of face-to-face, one-on-one marketing that is based upon pure research. Big Sky learned that skiers hate to wait in lift lines, so they've tailored their advertising message to emphasize the absence of lift lines at Big Sky. In fact, the whole resort was reengineered to help Big Sky live up to that prom-

Big Sky guerrillas

ise. Big Sky is certainly not a big spender. But it is without question a big success because its marketing department is focused on the cutting edge. I may meet you there on a chair lift, perhaps even in a gondola. But on a lift line? Never.

The guerrilla mindset: Most changes are *in your favor* and deserve advance scrutiny. This mindset enlists the cutting edge as an important ally in the advertising battles. Even with this attitude, you will not act upon all the changes. But none that can help your cause will escape your notice. For that reason, guerrillas always pay attention to the cutting edge.

13

Creating Advertising with Longevity

Among the most difficult assignments in advertising is the creation of a campaign that can be used for years, decades, even centuries. The rewards for developing a campaign with durability are:

- *Your advertising has a chance to work.* A lot of potentially great advertising never has the chance to strut its stuff because it is abandoned before it has a chance to take hold in the minds of prospects. If durability is a going-in goal, you'll stick with yours. **Give it a chance**
- *Your advertising gains strength as time passes.* Because people continue to see your message, they absorb it and integrate it in their unconscious mind, where purchase decisions are made. Eventually, your advertising becomes like a good friend. Isn't the Green Giant your friend?
- *Your advertising assures brand-name awareness.* The *Harvard Business Review* cautions businesses that if they do not develop an awareness of their name as a brand name, their chances for survival are sparse. Staying with one campaign emblazons your name, your offering, and your benefits in the minds of your prospects.
- *Your advertising falls in step with your strategy.* If the starting point for your new advertising is your past advertising, you are assured of getting off on the right foot by creating advertising that fulfills your strategy and does not wander off into tempting, but irrelevant tangents.

- *Your new advertising builds on your past advertising.* Many prospects who see your current advertising will be reminded of your past advertising, adding fuel to fire up the purchase decision. One, two, or three exposures may not do the trick. Fifteen or twenty exposures probably will.
- *Your advertising consistency nurtures confidence.* If you change your advertising campaign, it indicates that you feel you weren't doing the best job the first time around, undermining confidence in your company. By sticking to your advertising guns, you prove your reliability.
- *Your advertising patience saves money for you.* By far, the greatest amount of money wasted in advertising is that spent creating new campaigns. Money goes down the drain because (1) Advertisers are walking away from their initial investment too quickly, and (2) Unnecessary new advertising production costs are incurred.
- *Your advertising thwarts copycats.* Once you have staked out an advertising territory as your own, any copycatting by competitors or even noncompetitors will serve to remind prospects of your advertising, much to the detriment of the copycats, much to your enjoyment.
- *Your advertising can be used in any media.* Having created a campaign that is well-known to your prospects, you can gain even more prospects by running the campaign in media selected to enlarge your market. Your prior advertising adds a recognition factor so your magazine campaign easily translates to radio, your TV to newspaper.
- *Your advertising lends itself to merchandising.* The campaign stance you have taken can be carried from the advertising environment and right into the selling environment in the form of point-of-purchase signs, sales aids, promotion ideas, the full gamut of marketing weapons.

*   *   *

Now that you're convinced of the merits of longevity in advertising, what must you do to attain it without boring your prospects and customers?

Create your initial advertising with the concept of longevity in the front of your mind. This means you've got to allow for flexibility. While you will stay with your identity, theme line, visual format, and your primary media, you will be changing your headlines, photos or illustrations, case histories, offers, prices. You must be able to make those changes without changing your overall advertising campaign. **Flexibility is your ally**

Be sure everything in your campaign will wear well over time and not become tiresome, grating, or old-fashioned. When you prepare the first ad or commercial, have the second ad or commercial in mind, even the third. Have the advertising for next year in mind as well. Think in terms of the next decade, too.

As I've provided you with ten reasons to create advertising with longevity, let me inspire you with twenty advertising campaigns that have propelled their products into profitability over a long span of time and are still going strong. The first ten have stood the test of time; the second ten are still in the process of proving their durability:

1. The valley of the jolly — ho! ho! ho! — Green Giant
2. Come to where the flavor is — Marlboro
3. Fly the friendly skies — United
4. When you care enough to send the very best — Hallmark
5. You're in good hands — Allstate
6. I wish I were an Oscar Meyer weiner — Oscar Meyer
7. The loneliest repairman in town — Maytag
8. Sorry, Charlie, you're not good enough — Starkist
9. Snap, crackle, and pop — Rice Krispies
10. Be all that you can be — U.S. Army
11. Don't leave home without it — American Express
12. Just do it — Nike
13. I want my MTV! — MTV
14. I'm going to Disneyland! — Disneyland
15. Reach out and touch someone — AT & T
16. The Clydesdale horses — Budweiser
17. The lion — The Dreyfus Fund
18. The bull — Merrill Lynch

The longevity Hall of Fame

19. We do chicken right — KFC
20. We're a part of your life — Macy's

None of these campaigns seems old-fashioned, yet several of the first ten are from the thirties, a few from the forties and fifties, and just a couple from as recent as the sixties. The second ten were born in the seventies; some came to life in the eighties. But all twenty are doing just fine in the nineties. The campaigns are as fresh today as they were decades ago when they were created. And don't think that they were created for gigantic companies. Most were created for small companies that became gigantic. A consistent advertising theme certainly gets some of the credit for their growth.

Two benefits of "legs"   Advertising that can have this kind of "legs" is advertising that pays off in two ways — by working on its own and by eliminating the need to create new campaigns. Unfortunately, a great deal of advertising with potential longevity is deprived of entrance to the hall of fame because of an impatient attitude on the part of the advertising director and a ridiculous notion that advertising is supposed to change regularly. Guerrillas know that just the opposite is true.

The advertising graveyards are filled with marvelous campaigns that were tossed aside, many just at the threshold of greatness — just as they were beginning to take hold. Those same graveyards hold the remnants of advertising that never had a chance for longevity because its cornerstone was a joke that soon became tired, a visual or theme line that was too trendy to become classic, a spokesperson who fell from grace.

It is also true that the graveyards hold advertising that ran its course in less time than a decade because the advertiser, probably a *Fortune* 500 firm, spent as much in three years as most companies would spend in three hundred years. McDonald's "You deserve a break today" comes to mind. So does Coke's "Coke is it" and Pepsi's "You're in the Pepsi generation," not to mention 7Up's "The uncola" — which met with great success at the outset, then petered out, but now is resurrected. I know that Hamm's beer has been trying for years to improve upon their "Land of sky blue waters," but just can't seem to do it, try as they may.

Now that you have wrapped your mind around the idea of longevity being a major ally for your advertising, all of your future advertising will work better, and you'll recognize your task as improving it and moving about within its boundaries, rather than changing it and heading away from your original premise.

The problem with most advertising isn't so much that it is poorly planned or even poorly executed, but that it is expected to work wonders in a hurry, and if it doesn't, it is discarded. It becomes advertising litter. Guerrillas aren't in a rush to discard theirs because they created it with the idea of never discarding it, only improving it, expanding it, and adapting it to changes in the marketplace.

No littering, please

Your prospects, if not yet customers, won't be bored with your advertising. Your customers will appreciate your steadfastness as they justify the fact that they purchased your product or service in the first place.

Who will become bored? Maybe you will. Most likely, your employees will. Almost certainly, your co-workers will. And it's a good bet your friends and family will also become bored with your advertising campaign. But these are not your prospects or your customers. This "internal boredom" is one of the reasons so much fine advertising gets left by the wayside, often to be replaced by advertising that is clearly inferior.

Don't let this happen to you. Think of your advertising as a living, breathing organic entity that needs time and care to grow, flourish, take wing and fly. What a crying shame to nip it in the bud and deprive it — and your company — of the powerful and multiple benefits of longevity.

III

Maximum Profits from Advertising and Promotions

THERE IS NO WAY you could have read this far without knowing deep in your bones that the whole purpose of advertising is to energize the process by which you earn profits.

Those profits, an elusive figure because profits are whatever the business owner defines them as, come not only from effective advertising that is focused, creative, and capable of a long and healthy life, but also from spending the right amount of money without overspending and defacing your bottom line.

Many advertisers, in the righteous effort to cut their costs, also cut their quality. This is not necessary. Others feel left out of the advertising scene because they believe they can't spend enough to be noticed. The truth is that they don't have to spend all that much to be noticed by their prospects; they just have to spend *enough* in the right way — and that does not automatically mean a lot.

Throughout the world, advertisers miss out on potential profits because they are operating in their own world, which differs quite a bit from the real world. Or they are living in the past, which differs considerably from the present. It could be that they are employing advertising techniques that worked wonders during boom years, but now that a recession is upon the land, their techniques are inadequate.

A primary cause of lost profits is expectations that are too high for mere advertising, expectations that could be met, even exceeded, if the advertising were wed to promotions — a marketing weapon that can add new verve to advertising.

In the beginning of this book, I warned you that advertising all by itself usually can't do the selling job. It greases the wheels of the other guerrilla marketing weaponry, empowering all of your marketing, but is usually too limited to handle the whole sale, start to finish.

This is where sales promotions shine. They can use advertising as a springboard to glowing profits and can appear in the form of coupons, sales, freebies with purchase, incentives for larger purchases, contests, special events, and a galaxy of fusion marketing opportunities. If you are serious about maximizing your profits, you will take the whole idea of special promotions seriously and incorporate them regularly into your normal advertising.

When you plan your advertising — that's just when you should also be planning your promotions. That's when you'll see if your advertising lends itself to promotions, and if not, you'll be able to make the changes so that you have advertising that is promotion-compatible.

With the tremendous influx of self-service, superstores, hypermarkets, shopping malls, and discount houses larger than Rhode Island, merchandising and promotions are more important than at any other time in history.

Shoppers are more motivated than ever to take advantage of special deals and "value-added" offers that provide the product plus something of value — such as a discount, an extra package, a premium gift. They are more persuaded to purchase by point-of-sale signs, position of the product in the stores, clearance sales, any chances to save money.

Gone are the days when a clerk would recommend your product. Instead, that clerk is gone, replaced by a bar code and computerized scanner. Your product has to recommend itself with your own packaging, your own signs, your own sizzle.

The idea is to wring the last penny's worth out of your advertising investment by means of promotions and active merchandising. In many cases, much to the surprise of the advertiser, promotions result in higher profits than the advertising itself. Don't be shocked when this happens to you. Guerrillas are used to it.

They not only merchandise their offerings, *they merchandise their advertising.* This is the key to maximum advertising mileage — merchandising your advertising to your sales force, distributors, retailers, the media. More guerrilla insights for optimizing advertising begin on the next page.

14

Knowing How Much to Invest

There are numerous formulas for determining how much of your hard-earned revenues go into advertising. The guerrilla budget strategy is based upon investing a percentage of your projected gross sales — not your past sales, because no guerrilla is satisfied with the status quo — so that you can operate in a growth mode.

Typically, the average American business owner invests about 4 percent of gross revenues in marketing each year — and most of that is for *advertising*. The guerrilla, because she is aggressive and realistic, thinks more in terms of investing around 10 percent in *marketing*, and about half of that for mass media *advertising*. Some companies, especially cosmetics firms, invest up to 33 percent in advertising — because their image is the most important thing they've got to offer. A few publishing companies pony up 50 percent of gross sales. Home-based businesses with limited overhead and zero inventory may match that percentage. But all businesses, home or otherwise, have the need to channel their marketing funds in other than advertising.

How much do others invest?

Those marketing funds are channeled into weaponry such as direct mail, telemarketing, brochures, sales videos, a catalogue, a newsletter, infomercials, and research, just a partial list of weapons that give strength to advertising, which is the recipient of approximately 5 percent of anticipated gross revenues. That advertising will work better because of the other weapons, and they'll be more effective because of the advertising. Don't ever let me catch you investing *all* of your market-

Don't put it all into advertising

ing budget in advertising and none in the other weapons of guerrilla marketing.

A sensibly aggressive guerrilla with a three-year-old suburban bookstore, Book Universe, that grosses $2 million annually, might allocate $200,000 of that to marketing.

How a bookstore might invest

The owner of Book Universe would set aside 10 percent of the $200,000, a full $20,000, for the production of her marketing materials — her ads, TV spots, catalogues, and direct mail postcards. That leaves her with $180,000 to last a year. Because she already invested in the time of an expensive marketing consultant before she even opened her doors, she doesn't have to spend that money again. Her whole investment can go for marketing.

Half of that, $90,000, will go to advertising, costing $7,500 monthly for the year. The other $90,000 will go for other marketing materials, amortized at the same $7,500 for a year. The Book Universe $180,000 total marketing budget will be invested like this:

Advertising Media	Monthly Cost	Percent of Investment
Major newspaper	$2,200	
Local newspaper A	800	50
Local newspaper B	750	
City magazine	750	10
Cable TV	3,000	40
TOTAL ADVERTISING	$7,500	

Other Marketing	Amortized Monthly Cost	Percent of Investment
Catalogue	$5,000	66
Direct mail postcards	1,000	13
Twice-weekly events	800	11
Yellow pages	375	5
Customer gifts	375	5
OTHER MARKETING	$7,550	

When you do begin to invest in advertising, and let me remind you one more time that you *do that last* — after the other weapons are loaded and aimed — be prepared to burn into your mind these three important codes by which you must live:

1. Think of your advertising investment as *rent*, something **Codes to live by** you spend every month automatically because you have to, not something you can decide whether or not to invest in a given month. Your advertising is part of your monthly overhead, or you're deluding yourself about being a guerrilla.

2. Understand that your primary investment in advertising will be *at the very beginning*. The small ads and limited impact that can sustain you once you are established and have the benefit of repeat and referral business will not make many waves at the outset. So you've got to be prepared to spend big right off the bat so you can start obtaining the share of mind you'll need. You might even spend *twice* as much the first year as you will the second — but only if you're a pure-blooded guerrilla advertiser who wishes to make failure an impossibility. A big customer base is a glorious security blanket. The sooner you get it, the better.

3. Be prepared *to change your advertising budget* for the second year because of what you learned the first year. You'll probably eliminate some of the media you've been using because your tracking efforts proved that it wasn't pulling its weight. Most likely, you'll lean more heavily on other media because your tracking proved their worth. Maybe you'll be able to reduce your budget, not only because the first year is over and your awareness is high, but because you are gaining enough referrals and repeat sales to earn profits with less advertising. On the other hand, you might decide to increase your advertising budget because you're attracted by the idea of expanding or selling franchises. The first year is a year for profiting and for learning, with the accent on learning. Consider it a business venture *and* an experiment.

Frequently, you'll be able to maintain your growth and increase your profits during the second year by investing approximately the same dollar amount in advertising as you did the first year — taking comfort in the fact that the dollar amount, once 10 percent of projected gross revenues, now represents only 7 percent of your projected gross revenues because of your growth. The following year, if you go about things properly, it will represent only 5 percent of your projected gross. But if I know you, you're interested in growing even faster, so you'll increase your investment because you know what works and where it works best.

Earning more without spending more

Such is the nature of guerrilla advertising. It enables you to grow without necessarily increasing your advertising expenses. If you wish to expand, be sure to eliminate any mistakes that exist anywhere in your company or else your mistakes will expand as your company expands. Ugly thought. Be careful, there are guerrillas out there.

Is it ever possible to achieve a stage during which you require absolutely no advertising? Oh man, do I dislike telling you this, but it is possible, not to mention desirable, and also very rare.

A client of mine, another bookstore called The Booksmith on Haight Street in San Francisco, once called with that same question, telling me that the advertising we had created three years earlier brought him so many repeat customers that he felt he could discontinue advertising and exist solely from his current customer base. What did I think?

Going against my grain and my training and grimacing as I spoke, I told him to give it a try. It worked. While he once spent $18,000 a year advertising in four small newspapers, plus another $2,000 doing direct mail to prospects, he now spends nearly zero for advertising and that same $2,000 for direct mail of new books and tapes in stock — not to prospects, but to customers. He does hardly any advertising. And there is no doubt that his bookstore is becoming more popular each year.

Too dangerous to try

If you remember anything from this tale, remember that it is unique and probably too dangerous to try. Should you decide to eliminate your advertising budget, recognize that the only people happier than you will be your competitors. Quoting myself from an earlier chapter, "Stopping advertising to save money is like stopping your wristwatch to save time."

Most guerrillas determine their advertising budgets on the percent-of-projected-revenues basis. But before engraving their budget into stone, they take into consideration:

- The current economy
- The media they'll be using
- The competition
- The industry
- The nature of their offering
- Their short- and long-term goals

Unfortunately, most American businesses never really establish an advertising budget. After other expenses are covered, they spend whatever they have left over on advertising. Bad idea. Other companies automatically spend exactly what they spent the year before, whether or not their advertising worked.

The guerrilla remembers that although the average marketing investment is 4 percent, the average American business fails within five years and no self-respecting entrepreneur bases his decisions upon the behavior of the average business owner. I tell you the average as a guide, even as an inspiration to invest more, but not as a rule to follow.

Since 1972, Snapple was a tiny company in Queens, New York, marketing all-natural sodas, waters, and juices. In the late 1980s, it introduced an iced tea in a wide-mouthed bottle. This alone would have kept Snapple tiny. But Leonard Marsh, Hyman Golden, and Arnold Greenberg, owners of Snapple, decided to take the plunge into mass media — not only investing heavily in radio, but also investing big bucks in two usually controversial radio personalities named Rush Limbaugh and Howard Stern. The company had zero sales in 1972. It had $203 million in sales in 1992.

A juicy Snapple story

Did it all happen because of the name, the drinks themselves, the wide-mouthed bottle, or the advertising? We both know that it was the combination of these factors. And media insiders know that Snapple invested a cool $30 million in national advertising in 1993. Kirshenbaum & Bond, an advertising agency in New York, is masterminding the Snapple ad campaign. Are they the next Leo Burnetts? Can't say for sure yet, but they're sure off to the kind of start that would impress Mr. Burnett.

15

Staying Within Any Budget

Although it is dandy to stay within your budget, it is not mandatory for health and success. Your budget should be flexible enough to allow for the need to spend more to do battle with a particular competitor or the luxury to spend less because of an influx of business.

Once, I consulted to a business that made its debut with full-page newspaper ads. Once a week, for four weeks, huge ads ran in two big-city newspapers. I was delighted, indeed, to hear that the showrooms were packed and that customers were being sold in droves. It was music to an advertising guy's ears. Then I visited one of the showrooms and during a two-hour stay witnessed three phone calls and one in-person visit from customers canceling their orders because the deliveries were taking too long. Fingernails on the blackboard to an advertising guy's ears.

By all means, cut back your advertising if you are not able to keep your promises, if you will be late with your deliveries, if you risk losing *just one customer*. Reduce that budget immediately. Don't shilly-shally about waiting and hoping that customers won't be alienated. We're talking about your future — and satisfied customers are an integral part of it. Dissatisfied customers can cast a dark pall upon it.

Thou shalt not alienate

But increasing your budget to deal with new circumstances, or decreasing it for sane reasons, are going to be rare occasions in your advertising life. Instead, the idea is to maintain your budget while at the same time making it work harder because you:

- Eliminated wasteful media
- Used more of your proven media
- Improved your creative message
- Gained from the synergy of your other marketing weapons
- Established a trusted brand name

The true guerrilla is able to stay within a budget while improving the return on the advertising investment on a consistent basis. That is the way it is supposed to work, can work, and has worked. Although you may not achieve any results whatsoever from the first three months of your advertising, fear not. Within the next three, you will begin to see signs that your advertising is working. Yes, you will have clear indications that your other marketing is working as well, but I'm talking solely about your *advertising*. You'll no longer feel that it is an act of faith, which is what it often feels like. You'll know for a solid fact that it is generating profits — or attaining whatever goal you set for it.

Getting better all the time

Within those first six months, you should see that it is paying its own way, and each month after that — for the rest of the time you are in business — *it should work better than the month before*. If you are in a seasonal business and, for example, operate a ski area, each month should be better than that same month the previous year — all previous years in fact.

Resist the temptation to fiddle with your budget. Strive instead to keep it just as you planned and to get more out of it every month. Don't forget, we're talking about your rent. You wouldn't skip a month because sales are down, and you wouldn't increase it because sales are up. You'd pay it and go about the task of enjoying your life, accomplished partially because you are achieving success in business.

To stay within your budget, large or small, you must resist the talented media salespeople who urge you to invest in their media, often with good reason. Tell them you'll consider using their media next year because you are committed to the media you have selected for this year. Does this make you a hard-headed business owner who doesn't listen to reason? Not at all. It makes you a hard-headed business owner who does listen to reason but doesn't act impulsively, a valuable asset to any guerrilla.

Staying within your budget often means turning to other weapons of marketing if your competitors are outspending you in the mass media arena, as many of them often can. It means closing more sales, relying more upon existing customers, gaining the maximum amount of repeat business, obtaining the most possible referral business, and increasing the size of your transactions.

Rarely have I encountered a client who was happy for having increased or decreased their budget. But I have fond memories of clients who were grinning widely for having maintained their budget while increasing their sales. I know that took discipline, energy, imagination.

The more you realize that advertising is only 1 percent of the marketing weapons available to you, the easier it will be to stay within your advertising budget. But if you place too much reliance upon advertising, it will be difficult to keep to that budget when competitive or economic pressure is on. **It's only 1 percent**

By the same token, if you want to redecorate or add new equipment, don't use money that was allocated to advertising. What if dismal sales force you to lower your overhead? As I previously counseled you to do your advertising last, I now counsel you to *cut your advertising last.* **Do it last and cut it last**

If you abandon your advertising, people will soon forget it and your prior investment will have been wasted. If you move it to more inexpensive media, the same applies — your previous investment in the original media will have been wasted. The only time to switch media is if your original media, as proven by your careful tracking, has shown itself to be wasteful. Switch for reasons of ineffectiveness, not inexpensiveness.

Forever keep in mind that frequency in advertising will be one of your best allies. If you reach 10,000 of your target audience ten times instead of reaching 100,000 of your target audience one time, your advertising will be far more productive and you will earn considerably higher profits than with the one-time-shot approach. Don't undermine your all-important frequency by cutting your ad budget just because times are tough. Times will always be tough — and beautiful. Your advertising budget should reflect this reality of business and should not be characterized by the capriciousness of a follower. You want to be a leader.

Increasing your frequency but not your budget

You can increase your frequency, but not your budget, by running several commercials on the same TV or radio program. You can also gain frequency by making sure your radio commercial runs at the same time each weekday, assuring that you'll probably be reaching the same people every time, dramatically increasing their motivation to be customers. One great commercial aimed at zillions of people one time would probably not motivate as many to buy as a pretty good commercial aimed at thousands of people ten times.

The most powerful impact comes with time, not with size. When Apple Computer ran its famed "1984" commercial on the *Super Bowl*, showing robotic people acting in a robotic manner — thereby making the point that in computer matters you shouldn't act like a robot and should open your mind to the new technology represented by Apple — everyone and their cousin talked about it, but the commercial did not move many computers for Apple.

There is little question that it dramatically increased awareness of the brand and no doubt that it paved the way to future sales. But for aficionados of the fast buck, it was a flop. Today the computer industry knows otherwise.

If you are deadly serious about wanting to increase your sales while staying within your budget, get involved with fusion marketing and ask others to share advertising costs with you. These tie-ins with other advertising-oriented firms will increase your advertising exposure in a major-league way, but will not eat into those precious profits.

One of the greatest stumbling blocks to staying within a budget is the increasing cost of many of the print and some of the electronic media. If you have selected a major newspaper to be your flagship medium and it proves itself to be a winner, what do you do when the newspaper rep announces that rates are going up 15 percent? First of all, you don't fall off your chair, because many newspaper advertising rates are constantly rising, sometimes because the cost of paper and ink **Inflation happens** is also rising. You've got to expect that.

When it happens, your job is to *find a way to stay with that medium*. Never jump from a horse that is winning the race. What you must do is either reduce the size of your ad or pare down some of your other marketing costs. Just as I advised you to use other marketing weapons when your ads don't pull the way you want them to, I also advise you to get rid of some of them when your ads are pulling but the ad rates are going up. Staying within your budget should be a going-in goal.

16

Cutting Costs but Not Quality

To gain high profits through advertising, you have to do two things: *maximize income* and *minimize spending*. If you are advertising aggressively, you are spending money. That is a good thing because it gives you opportunities to *save* money, chances that most advertisers miss.

The cardinal rule in saving money is *not to waste money*. When you commit to one advertising campaign, don't waste money by switching to another. Unless you are prepared to stay with your investment, don't expect it to earn profits. You must stay with your format, your identity, your niche, your theme, and the media in which you are advertising.

It's okay to change your offers, headlines, copy, photos or drawings, and prices. But keep your same advertising personality, theme, and visual format all along. You have an investment in that personality, theme, and format. You have put money in the advertising materials and the media. You've invested in gaining that crucial share of mind that must precede a share of market. People don't just up and walk away from investments, letting their money disappear into nothingness because the investments didn't pay off quickly enough. People don't do that, do they? The answer is that they do, leaving potential profits in their wake.

The most common act of insanity in American business is abandoning advertising prematurely. Investments destined to bear fruit are uprooted. Seeds properly planted never get the chance to bloom. Like our calendar year, the guerrilla advertising process takes us through four seasons. The first is when prospects first notice you. Next is when they start learning about you. Then comes that long season when they keep an eye on you. Harvest time is next, when they buy from you.

Waiting until harvest time is the smartest way to cut your costs. It does not erode your quality one bit because you started with quality before you even started advertising.

To avoid wasting money, don't give one glimmer of thought to spending for advertising *until you've spent for the services of a track setter.* This is a marketing professional, probably a consultant, who knows your business, knows advertising, and knows marketing. He or she will set you on the right track at the outset — when most people get on the wrong track and waste money. More important, this person will help *keep* you on track.

Enter the track setter

This person is your marketing mentor. You find such people in the service directories of advertising trade publications such as *Adweek* and in the yellow pages under "Marketing Consultants." They charge by the hour, and no company can afford to do their marketing without one. I say this because of the vast number of companies that have failed simply because they never knew how to put their marketing on the right track or keep it on the right track. A track setter could have made the difference. The reason I refer to these people as track setters is because anyone listed under "Advertising Counselors" sounds to me like a person who would recommend advertising. What if all you need is direct mail? What if trade shows could do the job for you? Would an advertising counselor be able to help you? Maybe, but I'd opt for a marketing consultant and scour the service directories of *Adweek* and *Advertising Age* to find one. Regard the hourly fee you pay them as you did the fees you paid your lawyer and CPA before you started your business.

What size companies should use track setters? All sizes. The big ones usually have them on the payroll, often several of them. But even the one-person business requires the services of a track setter if the business intends to invest even a dime in marketing, if the business is designed to generate a profit, if the business owner is interested in survival, if the business wants the inside track on success.

You will use the track setter to help with your advertising plan and as a sounding board for ideas in the future. Advertising is far too costly to be left to amateurs, both the creating and the judging of it. If you're not a pro, get a track setter or you are almost guaranteed to run up unnecessary costs.

Can you have too much quality? Is it possible to have too much quality in your advertising? You bet it is. It happens every day, and you can see it on your tube every night. There is no need for some companies to spend $100,000 producing a television commercial when a far more profit-producing one could be produced for $10,000. The power, as you know, comes from the idea more than the production values.

Overspending is as big a mistake as underspending. Next to abandoning an advertising campaign too early, it's the most frequent cause of wasting money. How do you know when you are spending too much?

Your track setter tells you. This person may not be on your payroll — you probably couldn't handle the salary anyhow — but your track setter knows the relationship between advertising and marketing, how advertising lubricates the wheels of all your other marketing vehicles, knows the vampires that suck attention from your primary message, and knows when *not* to abandon an advertising campaign.

Guerrilla cost-cutting tactics Good track setters and serious guerrillas are in tune with a variety of ways to cut costs and not quality:

1. Use a track setter at the outset, a cost-cutting measure and not a cost, as it might appear on the surface.
2. Prepare to stick with a single advertising campaign.
3. Don't invest in unnecessary production style and pizzazz over selling substance; avoid both garishness and amateurishness in your production. Both are tempting traps.
4. Run regular small ads rather than irregular large ads.
5. Create brochures and print ads that will never be dated and/or can be easily and inexpensively updated.

6. Find multiple uses for quality photos and illustrations.
7. In color printing, be patient and wait for gang runs.
8. Use good acting-school students in TV and radio spots.
9. Plan ahead enough to secure media frequency discounts.
10. Negotiate and barter when obtaining TV and radio time.
11. Engage in fusion advertising with partners so you can spread the word more without spending the money more.
12. Be on red-light alert for anything in your advertising that detracts from your main message and wastes your money.
13. Learn about prospects with questionnaires before you advertise. Good data is good economics.
14. Advertise more to your current customers than to new prospects because you have already won their hearts.
15. Constantly measure the effectiveness of your message and your media so that you can eliminate any ineffectiveness. The best way to do this is to ask customers in person, by phone or by mail, where they first heard of you. If they can't remember, give them a list of where you have advertised so they can let you know which of those media captured their fancy.

Some money-saving tactics can backfire, so although I encourage you to save what you can, I urge you to save with caution. For example, if you're advertising on the radio every week, try experimenting with being on three weeks out of every four, "going dark" one week a month. Most people won't notice, and when you do come on again, there will be more freshness to your commercials. This can save you 25 percent of your radio expenditures alone.

Let's say you try this. It works out well. So you take the next step. You ask to be on for one week and off for the next. By alternating the weeks you run, you are never away from your prospects' ears for over a week, and you save a hefty 50 percent of your radio budget. Better yet, if you've been advertising for a year or more, your revenues probably won't drop anywhere near 50 percent. They will drop, to be sure. But not 50 percent. Of course, your bottom line should always be your guide here. If your revenues fall more than your advertising costs, you're cutting rather than increasing your profits. So put back the ads!

Be on the lookout for competitors who, sensing your absence from the radio limelight, have leaped into the light themselves with a saturation schedule of radio commercials. They are trying to win your customers away from you and they are succeeding at their task. But they won't if you find *the perfect balance point* in the frequency of your radio schedule. It might be three weeks out of four or three weeks out of five. You won't know until you experiment. Advertising never just takes care of itself. The delicate balance is just that: delicate. Be tuned in at all times.

Find the perfect balance point

During experiments, be prepared to observe the effects, the warning signs that sales may drop, whether that means tallying phone requests, in-store interest, mail response, even sales rep feedback. There's no point in experimenting with advertising if you're not prepared to measure the results — and measure them early, before you get a disappointing balance sheet. You've got to do this with all the media you employ.

Stay in the public eye. It is usually not well-advised to skip a weekly newspaper ad because that means you'll be out of the public eye for two weeks, and it doesn't take that public a long time to forget. They're very adept at forgetting. So don't give them any help.

Maintain awareness, but adjust the level of advertising down to a point where the economies dictate no more cost cutting. You must seek this perfect balance point on an ongoing basis — because it changes.

Competitors come on the scene, have the gall to advertise in your media, perhaps even mount a frontal attack on you. What to do? Stay cool is what to do. React if you must, but don't overreact.

The guerrilla mindset is one that is constantly scanning for new problems to solve, new markets to reach, new benefits to offer, new alliances to form, and new opportunities to exploit. This outlook in and of itself keeps costs at a minimum, but cost-cutting is never the highest priority. The goal is to gain the best return on an advertising investment.

17

What to Look For
in an Advertising Agency

You may design your business so that you never need the services of an advertising agency. You go this route by setting up an in-house agency, and your company will enjoy the same 15 percent discount on media granted to accredited advertising agencies. But in-house agencies, for all the economy they represent, are falling by the wayside because full-service advertising agencies and media-buying services have the technology not financially sensible for an in-house agency and the talent not ordinarily attracted to an in-house agency. Although having one is, indeed, an economy, this guerrilla considers it a false economy.

Should you have an in-house agency?

Or you could hire a designated guerrilla to handle your advertising — or take on the role of advertising guerrilla yourself — overseeing, masterminding, and activating your advertising by delegating the tasks to people who can bring your dreams to life. But you take the final responsibility for saying when the work is ready and when it is lacking.

The other option: You can hire an advertising agency, one that will handle all of your advertising — and if you are smart — *all of your other marketing as well.* I emphasized those words so that you wouldn't be negligent in this crucial area when teaming up with an ad agency. And teaming up is what it is. You should be prepared to give as much as you get.

Ask for more than advertising services

As a rule, if your ad budget is over $500,000 (and it may be someday), you should seriously consider an ad agency to make your life easier and more risk-free. If your budget is half that, $250,000, you may want to employ a free-lancer or, more likely, several free-lancers.

**What to give
your ad agency**

Give your agency or your free-lancers information, encouragement, feedback, company esoterica, details that might ignite the spark of the copywriters assigned to your account. Always see your task as helping the advertising agency. Usually, companies set up an adversarial relationship, gently and subtly criticizing the agency's ideas and work, stoning it to death with popcorn, as someone with popcorn scars once said.

Your most significant contributions will come in the form of data and judgment. Give data that advertising agencies can be creative about. Use judgment in recognizing just who is the advertising pro and who makes the products or services to be advertised.

Having spent a dozen enjoyable years in advertising agencies, I urge you to not select a big-name agency if you're a small-name company. The bigwigs of the agency will make the presentation that will win your heart — and your business. But the smallwigs will do all the work. Big agencies often assign the advertising work for small companies to neophytes. They don't see the necessity for having their most fertile minds help your growing company when they could be helping AT & T's growing company instead, justifying the stupendous media commissions they earn by placing advertising for AT & T.

**Agency rule
of thumb**

A rule of thumb: The smaller your business, the smaller the ad agency you should seek. The larger your company, the more services you'll need. A giant advertiser recently moved some of its business from its enormously successful Portland, Oregon, agency to a far larger one in Chicago — because the Chicago agency had more global services and this advertiser was seriously thinking globally. Global matters might not influence your decision on an agency. Their services and the quality of the people who will be doing the work on your business should be your prime considerations.

Before you go about the difficult task of choosing an ad agency, you should ask yourself ten questions:

1. What do we *need* from an agency — help in planning, researching, creating, producing, picking media, all of these or none of these? If you don't have a need, you don't need an agency.

2. Should the ad agency handle the media buying, will we do that ourselves, or should we use a media-buying service? Just because the agency offers it doesn't mean you have to use it.

3. Will the agency be compensated solely by the 15 percent commission they earn on the media they purchase and the 17.6 percent they earn on production, or will they require a flat fee that includes all services? Fees make sense. Ad execs are professionals. I never heard of a surgeon charging a commission on the cost of the operating room. But watch out for hourly fees. Agencies kill companies with these, and not on purpose. I would get a monthly estimate on these. Or I'd try to avoid them entirely by means of a flat fee covering specified projects.

4. Are we picking an agency because we want a specific kind of advertising campaign or because it's the best agency? Beware of agencies that specialize in one kind of advertising. Your company isn't like the others they've advertised. You're different and your ads should reflect that.

5. How important is it that we have regular and unlimited access to the president of the agency we select? If you get to see her and she's not involved with your account regularly, you're wasting your time. If you get to see someone from one management layer down and that person lives and breathes your business, the president means beans to you.

6. Does the agency have quantifiable prowess in direct marketing since that so closely ties in with advertising? If the answer is no, go directly to the next agency. Do not pass go.

7. Do we require an agency to handle our existing advertising only or our new product launches and grand openings as well? The correct response is "everything." How

Ten questions to help you choose an agency

adept are they at introducing new products and do they have access to public relations services? The two right answers are "great" and "of course."

8. Does the location of the ad agency matter to us? In these days of faxes, multi-purpose phones, and electronic mail, location is less important than ever. Nonetheless, personal contact is the best form of communication. Will you miss it if you don't get it?

9. Although we have the ultimate say-so in what advertising runs, who will really be in charge of all advertising details — someone at our place or someone at theirs? Do we respect that person?

10. The best for last: Do we love both the work done by the agency and the results it has achieved? Do we like the people? Do we trust them? Are they more concerned with awards or sales? Subtract ten points for everything they say about awards instead of profits.

※ ※ ※

Once you've decided you need an advertising agency, use this guerrilla checklist as a guideline for selecting the best possible one for your needs and goals. It is based upon criteria for the nineties and the twenty-first century, signposts a guerrilla seeks.

Agency guidelines for a new century

- *Be certain that the advertising agency realizes that advertising is only 1 percent of marketing.* The agency must demonstrate that it knows that there are many more marketing weapons to utilize and that it is capable of using or directing the use of all the appropriate ones in your marketing arsenal. Guerrilla businesses deserve guerrilla agencies. Don't settle for less.

- *Ascertain that your account will be considered important, special, and deserving of the agency's top talent.* Be sure you meet and talk to the people who will be doing your advertising — creative, media, research, anything. See what else the creatives have created. Avoid agency figureheads and get to know the troops who will be serving on your front line. Is the chemistry right?

- *Be sure that the agency understands your company's objectives and considers them reasonable.* This understanding will be reflected in their writing of your advertising strategy. If it's missing, go elsewhere.
- *Check to see that the people who will be working on your account have the right credentials, experience, and attitude.* If they haven't worked on a business just like yours, don't worry. Just make sure that they understand the critical relationship between profitability and creativity.
- *Be positive that the agency has a knowledge of your business, an interest in your business, and a knowledge of your competitive situation.* If they've done their homework by the time they present to you, they'll have these things. If not, you aren't interested.

If you do need an agency, just look at the ads they've created, the clients they've satisfied, and the profits they've won. Leo Burnett Advertising's greatest growth came from *the growth of its clients and their ever-increasing ad expenditures.* This is a better benchmark than growth coming from new clients attracted by work done for other clients. Such agencies are hard to find. But the search will be worth your time.

18

Getting Big Bangs for Small Bucks

Few things please guerrillas more than investing their advertising funds wisely, then profiting disproportionately from their investment. This pleases more than surprises these guerrillas, for they have made it their business to have few dollars do the work of many. This knowledge is essential to maintain profitability; it is amazing that it is so rarely practiced. But when you remember that most advertising is created and supervised by advertising agencies, it becomes less amazing. Saving the client's money is not their top priority.

Although the best advertising agencies have their clients' profitability foremost in their mind (after all, that's how they keep their business), even those — and most that are not the best — have at least one financial whiz in the agency whose prime purpose is to assure *the agency's* profitability. Many small businesses operate without ad agencies and are better positioned to concentrate on their own profitability.

Guerrilla bang increasers Just to get your big-bang blood flowing, consider these ten ways for increasing the bangs but not the bucks:

1. *Tie your advertising campaign into a public relations campaign so that both augment each other and many people are made aware of the advertising at the outset.* They will carry this awareness with them as long as you stick with the campaign. The ads will not have done the work all by themselves. The PR gets the credit here for directing the public's attention to the campaign concept, making it a newsworthy item, something worth remem-

bering. Long after the PR has taken place, the echo of its bangs will continue to reverberate through the advertising. A California firm buys used Levi's and sells them in Asia. It has advertised this fact regularly in the newspaper. But the ads took off, along with the profits of the company, when a publicity story about the enterprise appeared in the Sunday newspaper, complete with a photo of the happy owner. I'll bet whenever readers see the current ads, they remember the story and the smiling owner.

2. *Give yourself the benefit of synergy through cohesiveness throughout your marketing campaign.* Your advertising will serve as the star of this effort. Its theme and promise enters more minds and penetrates them deeply because you have featured the advertising in the standard advertising venues of the media along with the nonadvertising venues of point-of-purchase signs, a direct mailing, a special festival or clinic, brochures available at the premises of all your fusion marketing partners, as posters, as part of a sweepstakes, in seminars, in demonstrations, in the yellow pages, at a trade or home show, and in your sponsorship of a high-profile community or industry event.

3. *Be ultra-aware of any competitive advertising activity because people in the market at any given moment start their shopping using the ads currently running.* Guerrillas know they must aim their ads at people already in the market, rather than at those not quite ready to buy. These ready-to-buy people carefully scour ads before starting their purchasing foray. They study you. They study your competitors. If your advertising is based on what the competition did last year, you're in trouble. It should take cognizance of what they are doing at this very moment so that your ads can counteract theirs and win the sale. Being oblivious to competitive advertising is a good hint that you should be doing something new for a living.

4. *Think in terms of enlarging each transaction you make.* That means you should develop a deluxe version of your

Big transactions make big bangs

standard version, offer a package of services rather than a single service project, entice customers to make a multiple rather than a single purchase, do what you can to get people to "subscribe" to your offering. Perhaps you can offer a catalogue so that first-time customers have a reason to become lifelong customers. Your advertising costs will not increase with these tactics, but the payoff from your advertising will show a marked upswing, along with that ear-to-ear grin you'll be wearing. It looks good on you.

5. *Have copies made of your ads — black and white or full color — and post them wherever you can.* Well, of course you should post them in your own place of business — in the window, on the door, at the counter, on a wall. They should also be posted on the premises of fusion marketing partners, on community bulletin boards, in take-one boxes, wherever your target prospects congregate. Even though you may be advertising in a medium with a large circulation, increase the readership of your ads by exposing them to people who may not read the publication in which you advertise.

6. *Hold on a second and ask yourself if advertising is the intelligent way to reach your target market.* For example, recent statistics reveal that only 2 percent of the U.S. population rents a car ten times a year or more. Since there are no publications directed solely to car renters, does it really make sense to advertise a car rental company in general circulation media? After all, you want these frequent renters as regular customers, but 98 percent of the readership and viewership of the standard mass media *are not your primary audience.* Is there a more cost-efficient way to reach these people? If it were my Hertz, Avis, Budget, or Alamo company, I'd consider advertising in in-flight magazines, fusion marketing with hotel chains, and a direct mailing to businesses with over two hundred employees, offering company-wide discounts.

7. *Sales training to your own sales force or to anyone who*   **Bangs on**
will be selling your product will help the advertising pay   **the sales floor**
off right on the sales floor. Selling a product or a service is
almost always a team project. The ad makers are part of
the team, but not the whole team. The salespeople are
an integral part of the team as well. They must be informed of the advertising, the reasons for it, and the way
it relates to their commissions. This way, the advertising
won't just sit there; it will come alive at the point of sale.
Guerrillas know that it is sales training that often makes
advertising effective. If you see an ad for a book, you may
not purchase it while visiting your local bookstore. But if
the bookseller says something about the book, that recommendation *plus* the ad will probably make you a
buyer of that book.

8. *Hire a top professional to produce your advertisement.*
You may pay through the nose for this service, but the
wisdom of this investment expands when you use the ad
as part of a mailer, as a poster, as the innards of a brochure, as a sales aid for your sales force, as a page in a
flip chart, as part of a future catalogue, and as something
your fusion marketing partners will display for you. Plan
also to use the ad for many years, each year decreasing
the cost-per-usage of the ad. Because you used a pro,
your ad will have longevity, and the amortized cost of
production will soon seem like a piddling amount. This
is more than your own perception of it. This is the truth.

9. *Somewhere in the ad or commercial, give readers or viewers or listeners an opportunity to continue the dialogue.*
Perhaps it can be a toll-free number, a coupon, an invitation to contact you. Even though you want profits to be
the result of your advertising, sometimes those profits
don't come in a hurry. Bright prospects want to know a
bit more about you, about your offering. By inviting dialogue, you give them a chance to become more involved
with you and to satisfy themselves completely that they
should buy from you. Notice that more and more adver-

tisers are using this technique to increase both profits and the size of their customer and prospect lists.

10. *Use your package, invoice, or receipt to sell something else that will increase your profits.* Maybe you'll sell them something that you make, a product or service, a super-deluxe version. Perhaps you'll sell them something that one of your fusion marketing partners offers. The point is that when they have purchased from you and when you live up to and exceed their expectations, they will feel favorably disposed to do more business with you. They are hot and you are ready with your brilliantly worked package insert, side-panel copy, or double-duty receipt. Very few bucks are required to enhance the original bang. A local restaurant, India Palace, informs all patrons on its menu and with strategically placed signs that it has a room for private parties, caters parties at your home, brings its genuine Indian clay oven along, delivers, and even offers lessons in cooking Indian cuisine. Do profits increase with such inexpensive marketing? Is Indian food spicy?

Enhancing the original bang

These are but morsels in a whole smorgasbord of methods to increase the bang while decreasing the bucks. Although this should never be your top priority, it should rank near the top and not be overlooked.

Guerrillas capitalize upon every opportunity, and they know that when a person responds to their advertising, they've got a golden opportunity that they then seize with the follow-up that larger companies can't manage because of their ponderous size.

19

Never Losing Sight of Reality

Advertising will be a source of heartache instead of profits if you have unrealistic expectations. Don't expect it to be easily created. Don't expect to find the ideal media for it the first time out of the chute. Don't expect it to lead to a whole new world of profits unless you combine it with many of the other weapons of guerrilla marketing.

Reality is being aware that people do not pay much attention to advertising, regardless of its quality. Reality is knowing that even if people do pay close attention to your ad, they may not be able to afford what you are selling. Reality is competitors studying your every move, then trying to make those moves before you do. Reality is eager entrepreneurs doing their darnedest to woo customers from your customer list to theirs.

Unless you and your advertising face these realities and accept them as part of the territory in today's marketplace, get yourself a lifetime supply of Tums for your tummy — as they used to say but no longer do.

The parent says when comforting the distressed child at the theater, "It's only a movie." The adult mind thinks when exposed to any ad or commercial, "It's only advertising." Adults know that advertising is supposed to be taken with a grain of salt because all advertising exaggerates, doesn't it?

"It's only advertising"

Of course it doesn't — not all of it, at least. But because some of it does, all of it is taken less seriously than, say, the dictionary.

Reality means knowing that even with the greatest strategy, idea, headline, visual, copy, theme line, and offer, your ad may be ignored or, worse yet, not believed. However glorious, it will be one of many ads that your prospect has seen that day. Do you really expect that prospect to remember your ad? Do you expect the prospect to buy from you after only one exposure to your ad?

Guerrillas are realistic

Life does not work that way. Advertising does not work that way. Expecting otherwise is unrealistic.

There is no room for unrealistic expectations in the advertising process. Put something on sale, and before you know it, a competitor is offering the same thing at an even lower price. The owner of the now defunct Gimbel's department store in New York, a thriving retailer during its heyday, told his secretary that he was taking a business course one night a week. The secretary was surprised that such a successful businessman would be taking a course. "My employees know words and terms that I can't even understand," said Mr. Gimbel. "I have to keep up with them."

A few months later Mr. Gimbel entered his office with his head hanging down, a glum look on his face. "What's the matter, Mr. Gimbel?" asked his caring secretary.

"I flunked the course," said Mr. Gimbel. "The final exam was a one-question test that asked what you'd do if you bought 5,000 dresses and your competitor offered them at $5 lower than you could. The correct answer, according to the professor, was to lower my prices $6 to beat the competitor. But I flunked the test because I said I'd rip off all the buttons and send the dresses back as rejects."

Whether you're running a department store or selling hand-knit sweaters out of your home, you must be ready to head the competition off at the pass. They will do absolutely everything in their power to win business away from you. Not understanding and reacting to that is a failure to face reality.

Reality in advertising is knowing that advertising is constantly changing. During the 1980s, a study by researcher Daniel Starch revealed that black and white ads are about 20 percent more effective than black and white ads with one color. In 1992, a study reported in Cahners' Advertising Research Report showed that the addition of a second color to a black and white ad *increased* readership by 20 percent. Was the first report wrong? Nope. Times have changed. Realists in advertising keep up with those changes. Realists know that although a two-page ad costs twice as much as a one-page ad, readership goes up only 25 percent, that a half-page ad is two-thirds as effective as a full-page ad, and that a full-page, full-color ad attracts about 40 percent more readers than a black and white ad. **Realists keep up with change**

Never losing sight of reality also means never being in a rush. Speed diminishes the excellence that can be achieved with the creative process. If you ask your ad makers to create an ad in a hurry, expect less than their best.

The advertising industry has long been accused of being a brag-and-boast business, characterized by product claims that have no involvement with consumers' lives. Many of today's TV commercials are brilliant thirty-second *films*, but they are lousy *commercials*. There's an enormous difference.

How often have you watched a TV spot and asked, "What did they mean by that?" Someone has clearly lost sight of reality. Sometimes an even worse question is asked, "Who was that for?" If anyone ever asks that about your commercial, fire the person who created it. Questions such as those are proof that the person and reality are strangers.

If you are in the position to employ an agency to create ads and commercials, it's your job to provide the reality check. Don't let dazzling visuals or cleverness cloud your thinking. Reality requires that you stay very clear on what you're saying and to whom you're saying it.

Here's my reality checklist: **A reality checklist**

1. It's the state of the economy at the moment you are creating the ad.
2. It's the competitive scene, even if you don't come out on top.
3. It's the latest technology for producing ads and for exposing them to the public.

4. It's that airplane crash that dominated the newspaper on the day you ran your ad for a new vacation destination.
5. It's the advertising budget that dictates your reach, your frequency, and your ad production values.
6. It's the inevitable clutter of other ads, other commercials, other advertisers — all surrounding your ad.
7. It's the call of nature, causing your target audience to run to the bathroom during the commercial break, just when your commercial is running on the tube.
8. It's everything else on your prospect's mind, things that probably do not include your product or service.
9. It's a ho-hum public attitude toward advertising, if, indeed, the public has ever given advertising much thought.
10. It's knowing whether an ad is amusing, startling, boring, or motivating — be honest with yourself and you'll have the right answer.

When you learn that most advertising is created with one eye on winning an advertising award and another on a dream world, you should take that as wonderful news. It's an invitation for you to join the real world, letting your experience guide you toward creating reality-based advertising. It's a reminder that the competition isn't really all that tough in the advertising arena, in spite of how much I urge you to be on your guard.

A new business called the New Adventures Club was formed to give everyone the opportunity to engage in exciting adventures such as white-water rafting, hot air ballooning, skydiving, skin-diving, and soaring in gliders. The advertising stressed adventure.

The launching of the business was only a medium success in that the business earned a profit, but not a heady profit. The owner, however, noticed that the people who signed up for the adventures seemed to be far more interested in each other than they were in the adventures.

This was reality. The target audience wasn't really as fascinated by new adventures and fast-flowing adrenaline as it **Reality can be** was by new people and fast-flowing hormones. The club ad- **beautiful** justed to the real world and, while it offered exciting activities, the emphasis was strictly on the social aspects of taking them up. Profits skyrocketed. Thank heavens the owner took the time for a reality check.

20

The Role of Promotions in Advertising

As advertising is only one part of marketing, promotions are only one part of advertising. As advertising can give a major boost to all your other weapons of marketing, promotions can help you maximize the profits from your advertising. It's all one big, happy family: marketing, the grandparent — advertising, the parent — and promotions, the child. Direct response, trade shows, public relations: They're also part of that large family.

That means your mind must be attuned to thinking of marketing first, then advertising, and finally — promotions. And just what are promotions? They are *special efforts, such as sales, to generate profits and tie in with your advertising and marketing.* They are designed to boost sales and profits for the short term. By their very nature, promotions are short-lived.

All year, but not nonstop They can be used throughout the year, but not nonstop. And they are highly addictive. Because they work so well, business owners tend to repeat them too much.

When this happens two ugly side effects occur:

1. The promotions lose their impact over time. The repetition that is so important for advertising is counterproductive for promotions because it diminishes their importance.
2. Prospects don't patronize your business as frequently because they wait for you to have a special promotion. You've conditioned them not to buy unless you are offering something special.

Your job as a guerrilla is to find the optimum balance point between all of your marketing weapons, and especially between advertising and promotions. You should be promotion-minded to get the most from your advertising investment. But your advertising strategy calls for a specified number of promotions per year.

Hallmark has created and identified a number of promotion opportunities — everything from Secretary's Day to the most consumer-driven holiday of all — Christmas. Bing Crosby sang of it as being a *White Christmas*. Advertisers see it as a Green Christmas, and they aren't thinking about the environment. You're not Hallmark, so you've got to offer promotions that fit the needs of your target audience.

Promotions are undoubtedly on the increase. In 1969, expenditures for advertising were 53 percent of total marketing budgets, and expenditures for promotions were 47 percent. In 1991, the ratio had switched around to 25 percent for advertising and 75 percent for promotions. But research proves that while promotions can cause a sudden spurt in sales — not profits, but sales — the spurt is brief and often costly. **Promotions are increasing**

The *Harvard Business Review* calls this "The Double Jeopardy of Sales Promotions." They report that in most promotions, the sales do not increase enough to raise net profits. One sad case they profile is of a company that tried a promotion which raised sales 16 percent but resulted in a 104 percent loss in profits because of wasted marketing expenditures.

Overreliance on promotions can lead to long-term pains in the form of a product or service losing its identity and whatever it stood for to its prospects. Studies show that companies that commit only a small percentage of their marketing budgets to advertising and a large percentage to promotions are rarely market leaders. In fact, the smaller the ratio of brand advertising to promotion, the smaller the return on investment.

According to *The Wall Street Journal*, when only a quarter of a company's marketing budget is allocated for advertising, the return on the marketing investment is 18 percent; when the ratio is 50:50, the return is around 29 percent. These are numbers to keep in mind when you need that quick fix of cash.

Still, keep an eagle eye on *all* the media for promotions used by others. Perhaps the airline industry is having a promotion that you can adapt for your consulting practice. Possibly a supermarket is promoting in a manner that makes perfect sense for your software business. Your eagle eye will spot many cross-promotions where two or more companies have hooked up in an arrangement to benefit both them and their customers. If movie studios can cross-promote with fast-food outlets, if IBM can team up with NordicTrack and Nike, shouldn't your word-processing company pair up with a local copy shop?

Forms of promotions

Promotions take on many forms:

- Sometimes they are sales promotions with contests within your sales force. The sales force works harder than ever, but the public doesn't even know you have a promotion going on. That's cool — as long as profits rise.
- Often they are sales — all kinds of sales, from the humdrum Clearance, Fire, Grand Opening, Going-out-of-Business, One-Cent, and Red Tag sales to the more imaginative Cash Flow, Free-for-All, Midnight, Sherlock Holmes's Birthday, Good Buy, Hit the Jackpot, Honest to Goodness, Home Run, Touchdown, Anti-Inflation, Come in Your Pajamas, and For Customers Only sales. These have all been real sales, and I've just scratched the surface of the silliness that capitalists employ in the noble quest for an honest buck. What would the classic economists think of such goings-on? They'd love them because the dictionary defines promotion, among other meanings, as "something that aids in developing a business." Music to an economist's ears.
- They can take the form of coupons, the favorite of deal hunters, which offer discounts on products or future services, tastings or samplings, or special-offer discounts on products if you buy enough of them, maybe even giving away a freebie if the purchase is large enough or offering

a service such as free installation if the purchase is made by a specific date.

- More and more, promotions involve fusion advertising where the customers can save at one business if they patronize another business and vice versa. "If you patronize the Sage Cinema, you'll receive a coupon for a free dessert at Nicole's Healthy Eats." And "If you have dinner at Nicole's Healthy Eats, you can get free buttered popcorn at the Sage Cinema." Kinko's Copies had a fusion promotion with Pacific Telephone. Jiffy Lube fused with Pennzoil. Fusion promotions are growing in popularity because of the shared cost of the marketing.

- Beginning in the 1980s, airline promotions began to include the many frequent flier programs. Members immediately learned that the airlines had fused with car rental companies and hotels, even cruise lines. These days, frequent buyer programs are springing up like crazy. Even my dentist is considering a frequent filler program. "No way I'll join," I warned him. His guerrilla dental reminder postcards are bad enough.

- Many companies are now promoting by aligning themselves with worthy causes such as protecting the environment, saving the rain forests, boosting the U.S. economy, and feeding the homeless. Perhaps you can contribute a portion of your profits to research for AIDS, MS, cancer, or heart disease. These types of promotions are contributions to the planet as well as to the bottom lines of these cause-minded companies.

- Promotions also take the form of contests for the public such as Pillsbury's famous Bake-Off, the California Milk Advisory Board's Moo-Off, and Levi's "Tell us about what you do while wearing our jeans." These promotions have the value of built-in publicity. Yours should be designed to do the same. Many guerrilla promotions generate profits from customers and prospects as well as coverage from the media. **Bake-Offs and Moo-Offs**

- Frequently, promotions will be aimed at special segments of huge markets. Chrysler Corporation successfully introduced its LH cars with test-drive invitations to four or five million key prospects. Some even received promotional videos.

- Often promotions will offer membership to regular customers. After renting six videos, they can rent one for free — if they're a member of the video club. Video stores that run such promotions use their membership mailing list to let preferred customers know about new arrivals or sales on movies. They may even trade membership lists with a fusion advertising partner.

- Some promotions are keyed to popular sports teams. When the Oakland A's reigned supreme in major league baseball, they cross-promoted with an official chicken, an official jam, and even an official fertilizer. There have been promotions with dry cleaners and the White Sox, with shoe stores and the Cubs, with bottled water and the Yankees, with bratwurst and the Brewers, and with Gatorade and almost every sport, it seems. Have you ever considered a cross-promotion with a local sports organization? It's an obvious idea if you run a sporting goods store or uniform shop. It's an innovative idea if your business is landscaping or garbage removal.

An official fertilizer?

The keys to proper promotions are to plan wisely, to state your goals at the outset, to be certain you have attended to all the details, and then to advertise your promotion so that the world knows what you're up to.

Advertise your promotion in the mass media, to be sure. But also market it with signs at the point of purchase. Many of your customers will not have read of your promotions in the daily paper or seen them on TV. Herald your promotion with direct mail, with PR coverage, and with every reasonable weapon in your guerrilla arsenal.

The best promotions

Remember that the best promotions are time limited and have a clear cutoff date. "This special offer of a free Porsche with every tube of toothpaste is available to you only until May 18, 1995." The urgency you add with your ending date will lend a sense of urgency for customers to buy. Plus, you can accurately measure the effectiveness of your promotion by putting a cap on the offering. You'd know if your free Porsche promotion was successful on May 19.

Listen, I know you're going to love the results of your promotions. Just be sure you plan carefully and execute them properly. A bad promotion is worse than no promotion at all, as anyone who ever made a special trip to a store based on a free gift give-away only to find the free gifts were all gone will tell you. McDonald's never seems to run out of Happy Meals. With a kadillion burgers sold, they know there are no shortcuts to success — especially if profits are your benchmark, and they'd better be.

IV

Guerrilla Intelligence from the Front Lines

YOU HAVE HEARD, from me and from others who deign to teach others about something as smoky and vague as advertising, that advertising is not creative unless it is profitable. I stand by that belief, but I don't want you to feel guilty if your advertising fails to produce profits.

Perhaps you did everything right, but the price was wrong. Maybe the retailer hand-sold customers a competing product because he was getting a special commission, called a "spiff," for selling it. Possibly your ad turned people on, but the package turned them off. Maybe your ad was on target, but the salesperson was in a bad mood that day, losing the sale for you.

Although advertising is supposed to produce profits, sometimes it is sabotaged by some other factor. Guerrilla advertising people carefully check the terrain and all the minor details before they run any advertising; they eliminate barriers before they become insurmountable.

Recognize that whatever you are advertising exists not only as a product or service, but also as *an idea, a perception, maybe even a misconception.* Whatever is inside the box you are advertising must be matched in quality by the looks of the box itself. Your offering, just like you, has a personality. That personality is the combination of looks, marketing, advertising, media, competition, and reputation. Perhaps you are advertising the best closet-remodeling service in the universe. It's available at the lowest price in history, and installation is both free and instant. Does that mean you have an automatic winner if your ads and commercials stress your benefits?

It does not. Perhaps a year ago a closet remodeling service was launched and its employees proceeded to steal items from all of the households it served. Suppose the thievery made headlines throughout the community. Now here you come, all bright and shiny, not to mention honest to the core. But your prospects ignore you in droves. You run grand-looking advertisements and captivating commercials. Still, you are ignored. You can't blame folks for refusing to patronize you, and a great ad isn't going to change things around. You've got past history to contend with. Your predecessor's ethics have become part of your perceived personality.

Unless you know this data at the outset, you have an unseen enemy that may never be conquered by advertising. That is why you must always recognize that advertising is only part of a much larger scene. Your job: *to see the whole scene so that you can tailor your advertising to the reality of the situation.* Others have and you can, too.

A guerrilla might even run ads mentioning the sordid history and separating his company from the one from the past. At least a guerrilla would know that all playing fields are not level and that all advertising does not start at square one; some starts ten squares *before* square one.

Advertising great Fairfax Cone, surveying the entire communications scene, reminded his own people that advertising is the business, even the art, of telling someone everything that should be important to him. It should be viewed as a substitute for talking to that person.

The good Mr. Cone, a founder of the advertising agency Foote, Cone, and Belding, said that advertising must meet five requirements, all worth knowing if you're to be a guerrilla:

1. It must be *clear*; this is a prime requirement.
2. What is clear must also be *important*; it must have value.
3. What is clear and important must also have a *personal appeal* to prospects and customers; no one else matters.

4. The advertising should express the *personality* of the advertiser; a promise is only as good as its maker.
5. A good advertisement demands *action*. It either gets the order or an unspoken mental pledge to buy.

Fairfax Cone then said, "This, incidentally, is all I know about advertising." This section aims to show you what happens when advertisers know the same and what happens when they don't.

21

Your Position, Your Look, Your Personality

The guerrilla carefully selects the manner in which she presents her company to the world. She chooses a *position* that will afford her the most profits, the least savvy competition, and the greatest opportunity for growth. She picks a *look* that personifies her essence, that clearly communicates her position. She selects a *personality* that stems from truth and will appeal to her target audience.

These simple tasks are the making or breaking of a business. The right product with the wrong positioning can prove disastrous. If a product's visual manifestations don't look like what it really is, bad news looms ahead. If a company has an identity or personality that is attractive to different people than those in its target market and actually turns off the real audience, doom and gloom are on the horizon. The selection of these factors must be done with care. You must be prepared to live with them a long time. Changing your position, look, or personality in midstream is definitely not a good idea.

Don't change your personality midstream

Bruce Bendinger, in his *The Copy Workshop Workbook* (1993, The Copy Workshop, 312-871-1179), gives invaluable tips to copywriters *and* briefly traces the history of advertising. To enlighten you about the past so as to make yours a brighter future, I'll trace it here even more briefly:

• Sometime in the early nineteenth century, a farmer asked a local newspaper publisher to publish a notice that the farmer had a hog for sale. Thus, advertising was born. Well, not exactly, but the listing itself, most likely

The first ad

known as a public notice, took hold as a way of selling in Europe and the United States. Future notices began to be called "advertisements," from the Latin words *advertire*, meaning "unattested," and *ad vertere*, meaning "to turn toward." Both individuals and companies discovered that public notices meant business. Advertising began to be known as "keeping your name before the public," and a profession was born.

- In the early 1900s, Albert Lasker, another founder of Foote, Cone, and Belding, known then as an advertising "agent" instead of an "agency," realized that advertising was "salesmanship in print," proving that a guerrilla had been born.
- Claude Hopkins, a successful copywriter, cautioned writers not to think of people in the mass, but to think of a typical individual who is likely to want what you sell. This turn-of-the-century guerrilla advised advertisers to talk to people *one at a time*. Both Lasker and Hopkins are from the old school of advertising, but their concepts are as fresh as tomorrow, and don't go around forgetting them.
- Helen Lansdowne, also in the early 1900s, became a superstar writer for behemoth-agency-to-be J. Walter Thompson and said, "I supplied the feminine point of view. I watched the advertising to see that the idea, the wording, and the illustrating were effective for women." Her insights made brand names out of many no-name products. Her ads for Woodbury's soap increased their sales 1,000 percent by promising "A skin you love to touch."

"A skin you love to touch"

- Ray Rubicam, who founded the giant advertising agency Young and Rubicam, brought research into the limelight as an advertising tool, involved art directors in the ad-making process, and created ads with both sales and graphic excellence. Until he did this, ads were hardly ever pleasant to look at. And if you don't want to look at something, chances are you'll resist reading it.

- In the mid-century, Rooser Reeves, chairman of Ted
Bates and Company, developed a concept centering
around a product's *unique selling proposition*, instantly
known as the USP. He taught ad makers that each advertisement must make a proposition to the consumer and
say to each reader, "Buy this product and you will get this
specific benefit." He then warned that the proposition
must be one that the competition either cannot or does
not offer; it must be unique. His sales tools were television, theme lines, demonstrations, and repetition, then
more repetition. This mindset moved tons of Anacin,
Colgate, and M&M's, which, by the way, were coined
by Reeves to "Melt in your mouth, not in your hands" —
as if you didn't know.

   The USP and why you should love it

- Another mid-century man and my own personal mentor,
Leo Burnett, built a giant ad agency in Chicago, along
with a number of well-known advertising campaigns: the
Marlboro Man, Charlie the Tuna, Morris the Cat, the
Jolly Green Giant, the Pillsbury Doughboy, the friendly
skies of United, and Maytag's loneliest repairman in
town. Leo was a fervent believer in the *inherent drama* —
something fascinating that exists in every product or service. He believed that people involved with products and
services on a day-to-day basis took for granted in their offerings what others would find dramatically interesting.
He believed that inherent within every product or service
is something fascinating that should serve as the source
of advertising ideas. He studied the Maytag research,
which showed few appliance breakdowns, making "the
loneliest repairman in town" an almost natural idea. He
literally listened to Rice Krispies as they snapped, crack-
led, and popped. They almost dictated their own advertising to him, so it seemed. A true guerrilla, he spoke of
"the glacier-like power of friendly familiarity." I cherish
the five years I spent at his agency. When I left his Chicago office to help run his London office, Leo said, "I
wish I were you." When I asked why this titan would

   What Leo Burnett believed in

want to be a relative greenhorn, he said, "I just wish I
could start over again." Sounds like a guy who enjoys his
work, someone who has hit it big. One of the most in-
sightful things I ever heard him say was "Advertising today
is selling corn flakes to people who are eating Cheerios."

- The agency that breathed life into "soft sell" was Doyle
Dane Bernbach. Bill Bernbach had a simple philosophy:
"Find the simple story in the product and present it in an
articulate and intelligent, persuasive way." He also often referred to "the power of an idea." Guerrillas were springing up all over the place.

**Guerrillas
in our midst**

- As advertising moved from one age to another, the basic
truths of the past age remained the same, but new truths
were revealed. Jack Trout and Al Ries wrote about *positioning* in the 1970s and claimed in their book *Positioning: The Battle for Your Mind* that positioning was the
key to success. They said that you have a choice of four
positions. The *best or leadership position* is exemplified
by IBM, Hertz, and McDonald's. The *against* position
was best used by Avis when they found customers by in-
sisting that the underdog ("We're only number 2") works
harder, an idea most Americans trust. The *new* position,
which you occupy when you establish a new category,
was used with brilliance by Federal Express. And the
niche position, where you aim for only a small segment
of a humongous market, was utilized with genius by
Virginia Slims (another Leo Burnett creation).

**Positioning
comes of age**

- The 1980s were characterized by ads that made their
impressions on a visual basis and were more simple because an increasingly complicated society denied people
the time to critically examine the facts. Energizer's pink
bunny is a child of the eighties. It keeps going and going
and going. Successful advertising of the eighties was simpler and more visual. Advertising was moving from ver-
bal to visual communication. Ad master Julian Koenig,
who ran one of the best agencies of the eighties, said,
"The simpler the better. Till form and content are one
and the same." Jeff Gorman and Gary Johns epitomized

the eighties with their intensely visual campaign for
Nike, known as the brand of the eighties. The Mazda
Miata, propelled to greatness by an ad campaign that
reeked of nostalgia and a theme directed to right-brained
car buyers, "It just feels right," soon attracted a traffic
jam of competitors.

While advertising was changing, so were consumers.
They learned to ignore, or more precisely, to pay no attention. "Selective reception" is the term that describes
the process. Allen Rosenshine, president and CEO of
Omnicom, a multi-national agency, said, "Too much
of advertising isn't simply bad, it's simply irrelevant."
During the eighties the largest ad agency, Saatchi and
Saatchi, which was born in England and became large
by purchasing at least five major U.S. agencies, made
inroads into virtually all international markets. Visually
powerful advertising for Bloomingdale's, Winchell's do-
nuts, Chanel, Osh-Kosh, and Coca-Cola dominated the
print media. TV highlights of the decade, spurred by *Se-
same Street* and MTV, appeared in advertising for Bud
Light (which used the dog Spuds MacKenzie), Federal
Express (which used one of America's fastest talkers and
was extremely successful), Izuzu (which used famed liar
Joe Izuzu and was notably unsuccessful), Bartles &
Jaymes (in which Gallo, the parent winery, used two real
people, neither named Bartles or Jaymes), Pepsi (which
used Michael Jackson), Jell-O (Bill Cosby), and Wendy's
(which used Clara Peller, who asked "Where's the beef?"
and has been long abandoned in favor of Wendy's owner,
Dave Thomas). Advertising geniuses of the eighties included Hal Riney, who created the Bartles & Jaymes and
Henry Weinhard's beer advertising and often served as
the voice-over announcer; Joe Sedelmeier, who created
many of the Wendy's and Federal Express commercials;
and Jay Chiat, whose agency, Chiat/Day, gave birth to
that pink bunny.
• The nineties, characterized by immense downsizing
(actually the right word is "right-sizing"), saw corporate

**"Selective
reception"**

**Where's the beef,
indeed?**

America conserve its resources — except for those huge and wealthy corporations that paid millions for celebrity endorsements, especially those who could slam dunk — and small businesses began to employ guerrilla marketing techniques to combat the high cost of advertising. This

The integrated marketing program

means an integrated marketing approach where advertising is an important part, but not the only part, of a multi-weapon marketing program.

Along with an integrated marketing program, the nineties offer advertisers new marketing venues, forums that didn't exist in the days of Albert Lasker, Leo Burnett, and J. Walter Thompson, who, incidentally, married Helen Lansdowne.

An example of this kind of integration is Apple's introduction of the Macintosh computer. First Apple ran a now-famous commercial, "1984," during the *Super Bowl*. Meanwhile, PR whizzes for Apple were briefing the technical and business press with stories to break in magazines and newspapers at introduction time. Multi-page, full-color inserts, like smaller magazines within magazines, were produced for magazines read by target prospects. Naturally, the inserts were 100 percent Mac-oriented. New TV commercials lauded the benefits of the Mac. Three new magazines were published, thanks to expertise, encouragement, and financing by Apple: *MacWorld, MacUser,* and *MacWeek.*

Added to the marketing mix were posters, brochures, banners, even T-shirts. Special events were planned for prospects to check out Macs and take them on the computer version of a test drive. Interactive software was developed for use in computer stores. Was the product a success? You tell me.

Or ask SmartFood, now owned by Frito-Lay, which marketed with billboards, direct mail, radio, and sampling, utilizing guerrilla marketing techniques and proving once again how well they worked. One SmartFood guerrilla tactic: People clad in six-foot SmartFood bags distributed the product in malls and on ski slopes. How much money do you suppose that cost? Would you consider it traditional or guerrilla advertising? The choice of media was as creative as the advertising;

the healthy product for the nineties was matched with the marketing weapons of the nineties. Advertising reached adulthood.

"Today, I am a man"

Salvation for the American economy is going to be in small business. Sure, there will be room for the *Fortune* 500. But the continuing and growing presence of the free enterprise spirit will result not in the weak inheriting the world, but the entrepreneur. Watch out! These entrepreneurs are going to advertise like fiends. You've got to take steps now to protect yourself from their increasing sophistication. Or better yet, become one of them yourself.

The moral: Select your positioning, your look, and your personality wisely, then communicate them not only with your advertising — but with all of your marketing weapons, too. You've read of many big-name companies who did that, but keep in mind that once they were your size, too. Smart advertising and marketing put them up there in the *Fortune* 500. But with 40 percent of the 1980 *Fortune* 500 no longer in existence, there's plenty of room on that list for new companies. You can be sure they will be advertising their offerings with the skill and patience of the guerrilla.

22

Advertising That Worked and Why

What an ugly, depressing sight! The marketing battlefields are littered with dead advertising that *didn't work*. Some of it died too young, before it could mature and blossom. Much of it was thought of as successful for a brief time, then fizzled in a flash. "Where's the beef?" was superstar advertising one day, but one day isn't long enough to generate beefy profits.

Adland is Marlboro Country You already know that Marlboro is considered by many people, this guerrilla included, to be the best advertised brand in history. Too bad it's for a cigarette instead of a charity. But its success is unquestioned, and its longevity — it was born in the late 1950s — attests to its greatness, as measured by its ability to still move merchandise off the shelves and out of the machines in a hurry.

That one advertising campaign transformed Marlboro from the number thirty-one selling cigarette to the number one seller. It made Marlboro number one among men (no surprise there) and women (some surprise there). But Philip Morris, the company that manufactures Marlboro, isn't worried about the female market because it also makes Virginia Slims. That's another example of advertising that worked — and even faster than Marlboro because it was so focused on the female market. It came close to dominating that market. Only Marlboro ranks higher in sales to women.

Some ad experts explain Marlboro's success by saying it was aimed at the portion of a man's soul that is capable of the heroics we associate with cowboys. As generations pass, the cowboy, instead of fading, looms larger in legend. By connecting its identity with cowboys instead of something trendy, Marlboro continues to succeed.

Not long after the Marlboro cowboy's debut, Miller High Life Beer was effectively advertised in its "Miller time" commercials. It showed beer drinkers that what they do is important and they deserve a Miller break. Sales soared. Alas, because Miller's advertising didn't work fast enough to pass Budweiser's Clydesdales roaring around the bend, Miller switched to its own animals — young party animals — and "Miller time," along with Miller sales, faded from view.

Some big spenders abandon an advertising campaign after a relatively short time because they feel they've spent enough money on it in a year or so. It would take over a century for a smaller advertiser running the same campaign to achieve similar results. Saturation is expensive, but for the giants it is possible, at least in the minds of the people who direct the marketing. Coke has abandoned some classic advertising themes. They did it with "The pause that refreshes," "Things go better with Coke," "Coke is it," "Can't beat the real thing," and several others, probably a few while I'm writing this chapter. McDonald's used to say "You deserve a break today," and it sold a lot of Big Macs. These days, they say it no more. Don't homemakers deserve a break anymore? Of course they do, but McDonald's feels they've saturated the public with that campaign and are now busy saturating us with another.

Don't you still deserve a break today?

Lux toilet soap, a market leader before the mid-century, achieved its pinnacle with ads built around the theme "9 out of 10 screen stars care for their skin with Lux toilet soap" — cashing in on the truism that as cowboys are to men, screen stars are to women. If you think that's sexist today, ask any woman if she'd rather be a cowboy or a screen star. Yes, I know my daughter Amy would opt for the saddle, but many advertising home truths remain forever true. Lux was leaning on glamour, luxury, fame, and sex appeal. At last glance, these things were still around. In fact, I once learned that the true definition of an intellectual is a person who *sometimes* isn't thinking about sex. Today the top-selling soaps are Dove, which doesn't go in much for luxury or fame but does a good job of hinting at glamour and sex appeal. Dial, the number two soap, solves our real or imaginary problem of body odor, steering clear of the old appeals and assuring us of social acceptability instead.

One of history's most powerful ads was a long print ad, editorial-style and crammed with three columns of small type. Written by the famous ad maker John Caples, it was headlined

"They Laughed When I Sat Down at the Piano"

"They Laughed When I Sat Down at the Piano But When I Start to Play!" The ad ran for years and earned a fortune in profits for the U.S. School of Music every time it ran. These days, some folks believe that people don't have the time to read long copy, but hot prospects love every word of long copy. The longer the better. Just read the ads for Mobil Oil and Merrill Lynch.

Listerine, still a major factor in mouthwashes, achieved stardom by inventing a "disease" called "halitosis," meaning bad breath. Lifebuoy soap invented "B.O.," which stands for body odor. Head and Shoulders pointed out that unseemly dandruff. Certs showed how fresh breath can often lead to romance — the ultimate promise, according to many experts. Products positioned to solve problems are easy to advertise. But it requires the mind of a guerrilla to dramatize the problem.

While Alka-Seltzer was winning awards and laughs, but not profits, for its "I can't believe I ate the whole thing!" and "Spicy meatballs!" advertising, Anacin was racking up sales by promising relief that was "fast! fast! fast!" The TV advertising was visually ugly but financially gorgeous.

Forget the advertising; make the product interesting

Instead of making the *advertising* interesting, usually a stupid idea, it was making the *product* interesting, always a wise idea. Be sure this is true of your advertising.

David Ogilvy sold many expensive cars with ads headlined "At 60 miles an hour the loudest noise in this new Rolls-Royce comes from the electric clock." Ads were loaded with technical facts presented with a human touch. A true creative titan, Ogilvy did not write the headline that appears above. He found it in an obscure British magazine article that reviewed the Rolls.

Bob Edens of Leo Burnett Advertising didn't write the brilliant "Fly the friendly skies of United," but instead lifted it from the body copy written by one of his many writers. Who gets the credit? Edens does because he recognized it. The other guy didn't see the bright light at the end of an implied promise of safety and warmth at high altitudes. I was in the meeting when Edens said, "Tom, will you read that line about 'friendly skies' one more time?"

Ogilvy put an eye patch on a model and made Hathaway shirts a household name in the sixties. He used Commander Whitehead, a relatively unknown man with a beard and an English accent, to put Schweppes on the map. Was it positioned as a soft drink? Nope. It was positioned as the man: sophisticated, attractive, sociable, and a good mixer at parties.

Bill Bernbach made Levy's Jewish rye bread a big seller in the East by running ads showing models such as a Native American munching a sandwich on rye, with the headline "You don't have to be Jewish to love Levy's." He made the Volkswagen Bug a major success with ads showing only the car against a white background and headlines such as "Lemon" **Think Volkswagen** (referring to a glove compartment chrome strip blemish, requiring replacement of the strip), "Think small" (which revolutionized America's car-buying habits), and "Relieves gas pains" (which made the point about the impressive mileage delivered by the Bug).

Cheer detergent moved from a weak number five position to a strong number two by switching from a promise of whiteness to a promise that you can use Cheer in all temperatures. The new name, All-Temperature Cheer, was ideal for the new fabrics and brighter colors of the 1970s. The creative brilliance is manifested in the positioning rather than the headline and copy. Volvo is positioned as durable and safe, maintaining sales and profits in a new world of luxury cars that tend to sell exclusivity and power.

Was "The uncola" successful for 7-Up? It was great in the sixties and seventies, then dropped, and now it's back again as 7-Up continues to search for those heady profits from the flower-child days. The Energizer is still a success, starting

Absolut guerrillas

back in the eighties, and so is L'Oreal ("I'm worth it"), Absolut Vodka (visuals so powerful they are sold as posters, framed, and hanging in many homes across the nation), and Dewar's scotch with its famous and long-lived "profiles" campaign in which ads ask fascinating people about their lives and eventually get around to why the person enjoys a glass of Dewar's. But even Dewar's has just switched campaigns. You can bet the reason was declining sales.

The nineties? Well, the jury is still out. Several highly paid celebrity endorsers have been dropped due to unsavory private habits, but it's too soon to know which of today's advertising will stick in the public's mind. Some worth keeping tabs

Up-and-coming guerrillas

on are: Ralph Lauren Polo, Nike for women, Blockbuster Video, Ben and Jerry's ice cream, Häagen-Dazs ice cream (made in the U.S.A.), Ikea furniture stores, Home Depot, Office Depot, Staples, Ultra Slim-Fast, Nutri-Slim, Weight Watchers, Calvin Klein, Reebok, Fortunoff — The Source, Toys 'R' Us (which ran fusion ads with American Express), and Samuel Adams Beer. Pepsi's advertising seems to be especially powerful these days, and some of the best TV advertising may be found in spots on MTV for MTV and on the Nickelodeon channel for its late night lineup called *Nick at Nite*. As guerrillas know, time and profitability will tell the truth. Only when you have something like a three-day sale or a one-month promotion can you be sure your advertising worked. Otherwise, only time and profits reveal the answer. I predict a sad outcome for some of those athletic-shoes and jeans advertisers who cause me and others to wonder what the heck they are trying to say.

23

Promotions That Worked and Why

At first glance, and possibly at second glance as well, it would seem that one of the most successful promotions in history was inaugurated by the airline industry with its frequent flier programs. Although I've heard rumblings that the frequent fliers and their free tickets and upgrades erode profits, the truth is that they have become de rigueur for the airlines — talk about copycats! — and have made loyal customers out of many bargain hunters.

Notice how many advertisers are now starting *frequent buyer* clubs. They don't do that because the promotion idea was a bust. One of the best things about frequent flier and frequent buyer promotions is that they *breed loyalty*. Most promotions do exactly the opposite. They spur impulse shopping and discourage loyalty. People who buy for low price alone are famed for their disloyalty. Their only loyalty is to their own bucks.

Why frequent flier promotions work

But I am also heartily encouraging you to promote a few times a year, and to learn from examples that appear in today's media as well as in the upcoming pages. Just remember that promotions are part of advertising.

Some small advertisers who use radio for advertising take advantage of the radio's ability to conduct *a remote broadcast* right from the store itself. This means the radio station sets up broadcasting equipment and arranges for one of its broadcasters, more likely, a disc jockey, to do the radio broadcast directly from the store. To set it up, simply ask the radio station. Some do it frequently. Others never do it. The cost is reason-

Conduct a remote broadcast

able, though higher than an in-studio broadcast, and the aura of excitement attracts radio listeners in large numbers, especially those listening in their cars. After all, how many live radio broadcasts have you seen? I know you've heard them, but few people have seen one. That's why in-store traffic is high when the store hosts a remote broadcast. These usually last from two to four hours, but some last a full day.

If a known radio personality makes an appearance, you can reap both fame and fortune. An air of excitement is built up. People have the sense that something important is happening, something with a hint of urgency, something that compels them to visit the store and buy *this very moment*. I've often seen hundreds of people in a buying frenzy at remote broadcasts. If you have a retail establishment and use radio, look into this kind of inexpensive promotion.

Never overlook the power of a freebie

Free samples should always be considered with a promotion for either a product or a service. Palmolive gained national brand-name awareness back in the twenties with ads that offered a ten-shave tube of shaving cream free with the purchase of a can of Palmolive aftershave talc. SmartFood made the same idea work today. Got a newspaper you want to promote? There's nothing like a week of free home delivery to spoil and influence prospective readers to subscribe. Free services are often just the trick for convincing those prospects still on the fence.

Plymouth automobiles conducted a wildly successful promotion in the 1930s when they put Chevrolet and Ford cars into their own showrooms and advertised "Look at all three!" The strong sales reflected this confidence and positioning, which were demonstrated in ads bylined by Walter P. Chrysler himself. I wonder if Lee Iacocca, acting as spokesman for the very same Chrysler Corporation, knew about his company's grand tradition.

Howard Gossage, my first boss and the man who showed me how much fun it can be to work in advertising, ran a successful promotion for Irish Whiskey with a *New Yorker* magazine campaign. Readers were invited to vote for "Pride" or "Profit" and received a free pin saying "I'm for pride" or

"I'm for profit." The ads created a mock controversy between Irish Whiskey drinkers who wouldn't use ice, water, or mixers of any kind under any circumstance with those who drink Irish Whiskey with anything, especially coffee. This campaign sparked a demand for Irish coffee (made with Irish Whiskey) and a doubling of Irish Whiskey's distribution. Profits followed in due course.

A Denver furniture store ran advertising three days in a row on TV and in the newspapers announcing that the warehouse store *would be closed* for three days so that the store could get ready for its annual clearance sale. On the day the sale began, the line of people waiting to get in was two blocks long; *all merchandise was sold out* by the third day. It was a successful promotion, successfully advertised by Thane Croston.

They advertised they would be closed

He ran another promotion offering a free bedframe (costing him $25) with every purchase of a complete bed (costing around $300). This promotion was such a moneymaker that he repeated it eight times in two years before selling his warehouse and forty-two other stores and embarking on a solo sailing trip around the world.

Mike Lavin, a West Coast furniture retailer, had the most successful promotion in his twenty-year career when he advertised a free-for-all sale. With every purchase from a group of relatively pricey beds, he offered free delivery, free linen, and free pillows. This was an offer just too good to refuse. Few refused. It worked on TV, in newspapers, on the radio. When your offer is too good to miss, you can advertise it almost anywhere. This promotion would not have worked with inexpensive beds, but because Mike was making enough profit on the costly ones, he could afford the giveaways and still turn an honest profit.

Mercedes-Benz, knowing the value of a promotion in which all parties come out on top, diverted its usual institutional advertising dollars to a promotion for leasing, called a "Win-Win" promotion because both the dealer and the leaser got a good deal. It was repeated long after its proposed cutoff date because it worked so well for Mercedes.

A local restaurant, Le Petit Auberge, celebrated its twenty-fifth anniversary a few years ago by rolling its prices back to where they were twenty-five years ago. Was the promotion a success? It was more than a success because even after it was over, business has never been as brisk as it has been since that promotion started several years ago, reminding people of how good the quarter-century-old restaurant still is.

Most promotions are termed "value-added" promotions, meaning you get more than the product or service itself in the form of a discount or a freebie. Still, a non-value-added promotion that hit home with my wife and me was for a free in-home demonstration of a brand-new $3,000 cooling vest invented for people with heat prostration but also proven very effective for people with multiple sclerosis, a condition afflicting my wife. Ads in the MS newsletter heralded the promotion plus a free video and an 800 number to call to request the video. Sounded worth checking out. So we called the toll-free number, received within three days the video and printed brochure, and sure enough, got a follow-up phone call within the week attempting to set up the in-home demo.

A promotion that hit home at my home

We were impressed by the video, printed brochures, and the conscientious follow-up, but still $3,000 is a lot of money. So we arranged for the demonstration. My wife wore the cooling vest for only half an hour, all it took to convince her that she should own one. I, too, was persuaded that the cooling system (a vest, hat, and electric cooling unit) had indeed helped my wife take about twenty steps without a wheelchair — a very difficult task for her, one that I hadn't seen her successfully undertake in about five years. But since I had never heard of the new cooling technology, I was a bit hesitant to commit $3,000. But we made the purchase because the sales rep (who also had MS) said that all we'd have to pay was $100 and after thirty days only if we were satisfied with the system would we be billed the other $2,900. The thirty days passed. The bill came and we paid it in a flash. The cooling system did, indeed, work very well, and so, said the manufacturer (Life Support Systems, 1-800-929-9808), did the promotion. Notice that the company succeeded because it used a variety of guerrilla marketing weapons: a very carefully targeted ad, a toll-free number, a free video brochure, a free written brochure, a follow-up phone call, a special offer of an in-home demonstration, and then a thirty-day trial period for a fraction of the purchase price. As with most guerrilla advertising, this was more common sense than uncommon brilliance.

Digital Music Express (DMX) is offered by many TV cable companies as a way of pumping thirty channels of uninterrupted music into households with cable TV and an existing sound system. Not buying any more CDs and tapes appealed to me; freedom from commercials (heresy in a book like this!) was another benefit. I was seriously considering DMX when I spotted an ad for a special promotion run by my cable company. The headline? "Free installation if you order DMX this week!" Did I order DMX that day? You know I did. And many others like me did, too. All because of a promotion. Once again, the media wasn't great. The ad was no award winner. The copy wasn't especially cogent. But the offer at the heart of the promotion? I give it an A plus.

Another A + promotion

When Chrysler Corporation introduced its line of LH cars, the entire introduction was one gigantic promotion — as most introductions should be. Here's what Chrysler did:

How a big guy promotes

- Invested $35 million into teaching 115,000 employees better selling and human relationship skills.
- Paid bonuses of up to $500 a car to dealers with high customer-satisfaction ratings.
- Generated positive word-of-mouth advertising by getting 10,000 opinion leaders to try out the cars for several days.
- Displayed cars in museums, concert halls, and hotel lobbies, where upscale prospective buyers would see them.
- Mailed test-drive invitations to about five million prospects; some invitations came with a promotional video.
- Got maximum mileage from advertising by doing less on network TV and more on cable TV and unconventional advertising media such as on-line computer services.

The mass media advertising, coupled with this promotional activity, made the LH one of the most successful car intro-

ductions in history. Advertising alone wouldn't have done it.
It took a promotion to make the ads work so well.

How a little guy promotes

Smart promotions certainly aren't limited to the big guys:

- Many fitness centers have a promotion offering a one-month membership if you join now, along with a money-back guarantee if you don't slim down.
- Bowling alleys and large pizzerias attract kids' birthday parties by offering a free birthday cake.
- Some savvy bakeries offer free decoration of cakes for any occasion, then suggest occasions such as birthdays, anniversaries, holidays, and even Super Bowl parties.
- Several businesses have continuing promotions such as free grocery delivery for the elderly, free full-service for the disabled at self-service gas stations, free baby-sitting at the hairdresser, free ski lessons for first-timers at ski resorts.
- The Body Shop helps the environment by asking customers to bring back their lotion containers for refills. Union Square Restaurant donates food to homeless shelters at the end of each day. Ikea offers to mulch your Christmas tree if you bring it back.

Your job as a guerrilla is to open your mind to value-added promotions and to other ways that buying what you are selling gives the buyer more than the product or service itself. You've just read several examples. Now create several examples for your own company. Promotions do work, and guerrilla companies are constantly scouting for new ways to promote without hurting profits.

24

Why So Much Advertising Fails

Look up one dark night and count the stars if you want to find out the number of reasons so many advertising dollars are wasted. Beginning with the stars of greatest magnitude, you see:

- *Premature abandonment.* The most disheartening thought in this chapter is that most advertising that is discarded too soon had a good chance of succeeding in time if only the advertiser had enough patience. Few do. Patience should be a going-in strategy.

  Prepare to be disheartened

- *Silly positioning.* Products and services enter the market-place and advertise their pants off while not being posi-tioned in the marketplace in a way that tempts buyers. Whatever were those wealthly beer barons thinking when they introduced dry beer? Certainly doesn't sound like a market position that would appeal to beer drinkers. And clear cola doesn't sound very appetizing to those hordes of Coke and Pepsi lovers. Many people holding impor-tant marketing jobs seem to be operating under a phi-losophy that dictates, "If it ain't broke, fix it until it is."

  If it ain't broke, fix it until it is

- *Failure to focus.* Advertisers fail to make the essential link between the glories of their offering and how it relates to their prospects. The technocrats of the computer industry have long been guilty of failing to communicate with non-technocrats. Their advertising and especially their user manuals are living examples of this truth. Apple and Epson are innocent of this charge.

- *Beginning without a written plan of attack.* Writing forces you to be clear to yourself, enabling you to be clear to others. A written plan that plots month-by-month actions lets you see where you've been, where you are, and where you're going. You should always know exactly how much you're spending on advertising and if the profits generated are commensurate with your efforts. You can't see that in the stars. You need it *in writing.*
- *Picking the wrong media for the right audience.* The homework for guerrilla advertising includes a course in media availability and selection, conducted for you by a marketing firm, media-buying service, or advertising agency. They will steer you in the direction of the right media. If you can't afford these services, you probably should wait until you can. Guerrillas can't afford to advertise without first utilizing these services. Their cost of a few hundred dollars can positively influence your future ad investment of thousands of dollars. Still, keep in mind that the people who work for you can provide a great deal of home-grown research. Ask anyone who might be a likely prospect what radio stations they listen to, where they shop. If the prospects are kids, ask what they read and watch on TV. Knowledge is everywhere — if you know where to look. The job of the guerrilla is not to know everything, but to know *where to find* everything.

For the want of $100, $1,000 was lost

- *Picking the right media for the wrong audience.* Your market research, undertaken at the outset of your venture, has turned up the ideal prospects for your offering — or else. Unpleasant days await you if you are planning to advertise in *The Wall Street Journal* for your acne cream.
- *Being unclear to prospects.* It is a rule of both thumbs and all fingers that if your prospects aren't clear about what you're saying in your advertising, the lack of clarity will probably cause them to think you'll be the same if they buy. So they pass.

- *Not understanding customers.* They may not want all the things you're lauding to the skies, but they may want a few you haven't even mentioned. Even more important than what they want is what they need. People do tend to buy what they want instead of what they need. Nevertheless, your business will fare better if you're attuned to filling the needs of your customers instead of their wants. From such conscientiousness comes repeat and referral business. Guerrillas are always more interested in the long term than the fast buck.
- *Not understanding self.* There's an old Yiddish expression: "Don't act so big. You're not so little." Don't miss the point about your strengths. At first, McDonald's thought it was in the burger biz when it really was in the fast-food biz.
- *Exaggeration that undermines truth.* Several trillion ads died needless deaths because a zealous copywriter, probably fueled by enthusiasm and the adrenaline of competition, used a word in copy that undid superb market research, brilliant media selection, and inspired artwork. That word may have been "best," "biggest," "fabulous," "incredible," or any of a thesaurus-full of adverbs and adjectives that overstate a case past the point of believability.

  An amazing and astonishing truth!

- *Not keeping up with change.* The changes that cause much advertising to fall on its face occur on the competitive scene, in the marketing field, in the national or local economy, in the media, or in current events. On-line advertising is growing, as you'll see later in this book. The information superhighway is starting to come into place. People are losing their technophobia. Idols are toppling. Marky Mark says something controversial and Calvin Klein is forced to drop him from its ads. Bo Jackson gets an artificial hip, motivating some advertisers not to renew their contracts with him. Michael Jordan retires, throwing a damper on the ad plans of several companies. Michael Jackson is inundated with unsavory

  Bo knows rejection

publicity, causing Pepsi to drop him as spokesperson. Everything seems to be transforming, especially advertising, advertising technology, even advertising spokespeople. Keeping apace isn't enough anymore. If you're not moving ahead, you're falling behind.

- *Unrealistic expectations.* This is the primary cause of advertising abandonment. Impatient advertisers expect profits to come in faster and larger than reality dictates. Advertising accomplishes many things. But miracles are not among them.

Sorry, no miracles today

- *Overspending or underspending.* Advertisers often put forth a shah's ransom to run a full-color ad when a black and white ad would have done very well. Still, that beats saving bucks by running an ad with a black and white Polaroid shot by your kid sister.

- *Saving money in the wrong places.* Nothing against your kid sister — mine's a peach — but she's also not the person to write your ad copy, plan your media, do your research, or design your ad. Yes, I know she earned straight A's in art, but use a pro for these items.

- *Inattention to tiny, but nuclear-powered details.* If the photo is perfect in an ad, the headline hits readers right where they live, the copy motivates people to grab feverishly for their Visa cards, but the ad doesn't tell them where to buy what's being sold, send in the clowns. Has this ever happened? More than once.

- *Missing the point about profits.* Some advertising has attracted a herd of customers, most of whom purchased the least expensive items because the ad featured loss leaders with low profitability, if any. A loss leader is a product sold with a minimum profit and sometimes no profit at all, a loss — with the purpose of attracting a lot of foot traffic into a store. Be sure that profits are measured above and beyond traffic and sales. If people buy only your loss leader, you're in trouble. If they buy your loss leader, then several products with healthy profits, you've done a good job with your advertising and you've catered to your overall goal of profitability.

Loss leaders can win profits

- *Thinking it can be done without hard work.* The home-work that goes into knowing how to say the right things to the right people in the right place at the right time is formidable. If you think you can finesse the homework, don't. Find a guerrilla who will do it for you.
- *Unimpressive first impressions.* You may have a heart that's a gem, but if you don't have a headline that's a grabber, how can you expect people to read your copy, much less buy your product? Print headlines and radio and TV opening lines are the real name of the ad game. As Geoffrey Beene said, "You only make a first impression once."
- *Committees and layers of management.* Although committees exist to contribute to the probability of success, they tend to dilute great ad ideas. Layers of management should see their goal as preventing disasters and maintaining momentum, sticking to plans and budgets, and measuring profitability.
- *Not using the media to their greatest advantage.* Because a person can crank out a classified ad that earns five times its cost each time it runs, as I did for eight years, that doesn't mean the same person has the ability to create a powerful TV spot. Each of the media has a special strength all its own. Guerrilla advertising capitalizes upon it.
- *Not supporting advertising with other marketing.* Advertising that is not augmented by some of the other hundred weapons of guerrilla marketing has very little chance of pulling its financial weight. Yet millions are wasted daily because naive advertisers expect ads to do the whole job.
- *Starting out in the wrong direction.* A great deal of advertising fails because crucial market and motivational research did not precede it. The advertiser operated by dead reckoning instead of fact, not a good idea. Even more advertising bites the dust because it was never tested, a terrible idea. Research and testing set advertisers in the right direction and help avoid failures.

Dead reckoning can be a dead end

- *Allowing success to beget lethargy.* Because many advertisers did it right yesterday, they thought they were doing it right today, but they weren't. Sure, commitment leads to success. But it must be a dynamic commitment that allows you to keep up with the times, do it better, respond to competitors, and seize new opportunities.
- *Boring advertising.* I've saved the most obvious for last. You know why you pay no attention to most advertising. You know how it comes at you with waves of invisibility, looking, sounding, feeling, and acting like everything else in the sea of advertising. The guerrilla never allows a hint of boredom in advertising.

*   *   *

It's interesting to note that much great advertising was created by individuals, but killed by committees. The reverse is *not* true. Hardly any great advertising was created by committees, but killed by individuals.

If committees are to screen ads, which I do begrudgingly recommend, they should be on the alert for reasons they will fail and bounce back ideas to make them succeed. Shooting holes in advertising is too easy. Making it better is tough.

The "Elvis brands" Oftentimes, once-famous products lose their market share for a host of reasons. Do you remember: Brylcreem, Ovaltine, Lavoris, Lifebuoy, Chesterfield cigarettes, Solo liquid detergent, White Cloud bathroom tissue, Ajax, Rinso, Bosco chocolate syrup, Pepsodent, Sen-Sen, Post Toasties, Maypo, Viceroy cigarettes, Beeman's gum, Clove gum, Schlitz beer, Rheingold Beer, or Lorna Doone cookies? These brand-name products have all but disappeared from the public consciousness because of discounted products, improved products, niche products, company mergers, and increased competition for shelf space. Advertising alone can't save them, though some are bravely trying for comebacks. Recently dubbed the "Elvis brands" in a *New York Times* article, they were once thought dead, but keep coming back.

On the way to the advertising graveyard, along with many of the above, are Camay, Chun King, Michelob, Miller High

Life, Prell shampoo, Sanka, Tab, and Winston cigarettes. Maybe sales dropped because the advertising for these brands changed too frequently to ensure consumer loyalty, but more likely, it's because even market leaders can take nothing for granted in a world with increasingly sophisticated advertising techniques and a plethora of new products, not to mention guerrillas lurking around every corner.

25

Rolling Up Your Sleeves and Doing the Work

When I was living in England, a London cabbie, while driving me home, inquired in the midst of our conversation about my chosen profession, "You mean they actually pay blokes to write those things?"

Well, they do. And very handsomely. In fact, a top creative executive in a giant advertising agency can earn a salary in the six-figure range, and if he's good enough, in the seven-figure range.

But that creative hotshot often operates in a pressure cooker. Staying on top means delivering the goods on not just some occasions, but on most occasions. It's not easy, and not everybody can do it consistently and with excellence. That, and huge advertising budgets, explains the high salaries. Explaining the hard work is a different job and one that few people, even in advertising, ever understand.

Still, the fact remains that after the smart people in the suits — advertising account executives, researchers, and media mavens — have done their homework, someone has got to get down to the business of churning out an ad, though I doubt Michelangelo ever thought of churning out a chapel ceiling. Not that there is an obvious comparison between the Sistine Chapel and a newspaper ad or TV spot, but any ad maker worth a hill of Rice Krispies takes on the job of creating an advertisement with the same sense of challenge, spirit of enthusiasm, and ever-flowing creative juices as did the masters of the fine arts.

I assume that you run a small business, possibly even cre-

Someone's got to turn out an ad

ate your own advertising. But for you, as for the professional ad agency copywriter, the task remains the same: *Create an advertisement or commercial that will generate profits.*

Suppose you went out and retained the services of an advertising agency. Here's what it's like for that agency copywriter, a person who wears the same hat that you will wear when you get down to the business of creating a profit-producing ad:

Several people have pored over the numbers to come up with the exact demographics and psychographics of your marketplace. Others have used their M.B.A. training and Ph.D. skills to learn why your prospects act the way they do, spend the way they do, and want the things they crave.

This information has been spoon-fed to you in the form of a multi-page memo or research document. Other marketing and advertising wizards have looked beneath the veneer of your prospects' personalities to learn the underlying reasons for their purchases, their behavior, and their quirks. This data has also been supplied to you.

Bright, well-spoken engineers and technical types have filled you in on the product specs of your offering, meticulously and proudly pointing out all the features they have engineered into the product. The list of specifications and features are now in your possession.

The media masters have given you crystal-clear insights into the magazines and newspapers in which your advertising will run, the purchasing habits of the drivers who will hear your radio commercials as they commute back home from work, and the consumer profiles of those who will watch your TV spots as they unwind from their day. This information is placed neatly on your desk, maybe even into your e-mail.

Fact is, you've been data-fed to the max. What now? What now is that you've got to come up with a winning ad, that's all. One winning ad, although four would be better, is all that is asked of you. Piled in front of you is the prospect information that your supporting cast has supplied you.

Inside your head is more information than you know what to do with. Staring you in the face is a:

You've been data-fed to the max

1. Blank computer screen
2. Blank sheet of typewriter paper
3. Blank top sheet of a yellow pad
4. Blank top sheet of a pad of drawing paper

Well?

**Rolling up
the sleeves of
your mind**

You create the ad. You roll up your sleeves and do the hard work of turning out an ad that will produce profits for the advertiser. You know that every word counts. Sometimes a company is paying the media as much as $40,000 in TV time for each word you write. Make each one count. Make each one earn $80,000, $400,000. Make that advertising investment pay off. Sometimes even more than mere money is riding on your words — your entire company is. Be careful, this is for keeps.

Remember always: The starting point for a great ad is a great *idea*. Maybe it's the value of your offering. It could be the breakthrough technology of your product or service. Perhaps you offer a benefit such as speed, ease, beauty, freedom, the solution to a nagging problem. Possibly you can show people how to look younger, healthier, slimmer. You might be offering free installation, free delivery. You could even be selling a dream — a vacation, a new home, a promotion, a new way to achieve wealth and power. Got that idea? Get several. The right one will often scream out at you, "I'm it!" Run that idea past colleagues, past prospects. Once you've got the bare-bones idea, which is really the hardest part of creating advertising, you are faced with the next part — also a bear. You've got to state that idea in terms that will move prospects to purchase your offering.

You know about the importance of headlines and opening lines? Okay, then write one, which really means write one hundred, then select the best. Make it a surefire winner. Be sure it intrigues people into reading every single word of your copy or compels them to order your product right now. Tomorrow will be too late because people tend to forget advertising lightning fast.

Will your first stab at creating a winning ad or commercial

be the right one? It has happened. More frequently, you'll have to take a second stab, a tenth, a twentieth. And that's just for the headline. If you're creating a print ad, the subhead will take another ten or twenty. If you're developing a radio or TV spot, the sound effects and visuals are crucial.

Next comes another hard part: writing your copy. Don't be afraid to say too much. You must give people enough information for them to make an intelligent purchase decision. Anyhow, that's what editing is for. The more time you spend shaping your idea and refining your headline and subhead, the easier it will be to write your copy. If your idea is powerful, your copy will flow. If it is weak, your copy will be blocked by some censor in your brain prohibiting you from investing money in a lame idea. In your copy, state the features you offer and bring each alive with the benefit that results from that feature.

How much copy is enough?

Example: The feature is more space in your expanded clothing store. The benefit is a better selection of merchandise. Be sure you stress your competitive advantage. There are so many advertisers that many run the constant risk of being perceived as a me-too brand. Competitive advantages surmount that barrier. List them all at the outset.

Then the time comes when you edit — self-surgery is an apt phrase — and polish and cut. Don't forget, you are not involved in the arts, in literature, or in entertainment. Your job is considerably harder. *You've got to make people act, using only the brute force of your ideas.*

Using ideas to generate action

Harder still is judging what you have created. Just how likely is that idea of yours to catch the notice of that housewife in Iowa who is watching TV with one eye and two kids too young for day care with the other? You've got to answer that, and you'd better be right. As your words come across the car radio, how likely are they to capture the imagination of an accounting clerk driving home from work with his mind on pouring himself a good stiff drink? The only acceptable answer is "very likely." And how will your deathless prose or eye-catching graphics affect that entrepreneur who is speeding along in the crowded commuter train reading a newspaper report about an economic downturn and glancing at your ad positioned next to it?

The moments of truth   Those are moments of truth. Ad makers are exposed to millions of them daily. During those moments, people decide to pay rapt attention, to buy today, or to actively ignore your cogent advertising message. Yes, you might reach these people some other time and place, but right now is all that counts. You want to make the most of every moment of truth. You have to. As a guerrilla, you realize that advertising dollars are far too scarce and precious to waste.

You'd have every right to feel a chill when you consider the import of your words and the apathy of your audience. But doing the work means delighting at the import of the words, respectful of their power, and perceiving the apathy of your audience as a wall that you can climb over while others are kept out. Your optimism must fuel your creativity.

When you actually do the hard — and thrilling — work of creating advertising that will see the light of public exposure, it can often be akin to a social event. In brainstorming sessions, ideas flash, die, sparkle, live, get improved, get polished, get shot down, get partnered with another idea, appear in a different guise, then gain a consensus, become produced, run, and contribute to incredibly beautiful bottom lines. Don't imagine for a moment that you have to create an ad all by yourself, though I personally, and several people like me, consider the creating of advertising to be an extremely lonely assignment. But it need not be lonely.

Shall we dance?   The hard work is also often a two-person dance, one leading, the other following, then both switching places. Some of my best headlines came from art directors. Some of their best graphic ideas came from me, an inept designer. A team of two will bounce around an idea and give it wings as dancers whirling around an open space. The dancers' movements become a work of art. The ideas become an ad. It doesn't happen instantly, but if you work at it hard enough, it does happen and can happen to you even if you've never created an ad in your life. Creativity comes from duos and soloists.

We're all different. In my case, the hard work of creating

an ad or commercial comes when I'm alone. Don't think of darkness and burning midnight oil. Just think of solitude, of a task that must be done and of you as the only person working on the task. Most who have earned their keep in creative pursuits will describe their tasks as lonely. To me, the loneliness is the best part. It is in that special place that I alone occupy that I locate and create the best of which I am capable. I need the solitude. If all advertisements and books were written by teams, my career would have been spent as a cable car gripman in San Francisco.

But that's me. For you, the experience may be considerably different. For both of us, however, the nuts and bolts of creating advertising is a twenty-step process:

Guerrilla nuts and bolts

1. Study or engage in the research.
2. Study the advertising strategy.
3. Study the benefits you offer, then pick the best ones and those that are competitive advantages.
4. Generate a slew of creative ideas for your ad, then pick the best. Don't take too long; you're probably up against a deadline — even if it's self-imposed.
5. Create the headline.
6. Create the subhead.
7. Develop the graphic approach.
8. Incorporate the sound effects or special effects.
9. Write the copy.
10. Edit, edit, then edit some more.
11. Show the finished idea to others, especially to prospects; they're the real experts, not the ad makers.
12. Measure the finished idea against your strategy.
13. Sleep on it, letting the idea sink in deeply.
14. Review the finished ad in the light of a new day.
15. Improve the idea, headline, subhead, and copy if you can.
16. Improve the visual presentation of your idea.
17. Look at your ad in a real magazine; just put it in the magazine and see how it feels in the environment in which it will live.

18. See what you can do to extend the single ad into a campaign that can live a long time.
19. Be certain that your finished ad will be clear to your prospects.
20. Be absolutely honest in assessing whether or not your advertisement will generate profits.

That's all there is to it — whether you're an agency copywriter or an entrepreneur trying to save money by taking a professional approach to creating your own ads. If it sounds easy, read it again. It may be enjoyable, but it isn't easy.

Whether as part of a large group, small team, or as an individual, I hope you experience the opportunity and the pressure — to do the work. May you do it splendidly.

V

Headlines, Copy, and Graphics

UP TO THIS POINT, we've been involved in the inspection of a beautiful automobile. We know that it is powerful, sleek, capable of great speeds. It is comfortable, too, and makes us feel good as soon as we take the driver's seat.

We know that when we turn on that ignition key and listen to that promise of unbridled performance, our pulses will quicken. We know this car will get us anywhere we want. We've got a detailed, customized road map, designed expressly for our needs. It shows us the best way to reach our destination. The mere thought of that destination makes our eyes sparkle.

But what happens when we turn the ignition key and are greeted by the heavy sound of silence? Our map is clear. The tank is filled with premium fuel. The battery is fully charged. But the car won't run.

So we open the door, get out of the car, lift the hood, and we see that the car doesn't have an engine! What's going to make it go? Nothing is.

This part of the book is the part where your car gets the engine it needs. Here's where you learn the truth about the headlines that get the engine going, the copy that speeds you through traffic and to the bank, and the graphics that add the elements of style and dash to the ride.

The headlines, copy, and graphics — those are the parts that make up the engine. And you know they're not easy to hone to guerrilla keenness. This is where we capture the four A's that give wings to advertising.

The first is *attention*, because without it, nothing else in the ad matters. Nobody will even see the headline, let alone the copy and graphics. The second is *awareness*, which is one level up from barely being noticed, but beats the pants off inattention. The third is *attitude*, which comes from your identity and describes how people feel about your product or service. The fourth is *action*, which is the purpose of the whole exercise. As ad makers of the 1890s and 1990s have learned, your advertising, using the tools of headlines, copy, and graphics, must gain attention, build awareness, mold attitude, and motivate action.

As always, that advertising is geared to profitability and powered by an *idea*. Without the idea, your headlines, copy, and graphics dry up in the creative desert to nothingness. They must be nourished by a clear and strong idea. When they are, the headlines write themselves, one after another. The copy flows from your word processor or black pencil like a mighty river. The artwork appears on your computer screen or drawing pad seemingly by itself because it fits so well with the idea, headline, and copy.

When P. T. Barnum had the idea in 1835 of exhibiting an eighty-year-old slave named Joice Heth, claiming she was more than twice her age and a former slave of George Washington, a sign proclaimed the "fact" and the headline obviously wrote itself. When Crest toothpaste was the first to be recognized as effective against cavities by the American Dental Association, it didn't take a creative superstar to write the headlines, the copy, and develop the graphics. The idea was powerful enough virtually to create its own ads and commercials.

If you wait for inspiration before creating your ad, you'll usually be in for a long wait. Instead, start with something easy — like the idea and the benefits it offers or the inherent drama within it. Write as though you are talking to a buddy.

The guerrilla of the nineties operates, when possible, in

accordance with four important guidelines for creating great advertising:

1. Use a word processor so fear of errors disappears.
2. Don't be in a hurry.
3. Avoid perfectionism.
4. Do everything in your power to *get it right the first time* by doing your homework before you start creating the ad.

26

Developing Headlines
That Inspire Action

The action you want from a headline if you're greedy is for the reader to immediately order what you're selling. The action you want from a headline if you're a guerrilla is for the reader to read the rest of the ad, then immediately order what you're selling. This is more realism than greed.

Worth repeating is Golden Rule #30 from my book *Guerrilla Marketing Excellence*: "If you have ten hours to spend creating an ad, spend nine of them on the headline."

Let me clarify right here that when I say headline I mean:

- Headline for a print ad
- Headline for a brochure
- Opening line for a TV commercial
- Opening line for a radio commercial

Four kinds of headlines

It could also mean opening lines for direct mail letters, postcards, telemarketing scripts, and several other marketing weapons, but we're talking advertising here.

John Caples, a primary architect of advertising, said that the most important part of an ad is the headline. He believed that if you could think up a good headline, directed to the right audience, and you could offer them a benefit, you could almost be guaranteed of producing a good ad. After all, he reasoned, your copy could simply be a continuation of the idea you expressed in your headline. He also warned that if your ad has a poor headline, you've probably wasted your shot because people will not read on.

A zinger from the past

John knew that ads usually have a basic selling appeal and the place for it is in the headline. One of his zingers was "How I retired on a guaranteed income for life." The basic selling appeal was financial security after retirement. The headline clearly spells out that appeal, and Phoenix Mutual Life Insurance Company was the prime beneficiary.

The revered Mr. Caples would be unrevered by many of today's art directors because of his belief about the illustration for an ad: *He believed it was determined by the headline.* In much of today's advertising, you don't see any connection. The visual often is not related to the headline, and sometimes there is no headline at all. What would Mr. Caples do if he were shown an ad without a headline? In today's world, the illustration is determined by the idea — not by the headline or the copy. The idea is king. Even the almighty headline plays a subservient role to it.

The most important thing you say

I feel it is my guerrilla duty to give you guidelines about headlines because your headline dictates your positioning in the mind of your prospect — and attracts prospect attention or is ignored. *It is the most important thing you say to your prospect.*

The biggest problem with most headlines is they are boring, unclear, and do not invite readers to learn more. Let's examine headlines for a new product called Non. It's a breath spray with ingredients that can help smokers quit. Many of the following hints are culled from advertising geniuses of the past.

Twenty-one guerrilla headline hints

1. Realize that your headline must either *convey an idea* or *intrigue the reader* into wanting to read more of your ad.

   NOW THERE'S A BREATH SPRAY THAT
   CAN HELP YOU QUIT SMOKING!

2. Direct your headline smack-dab to the reader, listener, or viewer, *one person at a time,* even if 20 million people will be exposed to it.

   IF YOU'RE A SMOKER, YOU'LL WANT
   TO LEARN ABOUT NON ANTI-SMOKING SPRAY

3. Write your headline *in news style*. This is especially essential for newspaper ads where news is on people's minds.

> NEW ANTI-SMOKING SPRAY HELPS SMOKERS
> SPRAY AWAY THE DESIRE TO SMOKE

4. Use words that have *an announcement quality* — words like *"Presenting," "New,"* and *"Introducing."*

> PRESENTING NON — THE ANTI-SMOKING SPRAY
> THAT CAN MAKE YOU A NON-SMOKER!

5. Experiment with headlines that actually *begin with the word "Announcing."*

> ANNOUNCING THE BREATH SPRAY THAT
> CAN HELP YOU QUIT SMOKING

6. Experiment with headlines that *begin with the word "New."* It is one of humankind's favorite words.

> NEW! A BREATH SPRAY THAT
> SPRAYS AWAY YOUR DESIRE TO SMOKE!

7. *Put a date* in your headline.

> ON DECEMBER 10, 1994, QUITTING SMOKING
> BECAME EASIER THAN EVER BEFORE

8. *Feature the price* — if you're proud of it — in your headline. It need not be a low price for the ad to succeed.

> WOULD YOU PAY $5.00 TO QUIT SMOKING?

9. Stress your *easy payment plan* — people like low numbers far more than high ones.

> BECOME AN EX-SMOKER FOR ONLY
> $1.00 A DAY FOR FIVE DAYS

10. Announce a *free offer*.

> FREE! YOUR SECOND PACKAGE OF NON
> WHEN YOU BUY YOUR FIRST!

11. Offer *information of value.*

> SMOKING A PACK OF CIGARETTES A DAY
> SUBTRACTS SIX YEARS FROM YOUR LIFE.
> HERE'S HOW YOU CAN STOP SMOKING:

12. *Start to tell a story* — then continue it in the copy.

> GINA POPE USED TO SMOKE A PACK
> OF CIGARETTES A DAY. THEN SHE HEARD ABOUT
> A NEW BREATH SPRAY THAT COULD HELP HER . . .

13. Begin your headline with *"How to."*

> HOW TO QUIT SMOKING SIMPLY
> BY PRESSING A BUTTON:

14. Begin your headline with *"How," "Why," "Which," "You," "Your,"* or *"This."*

> WHY 5,000 CALIFORNIA SMOKERS
> QUIT SMOKING LAST MONTH

15. Begin your headline with *"Advice."*

> ADVICE FOR PEOPLE WHO SERIOUSLY
> WANT TO QUIT SMOKING

16. Use a *testimonial-style* headline.

> "I NEVER THOUGHT I COULD QUIT SMOKING,
> BUT NON ANTI-SMOKING SPRAY HELPED ME
> QUIT IN LESS THAN ONE WEEK!"

17. Offer the reader *a test.*

> WHICH OF THESE NEW PRODUCTS
> IS HELPING SMOKERS QUIT SMOKING?
>
> A. A PRESCRIPTION MEDICINE
> B. A PRE-FRONTAL LOBOTOMY KIT
> C. NON ANTI-SMOKING SPRAY

18. Warn the reader *not to delay buying.*

> WE HAVE NON ANTI-SMOKING SPRAY
> IN STOCK TODAY.
> BUT WE MIGHT RUN OUT TOMORROW.
> DON'T WAIT TO QUIT SMOKING.

19. Use a *one-word* headline. You can make that word very large so that it almost seems to leap from the page.

> QUIT!

20. Address your headline to *a specific person.*

> IF YOU SMOKE CIGARETTES,
> YOU NEED NEW NON ANTI-SMOKING SPRAY

21. Whenever possible, and it's not always possible, *use your company or product name* in your headline and opening line. It may be the only thing prospects read or hear.

> NON ANTI-SMOKING SPRAY —
> IT CAN BREAK YOUR CIGARETTE HABIT!

* * *

Figure it like this: If the reader or viewer isn't stopped by your headline, that reader or viewer will move on to something else, and it certainly won't be more of your advertisement or commercial. Your heart was in the right place because you were investing in advertising, but your investment was mismanaged by your failure to judge properly one of the most crucial parts of your entire ad campaign. **Stop them or lose them**

Headlines and opening lines are initial bonds to your prospects. As important as saying something enticing *is the manner in which you say it.* Your job may be to create headlines or to judge them. Consider it one of your most important jobs. Never let a boring or me-too headline sabotage the thoughtful copy and graphics that surround it.

27

Writing Copy That Creates a Desire to Buy

Good for you! You've developed a can't-miss advertising strategy. You have a superpowered idea. You've dreamed up a grab-'em-by-the-eyeballs headline. And you've presented your message in a startling visual format. Now your prospects are all set to read the copy and you're perched on the edge of getting the business and reaping the profits. Oh, happy day!

Not necessarily. What if your copy starts from a different place than the headline or subhead and readers fail to make the connection? What if your copy is so boring, readers rush to turn the page? What if your copy has one long word that's unique enough to scare off 20 percent of your readers (losing 200,000 people if your advertising is reaching a million). What if the copy has one word of hogwash that spills hogslop over all the other words and destroys your believability? What if you don't give enough information in your copy? What if it's too technical to get through to your audience? Or what if it's not technical enough because your prospects are science whizzes and they feel you are leaving many questions unanswered? What if readers read it but are left numb and unmotivated? What if the grammar is poor? What if there are misspelled words? What if it fails to involve the reader? What if it regales readers with benefits, but solves none of their problems? What if it simply is not persuasive?

There are trip wires to explode your advertising efforts in more places than you dare imagine. You've got to take extra care to trip none of them, set off no explosions, and let your

How to lose 200,000 readers

copy lead your prospects right to that magic moment of purchase. For example, your perfect ad for a trade magazine doesn't fly in the general-interest magazine you want to appear in. Your perfect cutout coupon pulls when it runs in your supermarket supplement, but draws nary a response when it's in your local newspaper. Your visual is hot for the women's magazines, but has readers offended in the Bible Belt. Mistakes large and small detonate the best laid plans. And sometimes they're not even mistakes. Procter & Gamble's logo is the symbol of the devil to some religious groups.

To make it easy for you, remember ten things that copy should always be:

What guerrilla copy should be

1. Readable
2. Informative
3. Clear
4. Honest
5. Simple
6. On strategy
7. Motivating
8. Competitive
9. Specific
10. Believable

If your copy is at least those ten things, you have a fine head start on creating some good, maybe even great, copy. You must also remember that certain words are "ear" words and are especially well suited for radio, while other words are "eye" words and don't ring when you hear them, but look excellent when being read. "Guerrilla" means one thing to the eyes, something very different to the ears.

Unfortunately, your formal education probably provided you with very few skills for producing effective advertising copy. Most schools stress grammar, vocabulary, and spelling rather than motivation and persuasiveness. You are required to fill a specific number of pages — or an entire blue book — with your writing, when the key to successful copywriting is brevity. That does not mean short copy. Instead it means short words, short sentences, short paragraphs. Brevity is scorned in school. It rarely fills blue books.

Never let your advertising sound like advertising, but don't hide the fact that it's an ad. You can even be proud of that fact, but demonstrate your pride with fresh, readable copy that gets people to take notice, read, then buy and recommend.

Jay Chiat, a modern-day John Caples and founder of one **What good** of America's top ad agencies, once said, "Good writers come **writers have** in all sizes, shapes, and ages. What they all seem to have in **in common** common is the ability to hear, to listen, to understand — and to distill what they hear and learn into something that's human and persuasive." I would add that good writers always seem to be curious critters.

The most exciting thing about copywriting is that anything goes. There are no formulas — in fact the fewer rules you have, the better. There aren't a whole lot of copywriting rules, anyway, but here are ten copywriting nuggets to set you on a true course:

Ten guerrilla 1. *Verbs activate your ads.* So write in the active voice. *Do* **writing rules** *it now. Write better copy. Pay close attention.* Those are short sentences with verbs that motivate action. They don't just sit there. Run, don't walk.
  2. *Use adjectives, but sparingly.* You must be selective in this area. Your adjectives must clarify, inform, excite, but never exaggerate. Adjectives tend to get more trendy than other words, and it's smart to avoid trendy copy. A thesaurus helps vary your copy, but contains many obsolete and unknown words, so use one with care — unless an obsolete word is just the ducat.
  3. *Don't overlook adverbs.* The original line for Federal Express was "When it has to be there overnight." Two adverbs made that theme line into a classic: "When it *absolutely, positively* has to be there overnight."
  4. *Create original clichés.* Turn a phrase in a way it never has been turned before, but don't resort to old-fashioned clichés. Campbell's soup once described itself as "tender

loving fare" — an original cliché. Your job: to create
new ones every time you write.

5. *Write with a positive attitude.* Almost any negativity becomes associated with your product. Avoid it. Avis said
   "We try harder" to turn the negativity of being number
   two into a positive attribute. A once-famous cigar once
   said in its ads, "No spit. No spittle." The readers remembered the spit and spittle, but not the cigar. That's why
   the once-famous cigar is now the long-gone cigar.

6. *Make every sentence lead to the next sentence.* This gives
   your copy "flow" and promotes readership all the way to
   the last word.

7. *Relate all you say to your headline and main idea.* People
   are too busy to follow you on your meanderings, so get to
   the point and stay with it. People will appreciate this by
   reading and understanding everything you say. Maybe
   they'll even buy what you're advertising.

8. *Watch out for rhymes, puns, and clever writing.* These
   may be fun to write, even fun to read, but they're beside
   the point and get in the way of your flow. Do you want
   folks to remember your pun or your offer?

9. *Don't worry about sentence fragments.* Sometimes they
   make for copy that is readable. And clear. And even
   motivating.

10. *After you've written the copy, get set to rewrite it.*
    Often this is when the best writing takes place. It helps
    you write tight (excuse the rhyme, but this is no ad;
    this is a book and I get to play by different rules) and it
    helps you cut copy mercilessly, which is usually the
    best way.

Mark Twain once said, "Eliminate every third word. It gives
writing remarkable vigor." Twain was not talking about advertising, but he had a good point. Your ad will be as good as its
weakest element. Never let that be the copy.

To help you write good copy, I borrow again from my book
Guerrilla Marketing Excellence to alert you to the magic words
and the tragic words in advertising copy.

The magic words   The magic words carry far more than the weight of one word. In advertising copy, they carry immense power. They are:

FREE	LOVE	SAFE
NEW	BENEFITS	RIGHT
YOU	ALTERNATIVE	SECURITY
SALE	NOW	WINNINGS
INTRODUCING	WIN	FUN
SAVE	GAIN	VALUE
MONEY	HAPPY	ADVICE
DISCOVER	TRUSTWORTHY	WANTED
RESULTS	GOOD-LOOKING	ANNOUNCING
EASY	COMFORTABLE	YOUR
PROVEN	PROUD	PEOPLE
GUARANTEED	HEALTHY	WHY

The tragic words   The tragic words, fewer in number than the magic words, can undo otherwise fine copy. That means they can blow the sale for you. Avoid tragic words such as:

BUY	DIFFICULT	DEATH
OBLIGATION	WRONG	ORDER
FAILURE	DECISION	FAIL
BAD	DEAL	COST
SELL	LIABILITY	WORRY
LOSS	HARD	CONTRACT

As life goes on and you write — or judge — ad copy for your company, I know you'll discover even more magic words. Just be sure that you're constantly on the lookout for more tragic words.

Copywriting is too disciplined a craft to allow itself to be sabotaged by a tragic word. And profits are too hard to come by for you to overlook the potential use of a magic word. If you're going to be writing copy, one of the smartest things you can do is to *read* copy. It won't take long for you to recognize words that push your hot buttons and make you want to own the product or service being advertised — and other words that turn you away from what might be a quality offering at a reasonable price.

Ever thought you'd read ad copy as a way of becoming better at your business? It's required reading for guerrillas.

28

Using Graphics to
Burn In Your Message

You've got a can't-miss advertising strategy, a headline or opening line that stops prospects in their tracks, and copy that
makes them long for your product or service. But what if your
ad or TV spot is so ordinary, so visually empty, that nobody
even notices it?

You've wasted a lot of time and talent if that happens. You
need powerful graphics to help that time and talent pay divi-
dends. And where do you suppose potent graphic ideas come
from? First, you've got to know where they *don't* come from:

**Where potent
graphic ideas
don't come from**

- They don't come from thumbing through copies of art
  director magazines, publications of award-winning ads,
  or from viewing TV prize winners from around the
  world.
- They don't come from seminars, art books, or art
  courses — though the good ones do show you how to
  think about advertising, a prerequisite for successfully
  creating it.
- They don't come from advanced computer software,
  special effects machines, or technology itself.
- They don't come from a starting point of art technique,
  beautiful design, or art for art's sake.
- They don't come from inspiration, so don't wait for it.

*They do come from the inherent drama of your offering,
your competitive advantage, an in-depth understanding of your
target audience, and from the details of life itself.*

You'll come up with winning graphic ideas by observing what's happening in the world, from watching TV newscasts, reading the newspaper, subscribing to a weekly newsmagazine, reading books on topics other than advertising, going to movies and the theater, and driving or strolling around with your eyes wide-open to observe the minutiae of life in today's world. You'll find excellent graphic ideas by exploring the depths of your own memories, your own experiences, your gut reactions, your intuition and instincts.

As long as you always remember that the purpose of any graphic idea in advertising is to create a desire for the product or service, you probably won't stray too far from the right *ideas* you need.

Stop right here, reread the word I've put into italics, and realize that there are *several* ideal graphic concepts that will serve your purposes. There isn't *just one* idea; there are always more than one. As there are many magnificent ideas, there are even more mediocre ideas. Your job is to visualize the magnificent ones and reject the mediocre ones. Don't search for the Holy Grail when there is a cupboard full of grails, each as ideal as the holy one.

Several great ideas, not just one

One of your prime purposes in the graphic presentation of advertising is to avoid being humdrum, or as advertising superstar Ray Rubicam said, "Resist the usual." Go out of your way to be extraordinary in a sea of ordinariness, but remember your purpose.

Get attention, but be sure it is positive attention directed at the benefits of your offering. Leo Burnett once said, "It's easy to get attention. Simply come downstairs with your socks in your mouth."

One of your most crucial jobs in the graphic telling of your story is to tell it visually with impact, described by Mr. Rubicam as "that quality in an advertisement which strikes suddenly against the reader's indifference and enlivens his mind to receive a sales message." The same, naturally, is true for TV, as visual a medium as there is in the ad world.

Another major task is to have the graphics work *with* the headline, opening line, and copy. The need for teamwork be-

Go team, go!

tween words and pictures is especially acute in advertising. Rembrandt, Dali, Renoir — they didn't have to worry about having their graphics combine with words to put forth a sales message. But as a guerrilla, you do.

In print advertising you must also remember the principles of good typography. Type isn't beautiful if you can't read it. Readability is paramount. That not only means type that isn't too ornate, but also columns that aren't too narrow or too wide. Forty characters of type per line is a good rule of thumb.

If you're going to run large space ads in the newspaper, you need not concern yourself with the border around the ad, but if you run smaller ads, a border can help your ad stand out if you have the right border and use it consistently enough.

Unlike copy, which can be long if necessary, graphics have the obligation to gain attention instantly. Again, Leo Burnett: "The art director is the difference between advertising that stands still and advertising that stands out."

The complete ad creator, that is, an ad maker who creates both art and copy, is about as rare as the dodo bird. Most of today's good advertising is a collaboration between an art director and a copywriter. Neither allows ego to get in the way, but each builds upon the other's contributions. Usually, the better the teamwork, the better the ad.

Advertising legend Howard Gossage said, "Ads generally receive a good deal better art treatment than copy treatment . . . there are unlimited ways of making a lousy idea look brilliant and almost any competent art director can do it and even win prizes with it. There is hardly any way at all to make a lousy idea read brilliantly; the most you can shoot for is writing it competently enough so it doesn't rot the paper."

Although he was a copywriter, he emblazoned into my mind the idea of writing and art teaming up — either in the mind of one talented individual or two individuals, even more if that's what it takes. Everyone involved must always focus on the idea and not on the art or copy.

Classic print graphic ideas   Feast your mind on some examples of classic visuals used in print media through the years:

- The mysterious "man in the Hathaway shirt" who will always be remembered for wearing an eye patch
- Kellogg's Tony the Tiger, who has sold cereals to America in gr-r-r-r-eat quantities
- The Marlboro Man working hard and puffing hard out there among the cattle and cactus in Marlboro Country
- A cat in a hat with a cigarette holder in its mouth, talking intimately with customers of Ohrbach's, a former New York retailer
- Baseball Hall-of-Famer Jim Palmer pitching Jockey shorts while wearing Jockey shorts
- Dancing fruit bringing to life the name of a Jockey competitor, Fruit of the Loom

Television, by its very nature, is an ideal environment for visual demonstration, and it's becoming more fertile than ever for dazzling visuals. Computer graphics and high-tech effects can energize your visual. People love to be dazzled, but be sure your special effects don't get in the way of selling your idea. If any viewer ever says, "My! That was the best-looking commercial I've ever seen!" take that as failure on your part. The response you want is "My! I want that product and I want it as soon as possible!" **Fertile ground for dazzling visuals**

A good exercise for ad makers, especially TV commercial writers, is to try telling the entire story visually. Of course, you'll eventually contribute the words and soundtrack, but if you can create a vivid TV script of exactly thirty seconds, describing the visuals that express your message, you probably have a dynamite TV spot with a crystal clear message. Because so many people, estimated at nearly 70 percent, mute their TV sets during commercials, if you don't tell your story graphically on the tube, you're not telling your story. Classic TV visuals have included: **Classic TV graphic ideas**

- The omnipresent Jolly Green Giant, who works as hard on TV and in print as he does in his valley (ho ho ho)
- The California Raisins, animated by a technique called

"claymation," dancing to "I Heard It Through the Grapevine" for the state's Raisin Advisory Board
- Spuds MacKenzie, a dog with a natural black eye patch, as much the life of the party as Bud Light
- A fresh egg being fried in a skillet to demonstrate the effect drug abuse has on brains, run by the Partnership for a Drug-Free America, a nonprofit organization financed in part by the alcohol and tobacco industries
- A gorilla committing mayhem on a piece of Samsonite luggage that suffers naught in the violence
- The sound fidelity of a Memorex tape is captured by a wine glass shattering suddenly as Melissa Manchester sings a high note
- Hundreds of kids on a hillside in Europe singing beautifully about world harmony and Coca-Cola, making viewers feel good about life and Coca-Cola

As TV increasingly becomes more a part of everyone's life — the average U.S. family has the TV on over seven hours a day — our society is being moved more than ever by visual stimuli. We are not proud of the number of nonreaders in America, but nearly everyone can be communicated to visually. Many graphic principles that have long been proven in print are now being followed successfully in television.

Ten things guerrillas never do

There are ten rules that all good guerrilla art directors, be they ad maker or graphic designer, live by:

1. Don't let the art overpower the idea.
2. Don't let the art overpower the headline.
3. Don't let the art overpower the copy.
4. Don't let the art fail to advance the sale.
5. Don't let the art fail to grab casual readers or viewers.
6. Don't let the art fail to get the ad or spot noticed.
7. Don't let the art fail to be different.
8. Don't let the art fight the product's identity.
9. Don't let the art be created in a hurry.
10. Don't let the art dominate the ad.

Many talents are required to create the finished artwork for an ad or the finished tape or film for a TV spot. The *graphic designer* usually creates the layout for the ad or, in the case of advertising agencies or entrepreneurs with time on their hands, a TV storyboard that shows the visuals with the appropriate sounds beneath each, somewhat akin to a comic strip. Guerrillas consider storyboards a luxury and an expense that can be avoided by a detailed script.

The cast of graphic characters

After the designer completes the layout, she either turns the work over to, or dons another hat and completes the task of, an *illustrator* or *photographer*. If it's to be on TV, a *producer* and *director* become involved. Possibly an *animation artist* steps in at this point. At the photo or TV shoot, expect to see a *hair stylist, makeup artist, wardrobe artist, set designer, lighting artist,* and *camera operator.* If it's to be print, be prepared to meet a *computer artist, paste-up artist, typographer,* and several other production and graphics experts who will serve on your team, but not be part of your payroll, for the term of the production project, be it print or TV.

By the way, guerrillas always have a still photographer present at any videotaping so that they can save on production costs of print ads and brochures without sacrificing quality. Getting double duty out of production sessions makes guerrillas happy. They'll almost always get at least two TV commercials out of one production session by using creative editing. They'll get at least two print ads out of one photo session by knowing ahead of time the upcoming ad ideas and headlines in their advertising campaign.

Remember that the world of advertising graphics is populated by many talented people, and unless you can surpass their talents, tap them instead. When working with them, be sure they know of your fervent belief that the ad should always be dominated by the idea, the competitive advantage, the benefits to prospects. It is the job of the graphics and the graphic professionals to accomplish these objectives. The graphics must give readers or viewers a central visual element to focus upon rather than having their eyes wander all over the print page or

If you can't surpass them, tap them

TV screen. People are bombarded with so many messages, advertising and nonadvertising, that confusion reigns.

Guerrilla graphics present an island of clarity in a sea of chaotic communicating. They visualize the benefits, give life to the words, involve the prospect, and are always viewed as the means to an end, never as the end itself.

29

Building Flexibility into Your Advertising

The single most important key to successful marketing and advertising is *devotion*. Your advertising campaign theme will improve with age as consumers gain confidence in you and your frequently run ads. They are impressed, on an unconscious level, with your consistency, and they begin to believe in your offering when they become aware of the belief you are demonstrating in it by means of your consistent advertising campaign.

But hold on a moment. Consistent doesn't mean unchanging. Devotion doesn't mean devotion to an unmoving, static idea. Unless you build flexibility into your advertising, you'll be devoting yourself to failure.

Guerrillas refer to this as an *organic* advertising campaign, an ad plan that lives and changes with the times, that bends but never breaks, that remains forever fresh.

An organic advertising campaign

The Green Giant's flexibility, effective for over half a century, enables the big green guy to sell beans or corn, peas or frozen veggies. It allowed him to relate to people in the 1930s, and with zero signs of aging, it also lets him connect up with folks in the 1990s. The concept is flexible enough to work its wonders on television and in print. Let's not forget signs, either. This dude has been one great green salesman, and he has resided in the same valley for over fifty years.

Budweiser has changed its theme line several times during the Green Giant's lifetime, but has never changed its Clydesdales. Those horses are as flexible as they are large. The same is true of Merrill Lynch's bull, which has been used over many

Bud's flexible Clydesdales

years in many ways — maintaining the company's show of commitment along with its ability to match its message to the events of the moment.

Bartles and Jaymes, the spokesmen for Gallo's once red-hot wine coolers, put forth the same message, but did it in a wide variety of commercials. Though long of tooth, those guys were flexible — and during the heyday of wine coolers, they ruled their roost. The roost, however, seems to have crumbled beneath them. Not uncommon in capitalism.

Seen any pink bunnies lately? Energizer's pink bunny has been used to inspire the idea of a long-lasting battery in a variety of ways and settings. The bunny's chief competitor, Duracell, has long showed two parts of a battery solidly snapping together while the TV voice says, "Duracell — the coppertop," giving the product an instant point of visual identification in the advertising and in the store. Although this organic and visual TV logo has been around for many years, the story that precedes it has been changing to demonstrate Duracell's own durability. It has passed the flexibility test because in showing how Duracell batteries don't get tired in a hurry, it still isn't a tired campaign.

Flexibility in advertising means creating a concept or character around which different stories can be related over a long period of time. Although new technologies, new formulas, new versions of the product, and new benefits may be offered, the concept or character remain the same.

They're flexible and they dance The California Raisin Advisory Board has been selling trillions of raisins while increasing America's awareness of raisins in a variety of ways. Employing a type of animation called claymation, those dancing raisins can dance well into the next century unless some creative hotshot sells the California Raisin Advisory Board on a new idea. It may be new, but it won't be better. Those raisins allow for a great deal of flexibility. And they've helped the profits of almost every California raisin producer.

When United Airlines started flying to Hawaii, the Far East, and Australia, it featured those destinations in its advertising in all the media, but it never abandoned the idea of the friendly skies. The campaign theme was flexible enough to stand the test of time.

Wells Fargo has leaned upon its trademark stagecoach as a visual format regardless of what it was hawking — its name, checking accounts, certificates of deposit, or credit cards. Only a guerrilla could create a flexible stagecoach.

Absolut vodka went from zero in U.S. sales to the number-four-selling liquor. With 1992 sales of $432 million, the brand's media expenditures of $14.9 million included extremely artistic ads and posters that always featured the shape of the Absolut bottle. On billboards in Chicago, crowds of people formed the silhouette of an Absolut bottle enhanced by only *two words* of copy: "Absolut Chicago." "Absolut Warhol" was the copy for an ad with a drawing of the bottle by the famed artist. "Absolut Generosity" graced holiday ads showing a multitude of bottles, all gift-wrapped together with a ribbon. Breaking all rules of grammar but blazing new trails in advertising, Absolut used its own name as an adjective. This is called a *name awareness* technique, and it worked wonders for the vodka, giving it that unbeatable combination of profitability and flexibility.

Breaking grammar rules and sales records

You don't have to worry about being flexible if you're running ads for a new movie, an upcoming concert, or a limited edition anything. But if you plan to advertise your offering for a long time, and if you want your company to keep up with current events, you'll have the flexibility of the campaign in mind long before the very first ad runs. You'll know if the concept will wear out in a hurry, become dated, be easily copied, or appear old-fashioned, and because you're a guerrilla, you'll switch to a different campaign before even launching the first one.

What I don't want to do is beat a dead horse, but speaking of horses, the Marlboro campaign has been flexible enough to succeed in many new product introductions, though denied access to radio and TV. Marlboro has introduced its fliptop box, a long version, a low-tar version, and even catalogue merchandise — all using the same flexible Marlboro cowboy.

Are there many other examples of flexibility? Nope. Far too few as far as I'm concerned. Most companies, lacking a flexible campaign, drop theirs altogether because it's too hard to change. Remember the Swedish bikini ski team? They advertised a beer, but for the life of me, I can't remember which.

Chanel has advertised its perfumes very successfully around Christmastime each year. Chanel uses different commercials, but the overall identity of mystique and glamour is always present. The campaign makes a good case study in organic advertising because the devotion is to an identity.

Guerrilla advertising critters

Other good examples of successful flexibility: Starkist is devoted to a tuna named Charlie, and 9-Lives lives by its cat Morris. The Pillsbury Doughboy is synonymous with homemade warmth and freshness.

Volkswagen's advertising for its Bug made it the import leader for many years, keeping the same lovable personality for the car (lovable for a car conceptualized by Adolf Hitler) while changing the executions of the campaign to meet the needs of the car-buying public — low cost, practical, fun, well-made, and economical to run. All the ads were unmistakably VW ads, flexible enough to introduce new models. Readers sensed the devotion to the campaign, which they unconsciously equated with devotion to the car.

Many of the advertising campaigns of the nineties are fantastically executed, but they're one-time-only ideas. What do you do to follow up a one-on-one basketball game between

Godzilla vs. Charles Barkley

Godzilla and Charles Barkley? Nike may still be wrestling with that one. But they're doing a good job of it as attested to by their sales figures, which show them as the leader in athletic footwear, followed by Reebok, Keds, and L.A. Gear.

Computer technology is changing so rapidly that it's easier than ever to create a campaign with flexibility. More and more companies are rising to the occasion, but some allow the technology to get in the way of the sales message.

When I talk flexibility, I'm talking longevity with a format that breeds familiarity. Flexibility never relies upon fads and trends, but may tap into them sometime during the life of the advertising campaign.

Is it easy to create a campaign with flexibility? It's almost as tough as breaking the law of gravity, but it can be done, has been done, should be done, and is done by guerrillas, large and small. For at least two decades a local jewelry store in the San Francisco Bay area, Sidney Mobell, has used small-space newspaper advertising with the headline "Internationally famed, but uniquely San Francisco," to feature everything from Rolex watches to hourglasses filled with diamonds to annual clearance sales. The advertising is as fresh today as it was the day it was created. Almost all ads show a drawing of a San Francisco landmark and a piece of Sidney Mobell jewelry. Alas, small-business America is not teeming with such happy case histories because most small businesses don't recognize the power of devotion and the necessity for flexibility.

Blend devotion with flexibility

But you do, and as a guerrilla, you should be delighted that they don't. While they are constantly reinventing themselves, you must invent yourself properly *at the outset* so that minor and even major alterations may be made without the need for a major overhaul of your advertising. Flexibility helps you attain your goals because it keeps down the cost of creating new advertising *and* it gives strength and vitality to your original advertising.

VI

Adapting Your Tactics to Your Media

THE FLEXIBILITY that characterizes your advertising will be demonstrated by your ability to adapt your campaign and identity to all the media — the advertising media and the direct marketing weapons.

Any strong advertising idea can be adapted to fit well into any medium. Some of the fast-paced, music-dominated TV spots might be tough to transform into print ads, but if they have a core idea — which they often do not because they're too wrapped up in show biz — they can leap off the page as adeptly as they leap from the TV screen.

If you can't turn your radio commercial into a newspaper ad, there's a problem somewhere. You don't even have to search to find it; I'll tell you now. It's because *you've put so much emphasis into the style that the substance is lost.* Blame yourself. You've got to shine more light on that substance. You've got to get clear on the basic selling offer yourself, then be sure it is communicated in your advertising. When it is, you'll find that the idea can be expressed with aplomb in any medium you select.

Don't think that you've got to make a literal translation of a TV commercial into a magazine ad or vice versa. You can't translate music to print, motion to print, sound to print. On the other hand, you can't have the luxury of long and intriguing copy in a thirty-second TV commercial. And you can't show convincing before-and-after photos on the radio.

All the media have their limitations and their special powers. Guerrillas learn how to skirt the limitations and take full advantage of the powers. You'll learn what they know in the upcoming pages. You'll discover how to unleash the persuasiveness of your selling ideas to motivate prospects from radios, TV sets, magazines, and the daily paper. Each time you express your idea in one medium, that will intensify the exposures you've enjoyed in another. Whether your message is in the form of a five-minute video or a five-word sign, you'll also need to create the momentum and maintain it with free publicity, but that's another book.

As always, you'll be using the media to increase your profitability. That means you won't overuse or abuse them, but will use them properly and cost-effectively. Your magazine ads don't have to be in full color. Your newspaper ads don't have to be full page. Your radio commercials need not have background music by Elvis. And your TV spokesperson need not be the president of the United States — though William McKinley appeared in Waterman pen ads while he was serving in the White House.

All you need is a simple, clear, compelling offer along with the smarts to adapt it as effectively as possible to the media you have selected for your advertising. As you can see in the media all around you, power-packed selling ideas are not in great abundance. Clever ads and entertaining commercials are common. But ads with ideas that move people to spend their money are scarce. Many of the giants have been known to fall on their corporate faces in the advertising arena.

But you can't afford such expensive mistakes — as all advertising failures must be described. When you are blessed with an advertising idea that works wonders in the newspapers, you've got to know how to send your profits skyrocketing by trying to make that idea work in magazines, on television, on the radio, in brochures, in the yellow pages, and at the point of purchase.

You've got to be able to give your winner the added support of a special promotion or two. By utilizing a mixture of media to bolster your ad campaign, you'll not only have the benefit of synergy, but you'll also *learn which of the media are doing the best job for you.*

This is crucial information. That's why this section explores how to get the most out of your (hopefully) adaptable advertising campaign and how to best use the media by capitalizing upon their inherent strengths. A guerrilla is equally at home in print and on the air.

30

Getting Results
from the Print Media

Start out by creating a headline that is so potent, so reader-stopping, so pertinent to your message, that the visual and the copy become immediately apparent to your mind. The starting point for every print ad is an idea, but by now you know that and have the idea. It's time to put it into print. You may already be experiencing the bliss of having married a visual idea to a headline, but that's so rare that I'll assume you're starting with a blank sheet of paper in your brain. The first thing to put there is a headline.

Some great headlines are short, such as in Volkswagen's wonderful "Lemon" ad; some great headlines are long, as you read in the U.S. School of Music's ad about the guy who heard laughs as he sat down at the piano. Almost all great headlines work with the ad's graphics to tell the whole story.

Team the headline with the graphics

Here are some other examples of excellent short headlines:

DIAMONDS AREN'T FOREVER

(Ad shows a photo of a baseball park and makes a pitch to raise the money to build a new ballpark. It intrigues the reader because it makes use of an old cliché, says the opposite of what he's always heard. The photo hits home with target prospects: fans.)

YOU CAN'T EAT ATMOSPHERE

(Ad shows a plate of delicious food as served in Horn & Hardart, a former East Coast chain of cafeteria-style restaurants.

The ad turns a potential liability into a money-saving asset that prospects can sink their teeth into.)

BUNK!

(Ad shows a tough man in a pose of disbelief, then goes on to say that it's Zenith's answer to people who say the American worker isn't as good as he used to be. One-word headings need fast payoffs. Zenith delivers.)

The following first-rate ads have long headlines:

REVOLUTIONARY NEW KIND OF
DRAIN OPENER INVENTED;
UNCLOGS DRAINS IN 1 SECOND

(Ad has a full page of copy, diagrams, and testimonials run by a regional product called Drain Power. If I had a problem with my drain, I'd buy this product. It promises three benefits: newness, effectiveness, and speed.)

MORE PICTURES IN THIS MAGAZINE
WERE TAKEN WITH NIKON LENSES
THAN ALL OTHER LENSES COMBINED

(Ad shows a photo of a Nikon camera with a long lens and copy that ties in directly with the headline. This involving headline talks to readers about the magazine they are reading and the photos they are seeing.)

WHY TIMBERLAND HAS TAKEN AN
APPROACH TO MAKING SHOES THAT'S
YEARS BEHIND OTHER COMPANIES

(Ad has two full columns of fascinating copy, photos of three shoemaking tools, and three styles of Timberland shoes. Even if you don't read the copy, you get the impression that there's a lot to say about these shoes and that much quality and tradition go into making them. An ad for their mud-repelling boots was headlined "Our name is mud." Although I warn you against too-clever headlines, I encourage you to use a light-hearted approach *if it's pertinent to the product.* Most clever ads aren't. They start with a stab at humor, then get down to serious selling. I call this the "Speaking-of-insects-how's-your-aunt?" school of advertising. Don't go to that school.)

Print ads that look like a newspaper story and have a newsy headline are another sage use of the print media. People read newspapers to get the news, and if you've got some, tell it. They read magazines so they can become involved with the stories. Let them become involved with your ad. Just be sure your news is real news and that you give readers something with which it is easy to become involved.

Print ads must have a focal point of visual interest. In most cases, that's the headline, but it could also be a photo, such as the Blue Cross ad that showed a terribly wrecked car under the headline "First he killed the bottle."

A focal point of interest

Howard Gossage, a master of print media, believed that ads should invite a dialogue. He said, "To encourage the feeling of accessibility, we frequently stick coupons or other response forms in ads. It is not so important whether they really send in the coupons, as they feel they can. A visible invitation to respond, whether it is used or not, adds another bit of believability to the characterization."

Many of the most successful print ads are long-copy ads with headlines that begin with the words "How to." Long copy certainly isn't recommended for all print ads, but if you must write it to enable prospects *to make an intelligent purchase decision*, don't hold back. Although readership falls off fairly dramatically after the first 50 words, it hardly falls off at all for the next 450 words. Prospects hang on to every word. Don't be deluded into thinking people won't read long copy. They will if it interests them. And they will if it solves one of their problems. The sheer quantity of your copy will impress many prospects who won't even read it, but will figure that if you have that much to say about your offering, it must be worthwhile.

The truth about long copy

As your headlines and opening lines are keys to great print ads, recognize that there are other focal points as well. Closing lines either restate the major benefit or, better still, make a call

Closing lines get action

to action by telling the reader what to do. The closing line for a home brewery called Beerland was "Just brew it! Call 1-800-377-3320 and order the Beerland Home Brewery. Do it now!" Readers know exactly what action they must take.

There are few hard-and-fast rules for print ads other than what I have already stated because good ad makers are constantly creating new formats for a headline, visual, and copy. Often that mixture also includes a subhead — which can help readers make the transition from the headline to the copy. Here's an example:

Headline: FREE!

Subhead: *Free bed linen with any new BioFirm Mattress!*

Copy: The BioFirm gives you healthy back support, a choice of 80 levels of firmness, and a 30-night sleeping trial. Better still, it gives you all that for half the price of brand-name mattresses. And this month only, it comes with free bed linen — topsheet, bottomsheet, and two pillowcases. So if you love healthy sleep and healthy savings, plus free bed linen, wake up to the BioFirm Mattress. Available *only* at the Berkeley Design Shop. *This offer is good until October 28th.* Bring this ad with you for your free bed linen.

Note: That final line of copy enables you to test the newspapers where the ad ran. It can't hurt and it can help.

You can see how the headline stops readers, the subhead explains the headline, leads into the copy, and the copy completes the sale. This proven print ad is not an award winner unless they give awards for profits. If you were in the market for a mattress and lived near Berkeley, would you consider BioFirm?

If your product is complex and requires an explanation, you might use the print media *to whet the imagination of your prospects,* then offer free data in the form of a printed or video brochure or phone follow-up. This is called a two-step sale. **Going for the kill** The alternative is *going for the kill,* using print to get the order by giving all the details — ordering information and visuals that prospects can study, refer back to, and show to others before buying. Going for the kill gets fewer responses than the offer of a free brochure. Then again, it simplifies your business because a one-step sale is twice as easy as a two-step sale.

The ten principles to guide all your print advertising — and these should be committed to memory — are: *attention-getting, dramatic, clear, involving, interesting, informative, believable, motivating, honest,* and *on strategy.* You can follow those principles all the way to the bank.

31

Creating Effective Radio Spots

Radio has nothing to do with print because it has no visuals, uses no headline, and can't put across a whole lot of information. Right? Wrong, wrong, and wrong.

Radio uses visuals by painting visual pictures in the minds and imaginations of your prospects. Music, jingles, and sound effects also help prospects remember you and even visualize themselves enjoying the benefits you offer.

Radio uses headlines in its precious first three seconds that either grab your attention or lose you into the ozone.

Radio can put across enough information for prospects to decide to buy, even to drive over right now and buy.

The most intimate of the media

Although studies show that radio spots have the least impact of any of the major media, they are *the most intimate* of the media and allow you to go one-on-one with your listener's mind. That listener is probably driving a car or doing something at home with the radio on. If the radio is playing the listener's favorite music, it is coming over what guerrillas call *a background station* because it is on in the background, rarely with active listening.

Background stations

Commercials for background stations would do well to use a musical background as listeners have intentionally tuned in to a music station. The music should, ideally, match the format of the station: country, rock, reggae, classical, blues, you get the point. Otherwise, listeners either mentally tune out the commercial because the music is inappropriate, or more likely, because there are words in the first place. They're listening to hear music, not words, if you please.

The prime advantage of background stations: *targeting your audience.* As stations aim their programming at teenagers, oldies freaks, rural types, women, Hispanics, seniors, office workers, classical music lovers, sports fans, rock fans, talk show fans, religious people, fans, news junkies, and a lot more, you can home in on your ideal station on which to advertise. There are thirty radio music formats where I live. You can hit bull's-eyes with every spot you run.

Commercials for *foreground stations*, when created properly, are usually more effective than those for background stations. Foreground stations — talk radio, sports, news, religious — require active listening and are rarely on in the background. When your words come on a foreground station, they are listened to more attentively than the same words on a background station. People are already listening to words. There's a very good chance they'll listen to yours as long as the commercial maintains the tone and mood of the programming.

Foreground stations

To tap into the immense power of foreground radio, *consider advertising on a show with a known personality.* Nationally, Paul Harvey and Larry King come to mind. Their six-figure prices boggle the mind. But rest easy, guerrilla. There are a myriad of local personalities. The ones that reach your target audience can be gold miners for you.

Simply arrange, through your media-buying service, your radio station sales rep, or even by yourself, for the radio star to try your product or service. Then instead of supplying him a taped commercial, as is usually the case, or a script, as is also done — *give him a fact sheet and ask him to talk from his personal experience.* Every commercial he delivers is an implied, or perhaps stated, personal endorsement of what you are selling. Every one will reek with sincerity, believability, the same credibility folks attach to the announcer, and more pure persuasiveness than the most elaborately produced and expensive radio spot, even the most hilarious ones. Those, as you know, may also be the worst.

As an unspoken bonus, although you may be advertising on the radio personality's show with thirty-second commercials, the radio host may be speaking for forty or even ninety seconds, because the words are spontaneous, using only your fact sheet for support. You get more than your money's worth in many ways.

The cost to use a station's radio personality is more than for supplying your own prerecorded announcer, but not much more — unless you want a nationally known personality such as Larry King. The cost of radio itself is based upon the number of listeners in the station's audience as determined by one of several independent ratings services.

There is no difference in cost between using background or foreground radio; the format doesn't dictate the price, the audience size does. But as a guerrilla you are far more interested in the quality of the audience than the size, in the number of prospects who will be listening. After all, if you're selling computer software on the radio, an audience of one million, most of them under ten years old, isn't worth as much to you as an audience of one thousand, all users of computers. Cost per prospect should be your guide, not cost per thousand listeners.

Producing commercials
The most simple radio commercials feature an unaccompanied announcer reading live from a script. The next level of radio production is a recorded, but unadorned announcer. Then comes a recorded announcer combined with music. Rights-free music (you don't have to pay for the publication rights) is inexpensive and many recording studios have large libraries of it. Add sound effects and that's one more element. And then you can add announcers, actors, and actresses, using one, two, or five, as you wish.

Remember that as you add elements to your radio production, simplicity is still paramount. That simplicity refers to your basic selling idea. Don't let your execution destroy the message. And don't, under any circumstances, let the radio station write it. If you do, your commercial will end up sounding a lot like other commercials on that station and will probably fail to convey the unique identity of your product or service. Get a pro if you can't write it yourself.

Radio is wonderfully flexible in that you can change commercials at will and don't need the long lead time required by magazines. Even newspapers and TV are slowpokes compared with radio's ability to let you alter your ad message. Many guerrilla advertisers use what is termed a "donut" when using radio (and even TV). This is a thirty-second commercial with a taped opening, say ten seconds, then fifteen seconds in the middle with music only — for you to have the announcer read anything your little heart desires — and then a taped five-second close. A variation of the donut is the "tag" where you have, say, a fifteen-second taped opening followed by a fifteen-second live close.

Although many radio experts, those who boast of radio as the theater of the mind, stress the importance of music, "it deserves one-third of the radio budget because it is one-third of the power of a radio spot," says Jerry Jacob, a successful radio advertising professional who has represented stations across the country. Be sure the music enhances and doesn't interfere with your message.

The sound of music

If you use the personality on a personality radio show, don't use music at all. Although music is flexible, original music is expensive. Although jingles work well for the big spenders, they seem to impede the small spenders who cannot afford a saturation campaign. Be sure, when making radio part of your media mix, that your mind is on profits and not entertainment.

The anatomy of a good radio commercial is the same as that of a good direct mail letter, speech, or ad: Tell them what you are going to tell them, then tell them what you have to say, then tell them what you've just told them. Be careful and don't stray too far from this time-honored dictum. It may be old-fashioned, but so is breathing oxygen.

Most thirty-second radio spots have 70 words. Most sixty-second spots have 140. But Columbia University studies prove that when more words are crammed in, *people listen more attentively and retain more comprehensively.* The best explanation for this is that the mind works much faster than the spoken word and people get bored amazingly fast.

70 words in a thirty-second spot

Is repetition especially helpful in putting across your point on radio? *Absolutely* and I'm thrilled that you even asked.

Repetition helps in all marketing, all advertising, and especially on radio. What do you repeat? Your name, your offer, your promise, your benefit, but not your joke. Don't be one of those people who repeat their punchlines . . . zzzzzzzz.

Use words that paint pictures, words that evoke color, taste, texture, touch, sensation. Use sound effects to set a mood, create an environment, stimulate the imagination. Great radio can even bring to life an idea that is hard to convey with pictures. So listen to your radio spots with your eyes closed, not looking at a script. And listen on car radio speakers, not fancy studio speakers. Reality should reign.

32

The Truth About
Advertising on Television

Now that television is so affordable, thanks to cable and satellite TV, you should be giving serious thought to advertising on television. The cost is about $20 or less for a thirty-second spot run during prime time — 8:00 P.M. to 11:00 P.M. — in almost any U.S. city, and producing a thirty-second spot can run under $3,000. Compare that with the roughly $200,000 cost to produce the average U.S. spot — due to the fast-food joints, the beers, the soft drink makers, and of all people, the shoemakers.

$20 per prime-time spot

Yes, I know you're not McDonald's. But wouldn't it be nice to be McDonald's? TV might help you in that quest. It certainly helped Ray Kroc, McDonald's founder, and he didn't have untold billions when he started. Like you, he was just one more guerrilla searching for unconventional ways to achieve his life's goals. He hit the jackpot with TV. His consistent food quality and service, along with low prices, get most of the credit, but how do you suppose people learned about that quality, service, and value? TV is how.

I told a client of mine, Med 7, an urgent-care center in Sacramento, that TV had dropped in price considerably because of cable. They were intrigued that their commercials, again thanks to the precision of cable penetration, could reach only people who lived in Carmichael, a section of Sacramento. Their goal was to obtain a daily patient count of fifty by the end of three months. They signed a contract to run one-minute TV ads on cable for one year. We produced two commercials for a total cost of $3,000 — that's $1,500 per spot, unheard of by ad agencies and the Pepsi-Colas of the world. The cost was low because of a tight script, use of Med 7 employees instead of professional actors, rights-free music, and a non-union announcer.

After the commercials ran one month — the two spots alternating to prevent that dreaded sense of sameness — at the rate of five spots a day, five days a week, three weeks each month, Med 7 did a postcard mailing to the citizens of Carmichael. At the end of the second month, patient count rose to thirty each day. At the end of the third month, it went up to fifty each day — our goal for the *year*.

Med 7 added new physicians as their patient count leveled off at eighty by the ninth month. They also cut down on their commercial frequency, running only two weeks out of four. Newspaper ads, planned to run after the TV ads had run for four months, were canceled. Cable TV and one postcard mailing did the entire job. This is only one of many stories of small businesses enjoying sensational results from cable TV.

Sensational results from cable TV

It sounds relatively simple and it is. That's why I urge virtually all my clients to give serious consideration to television. Invariably, they become addicts — not addicted to watching TV, but to advertising on it. There's a good reason that television is often referred to as "the undisputed heavyweight champion of advertising."

In spite of many stories with happy endings, TV is incredibly easy to abuse, and is horribly misused by most advertisers who use it. Some of their commercials are so ridiculously bad that they lose customers every time they run. This is true for the smallest businesses in town as well as for many of the blue-chip companies. Still, most folks think they're in show biz when they run a spot on TV. Guerrillas know they're in sell biz.

Secrets of a bad commercial

What makes a TV commercial ridiculously *bad*?

- It is *more entertaining* than motivating.
- It is *not clear* with its promise.
- It is *not visual*, but depends on words.
- It is *schlocky*, lacking in credibility.

- It is *high-pressure* or exaggerative.
- It is a *fabulous film* but a terrible commercial.
- It is *so clever* you forget who ran it.
- It is wrapped up in *special effects*, devoid of an idea.
- It is *too complex* for an idea to come shining through.
- It is *boring, boring, boring*. Yawn . . .

As long as we're on this topic, what makes a TV commercial ridiculously *good*?

Secrets of a good commercial

- It is more *motivating* than entertaining. If it happens to entertain, that is its secondary purpose in life.
- It is *very clear* about its competitive advantage. Not one prospect is confused about what the advertiser offers.
- It is *intensely visual*, great even with the sound off. TV is a visual medium with audio enhancement. Got that?
- It is *professional looking* and builds stature. Nobody pays attention to the production values — unless they are embarrassingly amateurish — only to the product.
- It is *believable and compelling*, but not high-pressure. It sells like crazy, but sells with velvet gloves and truth.
- It is a fabulous commercial because it *creates a desire*. No one comments on the TV spot; everyone wants the product.
- It is focused on *advancing the sale*, not being clever. The most clever thing about it is the product and benefit.
- It is *wrapped up with the product* and uses special effects sparingly and only to make the product look good.

Even though these components of good TV ads are really no more than common sense, as is much of guerrilla advertising, bad TV commercials are as omnipresent as sand on the beach. So here, in front of my word processor, I get on my knees and plead with you not to waste money on TV advertising in ways that defy imagination. Others will do it all around you. Good advice is hard to find, good examples even harder. A minefield is a grassy meadow compared with the terrain of TV. Yet TV is the king of the advertising hill, and when used with the genius of the guerrilla, it can be devastating — to your competition.

TV lets you demonstrate The primary advantage TV has over the other media is that it lets you *demonstrate*. It lets you use pictures, words, sounds, and music to burn home your point. It allows you to bring your competitive advantage to vibrant life. It facilitates appeals to logic and to emotion. It moves. It is a pure moment of time that can command 100 percent of a person's attention or lose that person completely. Most people have a going-in position of not paying attention to commercials. So you've got negative momentum to overcome. But you can — visually and verbally.

The infomercial age You can do these things with television in formats ranging from a thirty-minute infomercial, which is a program-length commercial, to a ten-second electronic billboard. With a powerful visual centerpiece, the ten-second effort will remind viewers of the sixty-second spots, of your print ads, of your radio advertising, of why the heck they want so much to buy whatever you are selling.

In addition to giving you free rein to demonstrate, TV lets you show your product or service in action, lets people who have tried your offering rave about it in public, lets you show before-and-after TV footage, lets you produce little playlets, called slice-of-life commercials, that dramatize the problem and solution, lets you tap into all of the arts — music, art, writing, dance, acting — to profit well and wisely.

If you have the benefit of a full-service advertising agency, they'll furnish or have access to everything you need to produce your commercial. But as a small business, you probably are working without an ad agency and using talented freelancers to fill in any blanks in your marketing program. You might hire a free-lance TV producer to oversee your TV production. Fine. But guerrillas know ways to achieve professional-looking, profit-producing TV commercials before they even meet with a producer.

Guerrillas avoid storyboards Once they do, in the necessary quest to keep costs down, they avoid storyboards (pictures from your proposed TV spot with words beneath them, like a comic book) because they hamper spontaneity. Instead, they work from scripts that detail both the words and visual elements, but are not locked into a particular look. They or their designated producer or director produce their soundtracks first, because they know that voices on camera add time and complexity, while inviting Murphy, who wrote the law named for him, to the TV shoot. They shoot their visuals to an existing soundtrack. All sound takes place off camera. This way, the roar of a jumbo jet zooming overhead or a truck rumbling past the shooting location won't mess up an otherwise perfect shot. With video playback, you get instant feedback on each scene. Then there are no surprises at the editing session when the sound is matched to the video or film footage. Surprises are frowned upon.

Guerrillas avoid live soundtracks

Such TV production tips were unknown to the entrepreneurs of the sixties and seventies. It wasn't until the eighties that TV became affordable to small business, and it was the nineties that found knowledge of TV production to be mandatory for right-thinking guerrillas.

These entrepreneurs are not intimidated by television. They realize that its price is low enough for it to be standard weaponry in a guerrilla's arsenal. A century ago, knowledge of newspapers was a competitive advantage to the practitioner of individual enterprise. Today knowledge of television costs, production, and utilization gives the guerrilla a head start over competitors who are destined to learn of it in the future as TV becomes even more widely used for advertising and audiences even easier to precisely target. Guerrillas, as you know, are not followers, but leaders who learn of ways to grow their businesses with the weapons of the day. Right now, that's television. The more you know about it, the more likely you are to capitalize upon its power.

When using TV, remember that most people will see your commercial more than once, so don't try to squeeze too much into one commercial. Patience will again be a virtue. As muscle-bound as TV may be, it still requires repetition of your prime selling points and commitment to your strategy.

With the cost of TV time and production so low, any business is a candidate for using it successfully, from retailers to

Anyone can be a TV star today

CPAs, from airlines to consultants, from banks to lawyers. Businesses and professions that never considered TV in the past now consider it the best advertising medium ever invented, and they are deeply grateful for the technology that gave them affordable TV, cable or otherwise, plus programming that hits their prospects right where they live — literally and figuratively.

The need to run a saturation TV campaign has diminished for most businesses that now realize the importance of combining media rather than saturating any one of them. The real experts to consult about TV for your small business are found in media-buying services. And you can find them waiting for your phone call right there in your yellow pages. They can remove all the complexities if they're good, and they can quickly help you reach a comfort zone with TV that is crucial if you're to achieve your advertising goals.

The secret to TV is no secret at all. It begins with a strong idea, evolves to a visual expression of that idea, combines with a compelling opening line or sound, then becomes further empowered with copy and demonstration. Finally, it ends with a call to action — telling viewers exactly what they are **Tell them** supposed to do now, verbally and visually. Be sure you are **your name** *telling them your name visually*, because with their ruthless **visually** use of that remote control, they probably won't hear it spoken.

If anyone ever tells you they loved your TV commercial, hang your head in shame. If they say they saw your TV spot, then went out and bought your product, glow inside because you succeeded at your job. It's a tough job, so you know in your heart that you well deserve pats on the back, but only those that come from your accountant or banker.

33

Developing Printed and Electronic Brochures

Advertising can whet prospects' appetites, but before those special people will spend their time and money, they'll probably have to learn more about you. They need answers to important questions about what you are offering. They want details and a feel for the identity of your company.

To guerrillas, this is a good thing, a chance to begin a relationship. Guerrillas relish people who want more data. They freely impart it in person, by phone, by mail, and in seminars. Prospects *who have requested the data* provide opportunities that don't get much more golden.

Brochures, whether in print, video or audio format, are your best bet for putting your advertising into hypersell. The five advantages of using brochures are:

1. *They enable you to tell all the details.* No need to hold back on information when supplying it to people who have requested information. In fact, be sure to remind them of this situation on the envelope in which you mail your brochure. Say, "This is the information you requested," or anything else to put that point across.

   Tell all the details

   Most likely, you can't afford the time on TV or radio or the space in magazines or newspapers to tell your entire story, to convince your prospects to take that hard step of becoming honest-to-goodness customers. But within the friendly confines of your own brochure, you can afford the space, or in the case of a video or audio brochure, the time, to say whatever it takes to convince

prospects to buy. The generous time and space granted
you by a brochure allows you to show photos, diagrams,
and electronic visuals that cogently demonstrate why the
brochure requesters should hurry up and get onto your
customer list.

You don't get this luxury with most mass media advertising. It is a luxury that money can buy, but it takes
a large fortune to purchase it in advertising space or time.
It takes a pittance, though, to purchase it in brochures.
If you've got a story that just doesn't squeeze down to
a thirty-second or one-magazine-column format, you
should produce, offer, and disseminate a brochure *to requesters* and to other potentially hot prospects — but especially to those glorious people who actually ask for it.
Both you and your prospects will delight in its ability to
cover all the details. This leads to the second strength
of brochures.

Brochures can close sales   2. *They close the sale for you all by themselves.* Printed brochures can have 800 numbers, coupons, or order blanks
that people can mail or, if you're serious about profits,
fax to you. Electronic brochures can close the sale by
means of a toll-free number that callers can use to buy
what you are selling. The purpose of most brochures is
to close the sale, though you wouldn't know that by checking out most brochures. Sure, they're supposed to explain, but there is a goal to that explanation — profits.
Be sure you create your brochure to attain this goal. Your
advertising sets the stage and might, by itself, close the
sale. But in most cases, advertising initiates the dialogue.
The prospect, by requesting more info, continues the
dialogue. And your brochure takes it to the closing of
the sale.

The dialogue certainly doesn't end there. It continues and can lead to mutual benefits for decades if you do
your follow-up work. But before you get to that threshold
of long-term profitability, recognize that deciding to purchase from you is a hard step. To make it easier, guer-

rillas create soft steps. That is one more strength of brochures.

3. *Brochures enable you to take the ideal soft step.* It is a high-pressure situation when you ask a person to buy. It is a no-pressure situation when you ask a person to request a brochure. No risk. No commitment. Why not request one? The hard step of buying is a whole lot easier after folks have read or viewed or heard your brochure. Of the many soft steps — sales calls, seminars, consultations, samples, demonstrations — brochures are the most cost-effective.

4. *Brochures let you do the two-step.* As all guerrillas know, the two-step is a process where in step one you run many small advertisements in a large selection of publications. In each ad, you say one wonderful thing about what you have to offer, then offer your *free* brochure. *The key to your successful response is that your brochure is free* — the most powerful word in advertising. Step two is where the big payoff comes.

   Guerrillas do the two-step

   Step two is where you send not simply your free brochure, but also *a personal letter* thanking the requesters for requesting your brochure in the first place. You know that people are bombarded with around 2,700 advertising messages a day. For someone to take the time to request your free brochure is a major act of intent. This is a person worthy of your attention. Show it with your brochure, personal letter, *and your follow-up note.* Most people aren't used to such caring attention. Watch them show their gratitude by becoming customers. They figure you run your business with the same attitude that you used in approaching them.

5. *Brochures let you reach many hot prospects economically.* Anyone who takes the time to find out more about you can be classified not only as a prospect, but as a hot one. To reach many prospects can be done fairly economically through the mass media. But to reach *hot* prospects is a costly endeavor — unless you use the guerrilla advertis-

ing weapons of a free brochure offered in your advertising, a personal letter to accompany the brochure, and a
follow-up letter. If you use brochures *as part* but not all
of a well-stocked arsenal, you can expect a well-stocked
bank account.

Print brochures

What guerrillas know about print brochures:

1. They should be generous with copy, color, or visuals.
2. They should look professional, but not lavish.
3. They can fold twice and fit in a standard #10 envelope.
4. They should make ordering extremely simple.
5. They should connect very closely with your advertising.

Ideal products for print brochures: stationery products, educational materials, computer hardware and software, most services.

Audio brochures

What guerrillas know about audio brochures:

1. They should be used when visuals are not necessary.
2. They can run ten to twenty minutes, but must be clear.
3. They will be heard primarily by business commuters.
4. Audio and print brochures can be the most inexpensive
   to produce.
5. 92 percent of U.S. motorists have cars with cassette
   players.

Ideal products for audio brochures: books on tape, financial
services, consulting services, music albums, CPA firms such
as H & R Block.

Video brochures

What guerrillas know about video brochures:

1. They should run between five and ten minutes, not
   longer.
2. They should tell your story visually and verbally.
3. They should have no trace of amateurism.

4. Production costs run about $1,000 per minute, $1.50 for duplicates.
5. They benefit from music and a first-class announcer.

Ideal products for video brochures: vacation packages, summer camps, medical services, hotels and resorts, furniture, clothing lines, real estate developments, cars, fitness equipment.

You can convert as many as 33 percent of your brochure requesters into paying customers if you use brochures in the right way, and now you know the right way.

34

Yellow Pages and Classified Ad Expertise

Here in the yellow pages is your opportunity to take on all the competition, head-to-head. You can be sure that anyone browsing your section of the yellow pages is a hot prospect, either that or David Letterman looking for a new gag. In fact, the only people who consult the yellow page directories are torrid prospects interested in buying, guerrillas interested in spying, or simply loonies letting their fingers do the walking.

Stay out of the yellow pages

Before you become too excited about what you can do in and with the yellow pages, realize that you need not run any advertising there. If people are not used to finding businesses such as yours in the yellow pages, stay out of them. There is no rule that says you *must* advertise there. One of my clients, a printing and copying firm called The Print and Copy Factory, gets 95 percent of its business from the yellow pages. They'd be nuts to skimp. I get less than 1 percent of my business from them. I'd be nuts to spend a cent there. If you think the yellow pages are a viable way of attracting prospects, you ought to know ten things about using them:

Do these ten things if you go in

1. Inquire about the *electronic yellow pages*, which provide a special phone number that lets prospects call for updated information. The printed yellow pages people offer this service and happily list your electronic phone number in your yellow pages ad. This technology isn't everywhere yet, but it is on the way in a hurry. And it's not expensive.

2. If you get enough business from the yellow pages or think

you might be able to, invest in *the largest ad* in your section or *use the color red* or both. Yes, I know that red increases the cost, but it also increases the responses. Some yellow pages directories now offer full-color advertising.

3. Give *a lot of information* in your ad. This is not a newspaper ad, so visuals count for less and specifics count for more. This is the arena where purchase decisions are made, so give many, many reasons to patronize your business.

4. Be sure your yellow pages ad *ties in with your other advertising* so that when people see you in the yellow pages, they'll recall seeing you elsewhere. They'll equate your ads with your logo, your sign above the shop, your stationery, your business card, your Christmas card, your local ads, and more — gaining confidence in you.

5. Have your yellow pages ad *written and designed by pros*, not the yellow pages people. Their ads tend to look like most of the other ads and put more emphasis on the phone number than your specific benefits.

6. *Study the yellow pages in other sections* and see what catches your eye. Pay close attention to the headlines, the words, visuals, use of color, borders, and the questions left unanswered by the ad. Do they take credit cards?

7. As in print ads, *the headline is the most important element* in your ad, but the number of benefits comes next because people need reasons to travel a little further or spend a little more. If you can convey service, quality, selection, and personal care, chances are you'll pique their interest. Be sure your identity comes shining through.

8. Generally, *copy in phrases, called "bullets," is most effective* in communicating a lot of information in a small space. This allows people to pick up your prime points by scanning and does not necessitate reading copy. And since scanning is what most folks are doing as they let their fingers do the walking, bullets are just the ticket.

9. *Tell people what they are supposed to do next*. Don't just let your yellow pages ad sit there and force people to fig-

ure out what they're supposed to do. Tell them to call
you, visit you, check out your operation. Be clear on this.
10. Make certain that *everyone who works for you has read
your yellow pages ad*. This is especially important for the
people who answer your phone. They must maintain the
momentum generated by the yellow pages ad and not
waste it. Make certain you have a fascinating message on
your answering machine for people who call when you're
closed. Tell them when you're open, invite them to leave
a message, and thank them for calling. Don't lose the sale
or inquiry after your ad has done its share of enticing.

Okay, pretty soon you'll be satisfied, even thrilled with your
investment in the yellow pages. You might even be tempted to
enlarge your ad, advertise in more sections of the directory,
spread your geographic wings to run in the yellow pages in
new locations. Guerrilla hint: If you've got a winning yellow
Want to expand   pages ad, *you can expand your business by using it*. Check
your business?   neighboring directories. If yours would be the dominant ad,
you might be able to double your profits! If so, you won't be
the first to do it.

As many businesses have achieved fame and fortune
through yellow pages directories, many others have taken the
unlikely path of classified ads. These appear in small local newspapers, large metropolitan newspapers, huge national newspapers, and in both local and national magazines. You should
be running your classified ads in the publications read by your
Ten classified   prospects. There are, as you might have guessed, ten things
ad insights   you should know about them:

1. They are read only by *honest prospects*. So direct your
ads to these people and no one else. There's no need to
waste precious space when you've got an identifiable audience already turning to a classified section with a need
in mind.
2. They are more powerful than ever because there are
more classifications than ever, letting you pinpoint pros-

pects. Plus, classified ads appear in *more magazines than ever* — in the back, where 61 percent of Americans start reading a magazine. This gives you an inordinately high readership for a fraction of what high readership usually costs.

3. They can motivate people with *simple, clear words,* few abbreviations, a touch of warmth, a human attitude, an absence of exaggeration, and a headline that separates your ad from other ads in the same section.

4. They are *a great way to test ads, prices, claims, media, headlines, offers, and copy.* They offer flexibility, zero-cost or minimum-cost production, and a relatively low running cost — especially when compared with display ads in the newspaper. As with those display ads, the more you run your ad, the less you pay per insertion.

5. The best places to run your classified ads are *where your competitors run theirs* — in the same publications and in the same sections. This is because prospects are used to finding businesses such as yours there. Be easy to find. This is one place where innovation would be a mistake.

6. Use copy that makes you *appear like a good company to do business with* or a person who would be pleasant to buy from. A touch of humor doesn't hurt if it doesn't get in the way of your primary purpose. Be sure to tell folks what to do.

7. *Don't be clever, fancy, or unclear.* People do not want to spend their time figuring out your ad. So go to great pains to keep everything simple. Your ad will be read by one person at a time, so write it that way.

8. Because your headline is so important, as always, *put it in all capital letters or in boldface,* or make it very short, then explain it instantly with your copy. Whatever you do, don't put all your copy in capital letters.

9. *Stay away from punctuation marks.* Exclamation points are deafening in a classified environment. Question marks slow people down. Use short words and short sentences. Read classified ads to see what attracts you.

10. Learn a raftload more about classified ads by calling Agnes Franz at *Classified Communication* (602-778-6788). She publishes a newsletter that contains more classified information than you ever thought there was to know.

The yellow pages and classified ads aren't large, but neither are diamonds. What they are is extremely valuable.

35

Generating Sizzling Sales Promotions

Sales promotions spice up your sales curve, intensify the public's awareness of you, and open the door to lasting relationships.

You already know that the kind of people who buy during a sales promotion do not exhibit much loyalty to the merchant; their loyalty is to the best value around, usually the lowest price as far as they're concerned. Your job, and it's a mighty tough one, is to *earn the loyalty of these fly-by-nights.* They may have called you or entered your door because of a promotion — and that's reason enough to have your fair share of customer-attracting promotions — but your task now is to keep them as customers because of the value you offer. You've got to assure them that while it's true you have attractive prices, your *value* is why each should become a regular customer.

Earn the loyalty of the disloyal

Prove that value by consistent follow-up, stressing value in all your efforts. Shower these people with attention and offers of products or services that are superb values. Tell them, when your prices are high, that you know they don't want to make a purchase mistake during a recession (and it looks to me like we're in a perma-recession), that your high prices mean high quality and durability, and that buying from you not only gives them freedom from making a mistake, but also provides them with the best possible value.

Still, if you go about things with your eyes and mind wide open, you'll do everything in your power to *get these people's names onto your customer list.* If you can put some information about the people onto that same list, by all means do it. Sizzling sales promotions bring a lot of first-timers to your place of business.

The way to maximize repeat business is to conduct a new study on your prospects, learning what is most important to them right now, then *create a promotion centered around their wants and needs*. Through questionnaires or good old-fashioned conversation, see what's on their wish list, then try to give it to them. This guerrilla basic training for promotions is frequently overlooked by modern business.

The focus of your promotion

Another overlooked source of sparkling sales promotion ideas is *the trade publications in your industry*. You ought to be subscribing to several of them, scouring the pages for sales promotions that have worked for others. Perhaps they worked their wonders in Tampa or Tacoma. Now let them energize your profits in your area. Reading your daily newspaper also gives you a fix on promotions that are working in your corner of the galaxy.

Many companies *do their sales promotions internally*. These companies conduct their promotions among their sales-people, having contests and giving generous awards to the salesperson who comes out on top. Sometimes they'll involve their telephone operators, rewarding them for extra-special treatment of customers. More than a few companies pay their direct marketing team — direct mail or telemarketing — a hefty bonus for surpassing a specified goal. The sales promotion is going on and the public doesn't even know it's a promotion. Internal sales promotions are economical because they need not be advertised.

Shake, rattle, and promote

A rich source of promotion ideas *will come from current events*. When San Francisco shaked and baked during the earthquake of 1989, many enterprising companies constructed promotions centered around earthquake damage, earthquake safety, the earthquake relief fund, and a celebration of earth-quake survival. When the paper is loaded with heavy-hearted tales of a sagging economy, design your promotions to help people weather the economy. When an act of God is un-leashed upon our nation, the media sees it as a sensation,

Hollywood sees it as a movie idea, magazines as a cover story, publishers as a book, and guerrillas as the basis for a new sales promotion.

Although *money-saving offers make up the bulk of sales promotions*, the phrase "50% Off!" has been used so long that the words are nearly invisible. Still, you've got to admit that if you were in the market for the item being advertised with that headline, you'd be tempted by the size of the savings. That's why the pure opportunity to save money is the underlying basis of most sales promotions. However this opportunity is couched — coupon, rebate, two-for-one — it is nonetheless an offer to save money, and people like doing that. They also love getting things for free.

Ranking up there with saving money is obtaining of *something of value for no money*. Often it is a free thing that they'd have to purchase anyhow, such as a free ream of computer paper when they buy a personal computer. Guerrillas are known to offer a year of free service with every purchase.

Look around your community for businesses that have the same types of prospects that you do, then try to put together a joint sales promotion. Frequently, discounts at one another's companies will do the trick. *Fusion advertising* promotions, as we have seen, let advertisers spread the word of their promotions beyond the usual capabilities of their budgets because they are sharing the cost of advertising with others. My gas station has a coupon for $2 off a car wash. The car wash has a coupon for $2 off every fifteen gallons at said gas station. **Joint sales promotions work**

Although you want your place of business to be known for its consistency, you don't ever want your competitors to consider you predictable. That's why you should annually create brand-new promotions and balance them with proven promotions from the past. The brand-new ones will attract customer and prospect attention, perhaps even publicity attention if you play your PR cards right. They'll keep your competitors off-balance while intimating to your customers that something new and good is always happening.

Brand-new promotions are very hard to copy. If competitors can't see you coming, they can't take aim. By repeating the best promotions *you've ever conducted* and blending with them the best promotions *you've never conducted*, you will strike that fine point where sales promotions, though not addictive to you, are definitely attractive to your bean counters, not to mention your customers and prospects. It's the duty of every red-blooded guerrilla to sizzle while promoting, but not to overdo either.

36

Guerrilla Signs, P.O.P., and Coupons

Guerrilla signs, point-of-purchase materials, and coupons have been undergoing their own revolution, in case you haven't been looking. I'm not talking about high-tech as much as *new tech*.

Check out the moving signs that deliver a message of up to umpteen words, right in your place of business or maybe in your window, or perhaps even in both. In the space taken by one sign, you put across the messages of twenty.

Moving goods with moving signs

Check into the video monitors installed in shopping carts. This in-store TV delivers a brief pitch to the person making her way down the aisle of the store. Microchips planted in store displays activate the TV unit to show the tape appropriate to the section in which the cart is located. Check into the video monitors that appear at checkout stands. This method of using signs is so potent that the Checkout Channel, delivered by satellite to stores but not by cable to homes, was created and brought to you courtesy of your local (if you count 23,500 miles away to be local) satellite transponder (a new tech word that means channel). The meaning is clear: video is the signage of the twenty-first century.

Video is the signage of the twenty-first century

As TV is to print — dynamic, capable of appealing to eyes and ears — video is to signs. You put across *more of your idea*, and you know how important that is. Begin to figure how to state your idea in ten seconds, in five seconds, in three seconds. Advertising hero Fairfax Cone said that the cornerstone of all advertising is what you'd say if you were a door-to-door salesperson, rang a doorbell, and faced a busy, rather intimidating housewife who opened the door and said, giving you five seconds to answer, "Well, what do you want?" *What you say will make the difference between her slamming the door in your face or listening attentively to what you will say next.* Think of signs in that context.

Sporting goods stores show athletic competition. Music stores flash snippets of MTV. Stop & Shop gives cooking tips. Department store shoppers view fashion shows. Videos pull browsers and serious shoppers alike. We're a nation transfixed by the screen.

Marketing expenditures are being transferred from advertising to point-of-purchase signs these days because of their ability to generate impulse reactions, which hopefully lead to impulse buys. When designing signs for in-store promotions, keep in mind:

Three goals of signs

1. A *sign will accomplish nothing unless it is clear.* Nothing else that you do correctly will mean a hoot if people don't know what the heck your sign says. As in much of advertising, signs must start with clarity as a goal.
2. A *sign should tie in with your advertising.* You've invested a lot of dough in your ads, but they won't pay off at the point of sale unless you remind people of your ads with the words and graphics on your sign. When Leo Burnett implored us to plan the sale when we planned the ad, I'm sure he had signs in his master plan. You should, too.
3. A *sign's prime purpose is to sell the product or service.* Of course, they should be clear, readable, and connected with your advertising. But their prime purpose for existing at all is to beautify your bottom line.

Guerrillas take full advantage of the two main purposes of signs — *to direct people to the things they came in to buy, and also to direct them to the things you have in stock that they hadn't planned on buying.* In doing this, signs increase the size of many transactions, enlighten people about your other offerings, and actually double many of your customers' worth to you. They may think of you as a source for one thing, but when visiting you, learn from a sign that you can be their source for something else as well. I buy stationery at the place that does my copying. A sign planted that idea in my head.

Sign location is of paramount importance to guerrillas. You might put signs on top of your trucks because your business is office equipment and supplies and your trucks drive through financial districts. You also know the importance of placing signs in windows, at front entrances, at checkout counters, and at the many other strategic locations that exist in most stores. Some of these locations offer shoppers that moment of pause in which they realize they want or need what you've advertised on a sign.

Sign location is crucial

My first book sold 30,000 copies in one city just because a simple sign for the book, containing only the title and the price, appeared at the cash register of many bookstores. Cost of the signs: a quarter each. Profit to me from each book sold: a quarter each. Man, I love signs!

Signs in windows turn many strollers into shoppers. If they're big enough — probably as a window banner — they also flag the attention of motorists. What you've got to realize is that if you can communicate with prospects who are in or near the location *where the business actually takes place,* you've got a lot of momentum on your side.

The point of purchase is where the blood is drawn, the money is spent, the sale is consummated. Revere that point of purchase and remember that it is very important to you.

All guerrillas know the pulling power of neon. One client, Alan Caplan, founder of Applause Video in Omaha and once selected "Retailer of the Year" by *People* magazine, fervently believed that a red neon "Open" sign is the best sign investment a business owner can make. He refused to open in locations that prohibited neon window signs. I know, because he bypassed some very enticing locations. The power of his belief, combined with his other marketing idiosyncracies, have created an incredibly high level of success. He was such a believer in guerrilla marketing that he conducted his sales

A red neon "Open" sign

meetings and industry talks wearing an army guerrilla camouflage uniform.

Speaking of signs, Alan once said to me that "most store owners spend more money on their 'Going out of Business Sale' signs than on all the other signs in the history of their business. If they spent wisely in the beginning, they would never have needed that final sign in the first place."

Guerrilla dumps   Point-of-purchase advertising doesn't always mean signs. It also means dumps, which are display bins with signs attached to them, merchandise displays, and display racks. Whoever can forget the brilliant introduction of Hanes pantyhose called L'eggs in plastic eggs nestled in rotating racks — and found in supermarkets and drugstores. Up till that day, pantyhose were only to be found at clothing stores. It took a guerrilla to dramatically increase the distribution of Hanes, and a point-of-purchase display was the ticket to profits.

To find out about point-of-purchase techniques that probably deserve a book of their own, contact POPAI — the Point of Purchase Advertising Institute — at 201-894-8899. You may not match the 119 percent sales increase they claim for one of their clients, but on the other hand, you may exceed it.

Coupons also influence shopping decisions. A 1993 survey revealed that 32 percent of shoppers said coupons often influence their purchases, 18 percent said coupons occasionally influence what they buy, and 50 percent said coupons never influence their purchase decisions. The biggest users of coupons are in the Northeast.

The sophisticated   Coupons are more sophisticated than ever. A company
coupon   called Checkout Coupon (1-800-955-9770) lets you turn the common bar code into your own exclusive competitive marketing tool. Using data from the checkout scanner, Checkout Coupon finds and converts users of brands competitive with yours by issuing different incentives to different kinds of competitive users. Right at this moment, Checkout Coupon's Catalina Marketing Network reaches over 80 million shoppers each week. And that's just *one* of the coupon-dispensing technologies now at the disposal of guerrilla advertisers.

Another is offered by Actmedia (203-845-6200), whose Instant Coupon Machine, launched in 1991, unleashed average sales increases of 35 percent and more in participating stores. It's now the fastest-growing couponing medium in the marketplace. Stay tuned. These in-store advertising technologies are changing rapidly.

More and more business owners are finding out that coupons also do nice things for profit and loss statements. They enable you to promote without spending many promotional dollars. Your prospects can get your coupons from a variety of places: from the mailbox, from newspaper ads, from your fusion advertising partners, who freely give them away for you and, hopefully, vice versa, and right there at the point of purchase, where they can use them instantly.

Coupons in the nineties

Most coupons give a discount. Others give advantages such as a discount or a freebie if you buy in bulk or if your purchase is large enough. Some Americans toss away all coupons. Others save them and swear by them. As the perma-recession becomes understood for what it really is, coupons will have more power than ever as more people become coupon clippers. Almost any business — not just retailers — can benefit from the extra salespower of coupons. I suggest you experiment with them.

37

The Guerrilla PR Kit

The guerrilla PR kit is never sent to the media until everything in the company is running smoothly. As I counseled you to do your advertising last, after all your other ducks are in a neat row, I counsel you to obtain your publicity *even after your advertising*.

The disaster of premature publicity

Premature publicity has given many companies a great deal of business, but they weren't ready to handle it, people had no place where they could buy the product, prices were unclear, and worst of all, the publicity story could not be repeated.

Publicity brings in many one-time customers. Your job is to make them fifty-time customers. Customers who learned of you from a PR story in the newspaper or who heard about you on a radio talk show are not very likely to be loyal customers. The repetition so necessary in advertising is just not possible with publicity. Another disadvantage: You have no control over the publicity — when it will run and even what it will say. It may leave out the most important thing about your business and say something negative instead. This is called freedom of the press, glorious for a nation, potentially disastrous for a business owner.

Guerrillas are interested in saving money, but will wisely spend money to talk to a PR pro. The truth about publicity is that it comes to those who have PR contacts, people in the media you know on a first-name basis. PR pros have a myriad of these contacts. That's why I recommend them.

I also recommend that you absorb these guerrilla PR facts:

- CNN interviews an average of twenty-five people on the air each day.
- There are many newspapers that can help you — 16,000 dailies, 5,800 weeklies, biweeklies, and monthlies that cover the metropolitan, suburban, and rural American population. Some PR pros mail only to the top 300 papers, but many guerrillas don't mind the 21,500 others with circulations of under 125,000.
- There are over 350 general-interest magazines. PR pros service only about 50 of these — those with circulations over 500,000 — unless they are targeting a specific audience. Guerrillas don't need 500,000 people to read their PR story — 499,999 will do very nicely, thank you.
- There are 650 TV station outlets and over 3,000 radio talk shows. Do they want you as a guest? If you have news that will interest their viewers and listeners, you can be sure they will.

Guerrilla PR facts to absorb

As with many topics in this book, publicity deserves a book of its own. A good one is *The Zen of Hype* by Raleigh Pinskey (Citadel Press, New York, 1991).

Publicity can give your business credibility and awareness. It can get people talking about you because, after all, now you *are* the news if you're getting publicity. It can help establish you as the expert. And you can get started, after talking with a PR pro, by preparing a guerrilla PR kit. A basic kit consists of:

- A *folder to serve as a cover* and show that you are a professional about your business. Don't forget, the media are besieged by businesses that want free publicity. Yours can stand apart from the rest if it is presented in a way that does not make it look like a candidate for the wastebasket, where somewhere between 50 percent and 90 percent of press kits end up.

Components of a guerrilla PR kit

- A *feature story about your business* — containing an "angle" — a newsy reason to give you the coverage you want. The media is starving for news, and if you can come up with honest news and a fascinating angle, you stand a good chance of receiving the coverage you deserve. By the way, be sure to make a zillion copies of that coverage when a story appears. Blow up several copies and mount them on a press board or frame them handsomely. These are your Picassos, one-of-a-kind masterpieces.
- A *press release which can be a feature story or can lead to one*. A good press release starts off with a headline, which serves as an abbreviated version of what the story will be about. It should be punchy and brief. The first paragraph of the release tells the who, what, where, and when of your story. The second paragraph gives the how and why. These two paragraphs contain the most newsworthy information in your PR kit. Often they are the only paragraphs printed. If you're lucky, or have a good PR contact, the other paragraphs will also be printed. They'll give statistics, quotes, and general background data. Perhaps they'll lead to an interview. Bull's-eye!

     Most newspaper editors begin at the bottom when cutting a story. That's why PR guerrillas put their important stuff at the top. Releases should be written in journalistic style with no opinions or glowing adjectives. They should be exact, specific, and accurate. At the top of the release, if you want it published immediately, you should say: FOR IMMEDIATE RELEASE. If you want it to run later, say: FOR RELEASE ON FEBRUARY 10, 1995. Beneath that you should say CONTACT, then put your name (or PR pro's name) and phone number. Of course you should double-space and leave wide margins. End your release with a symbol such as ### right beneath the last line.
- An *8 × 10 black and white glossy photograph*, in clear focus, with no background detail. Smaller newspapers will accept 5 × 7 photos. Be sure to mention at the end

of your press release that a photo is enclosed, and don't forget to label the photograph with a caption and the photographer's credit line. It may be a photo of you, your product, your store, the results of your work, the mayor shaking your hand, or the President giving you an award.

Once you have the right press kit with the right components, and I'm assuming you have hot news in your kit, be prepared to expend lots of energy following up with innumerable phone calls, even personal visits, to get your story printed. The more contacts you have, the less determination you will need.

The more contacts, the more PR

Guerrillas turn up regularly on radio and TV talk shows because they opened the door with a great press kit, then proved that they're worthy guests. Let's say you're invited to do a radio interview. Perhaps you've even pitched the idea of offering free gardening advice on a question-and-answer listener call-in show. What better way to get folks to come to your nursery for the fertilizers you recommend? Naturally, you must rehearse and prepare, speak in sound bites offering ideas and advice that listeners can easily grasp. Project your expertise.

If you'll be on television, you can take advantage of many visual aids: slides, diagrams, demonstrations, charts, and the actual product, when possible. You know that TV is a visual medium. If you can get the TV crews to visit your store or cover your event, be sure every inch of your place of business is sparkling sharp and running smoothly. If you get on a show — make sure you're the same. There are coaches who can refine and focus your TV skills. They will use video and acting exercises to help you improve your public persona. Ideally, you'll be a merciless critic of yourself and will improve your presentation each time you're on.

Use visual aids on the tube

The best publicity is the kind that ties in with advertising and is part of a marketing strategy. When this is the case, the business opens its doors, addresses any unforeseen operational problems, and trains its staff thoroughly. *Then it finally seeks to obtain the publicity.* Usually, the coverage first appears in the newspaper, then spreads to radio, and finally to television.

Eventually, magazines with a longer lead time may want in on it.

Guerrillas know that publicity can happen anywhere and are prepared to greet the media in any of its guises. We've all heard of media fiascos and publicity disasters. How many could have been averted with proper planning and preparation? Take a guess.

For future PR, you still have to furnish intriguing news to the media, but this time, because you are a known quantity, it can be about an event you are staging or even a special promotion. As you and the media get to know each other — as they know the major PR pros — it is much easier to get more publicity. Some guerrillas have become such notable spokesmen for their industries — not only their companies, but their industries — that the media come to them for quotes and comments on current events. It's a good deal for the media and for the guerrilla.

To position yourself to get in on this deal, send regular releases to the paper, telling them facts of interest to their readers. Don't do any selling, only telling. In time, they may publish almost all of your releases, and you'll become known as the expert in your industry. Just remember that it all starts with a guerrilla PR kit.

What can get good PR for you? Just what kinds of newsy items would make good PR for you?

- Helping a charity or a community organization
- Hosting your own public or leased-access cable show
- Holding a free seminar on your topic of expertise
- Getting married in your place of business (a bit extreme, but it has happened, and the PR coverage was very comprehensive, even showing the wedding on the news)
- Offering lessons in hair care if you run a salon
- Taking some animals to visit a senior citizens' home if you run a pet store
- Letting children plant the saplings you furnished from your nursery in their new public playground

- Setting up a free or low-cost lending library for a children's hospital if you run a video store
- Giving free music lessons to the disabled if you run a musical instrument store
- Donating money, time, or expertise to any worthy cause
- Writing and publishing a book, even if you do it yourself

The ideas are legion. Just remember the words of Mike Hughes of Publicity Express (1-800-541-2897), "Without publicity, a terrible thing happens: nothing."

VII

The Guerrilla Advertising Attitude

BOOK LEARNING JUST WON'T cut it if you're going to be a guerrilla. You must supplement that knowledge with street-smart tactics in your advertising, with a mindset that differs from the corporate frame of mind — and with the common-sense attitude of a guerrilla. This attitude differs from standard attitudes about advertising in five major ways:

1. You see to it that all of your advertising *ties in very closely* with all of your other marketing. A lot of advertising has no connection with signs or mailings for the same product or service. What a waste of potential synergy!
2. You never abandon your advertising *before it has a chance to work*. Most advertisers view advertising as an act of faith, and are quickly unfaithful if they fail to get quick results.
3. You want to get *more for your advertising dollars* than instant sales: You want to build long-term relationships that can be converted into consistently growing profits. Most advertisers are out for instant gratification. You want a whole lot more: name recognition, connection with customers, conveying of your identity, customer loyalty that leads to repeat and referral sales.
4. You are a near fanatic when it comes to *measuring the effectiveness* of each advertising medium you use. You

take nothing for granted and always find out where every caller and every customer first learned about you.

5. You enjoy advertising, look forward to using it with force and precision, but *realize it's only part of the marketing process* and can't do the whole job by itself. This perception enables your advertising to contribute to the success of your other marketing vehicles.

If you don't have this attitude, I'm not optimistic about your chances for success. If you do, I hope I can look forward to reading your company's name in a future listing of the *Fortune 500*.

The guerrilla, unlike his counterpart, the traditionalist, has *realistic expectations* about his advertising. Guerrilla heads are not in the clouds, but buried in advertising media, checking out the competition. Guerrillas are far more interested in trends than fads or flashes in the pan.

Guerrillas are also *more aggressive* in their use of advertising. They stick with their media, select one or two flagship media to carry the brunt of their advertising, and continue to hammer in their message, knowing that most of their competitors are aggressive only in short spurts. This is not enough to sustain a growing business.

The guerrilla attitude is characterized by a *keen awareness* of the competition, the economy, the industry you're in, current events, and the marketing scene. It is the attitude of a visionary, taking *the long view* over the short view every time and knowing that time is the guerrilla's ally. Only those capable of the long view can practice commitment.

Guerrillas of the nineties and beyond can be described as *"information-crazed"* — dazzled by the power of data and able to access it at the push of a button. They know darn well that data, just like time, is more important than money, and their passion for information is inspiring. Are they actually compulsive about data? Frankly, yes, they are.

Even when empowered by data, guerrillas are very careful before they do an iota of advertising or spend one cent. Although you may think of guerrillas as being the very essence of derring-do, instead, they are *the essence of caution*, testing and experimenting with ads before committing to any. Even when they come up with a doozy of an idea, they are not content to kick back with a contented grin. They do kick back, do grin, . . . then try like crazy *to improve upon the results* of their advertising. They never stop trying to improve. They *never compromise*, either. When someone tells them that their advertising can be either visually pleasing or highly motivating, they demand — and get — both.

The most dramatic characteristic of the guerrilla attitude is the *penchant for action*. Action means creating, committing, measuring, and improving. Guerrillas know this action is the soul of guerrilla advertising.

38

The Importance of Research

Think of your mind, or better yet, your customer database, as a bank. Your job is to constantly make deposits into your account. You make the deposits in the form of information that you garner from customers, prospects, your employees, and your competition.

You do this because you know that in businesses that wish to thrive well into the twenty-first century, information is more important than money, and your desire for it is insatiable. You also know that satellite television is transforming the world into two classes: *the information elite and the clueless.* You are determined to be in the information class because you realize that information will be the key to survival, not to mention prosperity and even freedom from stress.

The elite and the clueless

You are well aware that cable TV companies, computer firms, telephone companies, and entertainment organizations have combined to form an information superhighway. These merged technologies are putting millions of people in touch with one another as well as with the information they crave. The last presidential campaign was characterized by electronic town hall meetings, information bites, and savvy spin doctors — the high-tech name for PR pros.

Your on-ramp to the information superhighway requires that you have access to a computer, a modem (which allows you to communicate with other computers, using phone lines), telecommunications software, and a telephone line. Today's guerrillas use high-speed modems, usually 14,400 bps, now easily affordable. Many modems come with software. The

Your on-ramp to the information superhighway

major data banks are accessible to all types of computers. Most smaller, local computer on-line bulletin boards are accessible only to IBM clones and MACs.

Right now, the information superhighway is a dream that is turning into reality. Our interstate superhighways were a dream twenty years before they became a reality. The data highway is here *now* and definitely in every guerrilla's future, along with CD-ROMs — which stands for "computer disc, read-only memory" — that can store almost limitless data and images. Computer networks will be discussed more fully in chapter 40. For now, just be aware that you have more access to information than ever before.

Ten gathering grounds for guerrillas

But you don't soak in just any information. You are selective in your pursuit of it. These are the ten areas in which you are the most active in information gathering:

1. *Your own business* — because you are obligated to be an expert on your products, your services, your employees, and yourself. You are always learning about your offerings to gain the power of internal insight, getting past blind spots most business owners have when viewing their own business.
2. *Your customers* — because they are what make your business tick, and without them, you'd have no business. The more you know about these marvelous people, the better equipped you are to advertise to them, market to them, and establish lasting relationships with them.
3. *Your prospects* — because they fit your customer profile but aren't yet customers. If you learn why they aren't yet your customers, you'll be able to make the proper adjustments in your advertising and switch them from your prospect list to your customer list.
4. *Your competitors* — because these people weren't born last Tuesday and they're out there trying to woo both your customers and your prospects. Will they succeed? Not if you always know what they are up to and what they are offering. Ignorance of the competition is unforgivable.
5. *Your industry* — because you can always learn from oth-

ers within it, regardless of where they operate. A global awareness is crucial as satellite TV transforms planet earth into a global village. Studying foreign versions of your business can be an exercise in enlightenment and profitability.

6. *Your geographic area* — because you've just got to know what is on people's minds at all times. This is necessary for your advertising to be timely and connected with the exact concerns that people have at the moment. If you're out of touch, you'll soon be out of luck — and money.

7. *The advertising world* — because it is changing at breakneck speed, and unless you are keeping up, you are falling behind. You've got to be aware of new advertising tactics, psychological findings, new studies of purchase patterns, and new advertising trends.

8. *The media world* — because it is becoming more accessible to small businesses every day. Cable TV, infomercials, regional editions of national magazines, zone editions of metropolitan newspapers — they all are lower in cost than ever, but ultra-potent when used by a guerrilla.

9. *The future* — so you can see what's coming before your competitors do and before it passes you up. Keeping abreast with the present gives you ample opportunities to learn about the future. Keep in mind that the rules from the past will not apply to the future. Don't let it take you by surprise.

10. *Your company in the eyes of your audience* — because your company exists for them. You've got to find out what they like about you, what they don't like, who they perceive as your competition, where they'd expect to find your advertisements, and what you're doing right — and wrong.

Research into these ten areas will always provide you with the ammunition you'll need for your guerrilla advertising attack. It will help you avoid errors, exploit opportunities, spot unfilled needs, and react to what your prospects and customers want. It will remove the guesswork that guides most advertis-

So long guesswork, hello certainty

ing. It will give you a degree of certainty that will make you a giant among your competitors.

Guerrilla advertising is like a sleek, new jet plane that gets you to where you want to be. Information obtained through research is the fuel that powers the jet. You've got to view research not only as a significant task at the outset, but also as a continuing need. While on course to your chosen destination, you wouldn't want your plane to run out of fuel. But it will if you cease learning about the ten areas so important to guerrillas.

Some companies prepare an excellent questionnaire, put it in the hands of customers and prospects, tally up the findings, alter their advertising to reflect their new knowledge, set new records for profitability, then eventually fall flat upon their derrieres. How can this happen?

The speed of change   It can happen if you fail to come to grips with *the speed of change*. One great questionnaire isn't enough of a data foundation to support your company over the long haul. Customers change, die, and move. Their needs and wants change. While 20 percent of the population has an address change every year, 50 percent of top management changes titles or companies annually. In addition, the competitive scene changes. And let's not forget technology, which is changing in all areas at all times. Opinions held by your customers three years ago probably aren't valid anymore. They've changed their minds about a lot of things, including you.

The only way you're going to find out about these changing attitudes in the minds of customers and prospects is by viewing research as an ongoing process and sending questionnaires to your customers on a regular basis. Once a year is probably too much to ask of them. But once every two years is **A guerrilla prediction**   reasonable and prevents you from falling too far behind. Prediction: You'll be floored at how much your data changes from questionnaire to questionnaire with a two-year time span between them.

An article in *Adweek* points out that since the beginning of the nineties, research has turned up several unmistakable signs of consumer pessimism:

- There's been a steep drop of those who say they're usually the first to try new products or buy new things.
- There's been a sharp rise in those who dread the future and find it hard to get a good job these days. Many college graduates will not find jobs in their field.
- There's been a gradual decline in those who say their greatest achievements are still ahead of them.
- There's been a steady increase in those who say they would do things differently if they could live their lives all over again. In the past, people said the opposite.
- There's been a big drop in the number of people who say that TV is their primary form of entertainment.

Those are just a few of the changes that should influence your advertising decisions. I'll bet your customers can add even more data that might shock you. Keep up with them. For example, what do you suppose today's consumers consider the most important things in their lives?

What's important in life?

Here are their answers, in order of their preferences:

- Being satisfied with my life in general
- Being able to afford things that are important
- Being in control of my life
- Traveling for pleasure
- Being able to take off any day I want
- Having a million dollars
- Owning an expensive car
- Having a successful investment strategy
- Having live-in help
- Having a gold credit card

You can be sure this information can add potency to your advertising, and you can be equally sure that the answers to this question will change within the next three years. Will you know the answers then? You will if you realize the importance of research and make it a continuing task. Only then can you engage in guerrilla advertising.

39

The Necessity for Testing

The test has never been devised that could accurately predict the results of advertising. If you have one, put down this book and go out and sell it for a billion bucks to the *Fortune* 1000. They've been searching for one for over a century.

A mental bungee jump Because much of advertising, regardless of how intelligently planned, is still a mental bungee jump, you've got to add as much certainty as you can to a smoky situation. Many tests have been created. Some test how much the reader, viewer, or listener recalls of advertising. Others test how much people "like it" — not an important criteria for guerrillas, but very important to Kellogg's, which tests advertising for "favorable association." Still more measure people's inclination to buy what is advertised. A few even electronically track eye movements of prospects as they view ads, packages, supermarket aisles. All can help. None are perfect.

That's the current situation. Here's how you as a guerrilla must handle the challenge of testing your advertising effective-
What to test ness. If you have the required patience, you'll test *everything*, including:

- The *quality* of your offering — it's got to be there.
- Your *price* — it should leave ample profits for you, but also not exceed the price point for the majority of your prospects.
- Your *advertising message* or offer — it must pull.
- Your *packaging* — it must express your equality and quality. It can also herald your benefits.

- Your *media* — they must reach your key prospects.
- Your *employees* — who must demonstrate expertise to match their enthusiasm.
- Your *follow-up* — to be certain it ensures the quality of all the efforts just listed.

The best media for testing, apart from direct marketing methods such as direct mail with a cutoff date, are newspapers and radio, followed closely by television. Point-of-purchase signs are also valuable. This is because of the speed and relative economy of changes in these media. See how the media are used in these examples:

•

Testing Quality

You test quality

G. Thomas Home Brewery wants to test the quality of its ingredients. It lets home brewers brew delicious beer whether it supplies them with fresh, whole hops, priced at $50 a pound, or dried, crushed hops, priced at $15 a pound. Would the home brewers re-order if they used the cheaper ingredients, but could pay less? Almost identical newspaper ads are run in matched newspapers in two cities. Ad A prices the brewery at $129 and stresses the fresh hops. Ad B prices it at $99 and skirts the issue of freshness. By carefully tracking in-store sales, G. Thomas learns that Ad A helped sell 59 home breweries at $129, while Ad B sold 74 of them at $99. Two months later, G. Thomas sees that 48 of the 59 sales from Ad A result in re-orders of ingredients, while only 16 of the 74 lower-priced breweries ended up re-ordering. G. Thomas Home Brewery was testing quality, using newspaper ads as the testing medium. They now know that home brewers want quality and are willing to pay for it. Testing proved it.

Testing Price

You test price

Non anti-smoking spray wanted to test price, so it created point-of-purchase signs placed at cash registers in three different cities. Each had Non at a different price. One TV commercial was produced in three versions to run on cable TV in the three locations. Version X had the announcer and superimposed graphic say the price was $4.99. Version Y priced Non at $3.99. Version Z priced it at $10. After one week, 500 Nons were sold in the Version X city — with total sales of $2,495. A total of 700 Nons were sold in the Version Y city — total sales, $2,793. And 150 Nons were purchased in the Version Z city, racking up $1,500 in sales. TV and point-of-purchase testing indicated that Non should be priced at $3.99. Even with the price of Non to the company factored in, the $3.99 price tag was the most profitable.

You test messages

Testing the Advertising Message

Nikki and Gina's Spa Showroom ran radio spots for one month on WDAB, featuring the pleasure and fun of taking a hot tub after work each evening. The next month, on WTRW, a station with a similar listener profile as WDAB, the spots stressed the health and stress reduction benefits of owning a spa. During the "pleasure month," they sold 32 spas. During the "health month," they sold 55 spas. Nikki and Gina now focus on health in their ads and sales talks. Small wonder their profits keep climbing. (Remember what guerrillas know about selling the solution to problems?)

You test media

Testing Media

Robert Michael Vineyards is introducing its cabernet sauvignon wines in several areas of California. All stores that carry the wines have a powerful point-of-purchase piece that ties in with the Robert Michael theme of "So fine, only 5,000 cases are produced each year." In Bakersfield, $5,000 worth of newspaper ads introduce the wine. In Fresno, $5,000 worth of TV time take on the job. Fresno sales are nearly double the sales in Bakersfield, though cabernet sales are equal in both cities. Robert Michael proves his common sense by using TV to introduce his wines elsewhere in the West.

Testing Employees

You test employees

Educational Enrichment helps schools raise funds by using advertisements in educational newspapers to secure leads for their sales reps, then telemarketing to set up appointments for their reps to call on schools. Myrna Lynne Ritchie's territory is Northern Ohio. Nicole Denise Gunnison's territory is Southern Ohio. After four months, Ms. Ritchie set up fundraising projects with 318 schools and has 52 more scheduled. Ms. Gunnison has set up projects with 261 schools and has 88 more scheduled. Educational Enrichment keeps both employees, but increases sales training for Ms. Gunnison. Sometimes the results of a test are not clear and choices aren't as apparent. This obviously was a case of having two good employees, one better than the other. Both were able to capitalize on the newspaper advertising and telemarketing investments.

Testing Follow-up

You test follow-up

Peggy Clancy's gift shop wants to see if follow-up is all it's cracked up to be. Her cable TV advertising attracts customers to her store. To every second customer, she sends a thank-you note within forty-eight hours. Keeping careful track of repeat purchases, she is dazzled by the fact that 78 percent of customers who received the notes came back within thirty days and made another purchase. Only 12 percent of customers who received no such note of gratitude made a second purchase within the month. The power of cable TV wasn't nearly as impressive as the power of follow-up. Today, if you buy anything from Peggy Clancy's shop, you get a thank-you note.

*   *   *

While it's only natural that friends and family may be your first guinea pigs for many of your ideas, you haven't tested those ideas until you've gone outside your loving circle of admirers. You need to test in the real world with total strangers who are more interested in their needs than your feelings. Your own gut feelings mean a lot, too. You have life experience and judgment. Back your intuition with testing. Know how to get the best of both.

Be sure to avoid the trap of using test results as commandments when in truth they are merely smart suggestions. You are in charge, not the results. They guide you, but do not rule you. Test results can send amateurs down garden paths, so be sure you analyze them with eagle eyes. Or enlist the aid of a professional.

You never stop testing *Always remember that you should constantly be testing your advertising* by keeping careful track of your profits and comparing them with the day before, the week before, the month before, the year before. Be certain that the magazine, newspaper, or radio has maintained the profile you originally selected it for. Small adjustments can make big differences. A new headline can cause an ad to leap from the page. A dramatic visualization of a problem can bring it to ugly life right in the minds of your target prospects. An offer can take on added impact when blended with the news of the day. Although you remain committed to your campaign, you make adjustments as you go along. If the adjustment isn't an improvement, don't change just for the sake of change. That is expensive idiocy.

Making a buying decision is a very intimate process for a consumer. That is why you cannot impose your beliefs and perceptions upon your prospects. That's where psychology helps a little and testing helps a lot. Data now exist about the purchasing and spending habits of various demographic groups. You can easily access this information through some of the databases I'll be covering in the next chapter.

Naturally, your profit and loss statement contains the definitive test results. If your income doesn't outweigh your expenses, sales and media excitement mean beans.

A rule of testing is to test *only one thing at a time.* Once you're satisfied with your quality, which means that your prospects are satisfied with it, you want to know the best offer, price, and media. If you test all three factors in three media, you won't know why the best ad was good: Was it the offer, the price, or that particular medium? But if you test the same offer of a free brochure for a product or service at the same price in three different magazines — and you have a coded coupon, which means a separate address and phone number on each magazine coupon — when the people call or write for your free brochure, you'll soon know which of the three magazines is your best bet.

Test only one thing at a time

Once you know that, you can test prices and offers. In direct mail, the 60:30:10 rule has been proven valid; it should be taken as instructive to guerrilla advertisers. Sixty percent of your success depends on the right mailing list, meaning the right advertising medium for you; 30 percent depends on the right offer; and 10 percent depends on the creative package, meaning the overall advertisement, visual, and copy.

The 60:30:10 rule

When you do pick a publication after testing, don't base your selection on the high response rate. Profits, remember — *profits* are the yardstick. See how many brochure requesters eventually place orders. Determine how much profit you earned from each order. Divide the cost of the magazine ad and brochures mailed by the profits generated by the magazine ad and you'll know the profit per dollar invested. *That* tells you the best magazine.

Guerrillas often test their offers in matched, but inexpensive media. That means they'll run, for example, the same ad, known as the control ad, in two newspapers with a circulation of 5,000. If the newspapers are truly matching, their response rates should be even. Then they can run Ad A in one newspaper and Ad B in the other, testing their offer. Once they've hit upon the right offer, they can test the same offer at one price in one paper and another price in the other. In this manner, the inevitable errors that one makes during testing are not too costly.

Offers of brochures and free gifts may not be part of your long-range plan, but they are excellent measuring weapons. You offer the same gift in five matched media such as newspapers with similar circulations reaching similar audiences in five different cities, asking people to mention where they heard of the offer when they request their gift by phone, mail, or at your store. In a jiffy, you learn which medium pulled the best. Then you pay close attention to the purchases made by the respondents. Sure, they'll be coming in to you for the freebie, but most will make a purchase.

Freebies as measuring devices

The cost of this type of testing is quite low compared with the cost of running an untested and ineffective ad. Just remember that profits, not responses, are the yardstick. A plant store attracted only 52 customers to its $500 ad for a free plant in one newspaper, *The Review*, but 77 visited the store in response to the $500 ad it placed in a different paper, *The Guardian*. It's a good thing they didn't stop with those numbers. The average *Guardian* customer spent $23, for a total of $1,771 — a $584.43 gross profit, slightly more than the cost of the ad. The average *Review* customer ran up a bill of $192, for a total of $9,984 — a $3,394.72 grand profit, far more than the cost of the ad.

The money, frustration, and time necessary for testing are the dues you must pay to run proven advertising in proven media at prices that keep your profits high and mighty. They take much of the uncertainty out of advertising.

The idea of testing is to find a horse. That horse is your media and your message at a price that makes sense to you. Then you've got to ride that horse and, as a guerrilla, find ways to make it go faster because other horses will always be trying to pass you.

Unless you invest the time and money to test, you won't know which horse to ride. It's hard to be a winner under those circumstances. Test results, along with your analysis of what to do with those results, give you something solid to work with at the beginning. In a universe of groping, testing gives you a firm grip. Ready . . . test . . . profit!

40

The Obligation
to Improve Constantly

Some people are going to take the advice in this chapter as
encouragement to change. That is not the advice being ren-
dered. Change is easy. Improvement is difficult. You'll be presented with a wide variety of opportunties to change as you
nuture and grow your small business. Beware! Many of those
opportunities are invitations to bankruptcy.

You cannot ignore change, and you must embrace those
that will make yours a better company — better in the eyes of
your customers and your accountants. Staying the course in a
changing world is reckless. Your job is to balance your devotion with a willingness to adapt.

To do that, start out by realizing that you are on the
threshold of, even in the midst of, something really big, something that will affect marketing, advertising, and the way business used to be conducted in the past. That something big is a
brand-new wrinkle in capitalism, one that dangles in front of
you a stunning array of advertising options from *interactive TV.*

Guerrillas view this not only as the source of fun and
games that it certainly will be — but as a vast video shopping
mall that puts at their prospects' fingertips a boggling selection
of home shopping channels. Guerrillas will be given the opportunity to do some seriously targeted advertising — such as
running their pet store commercial only to cable subscribers
who have pets. An improvement? Sounds like one to me.

New technology will assure that every click of a remote
control will be recorded on a computer, and you'll be able to

*Something big
is happening*

be faxed a printout showing you how many viewers saw *your commercial* rather than how many watched the show upon which you advertised. Big Brother will be watching you, and big brother can be the guerrilla's friend.

Big Brother is the guerrilla's friend

Methods of improving advertising are springing up like mushrooms, and it's your job to be aware of them, if not to employ them for yourself — yet.

Several advertiser-supported electronic magazines were launched late in 1993, allowing advertisers to zero in on prospects through a global computer network known as the Internet — an amalgamation of 30,000 computer networks connecting 15 million users. It's the largest file cabinet of data in the world, operating in 106 countries.

You don't have to be a computer genius to tap into the Internet, but you've got to have a computer and modem. A company called Delphi is the only major on-line service to offer full access to the Internet. You can "talk" with people all over the world using Usenet News, the world's largest bulletin board. You can be sure that your industry is among the 5,000 topics it covers. Learn more about Internet by calling Delphi Internet at 1-800-695-4005.

Internet and you

Although many people consider our information highway the precursor to the interactive 500-channel cable TV systems coming up, it's developing a traffic jam as a clamoring horde overwhelms the computer databases. Rush hour is upon us. It's good to know of alternative routes. Other on-line services worth checking into are:

- America Online — 1-800-827-6364
- CompuServe — 1-800-848-8199
- Genie — 1-800-638-9636
- Prodigy — 1-800-776-3449

Connecting up with Internet or any of the on-line services is simply a matter of calling them to determine the software you'll need and the rules for joining, along with their rates. In 1994, Internet offered two plans, one at $10 per month which covers four hours of on-line time, with additional time at

$4 per hour; or $20 per month which covers twenty hours of on-line time, with additional time at $1.80 per hour. There's an additional $3 per month for evening and weekend use. Will these rates change? Of course they will.

Meanwhile, once you've joined, you dial Internet's computer phone number with your computer, conveniently hooked up to the telephone lines by means of your modem. You'll have to press a key on your computer, type in a password — and then enter a new world.

Warning! On-line services may be addictive

Warning! Use of Internet and other on-line services may be addictive. Caution is urged. Excessive use of these services can prove to be injurious to the health of your business and the availability of your time. Use with care and only to improve your business. Have fun on your own time.

Larry Chase, president of The On Line Ad Agency in New York, is very hot on the potential of on-line advertising. He says that if you've got a computer and a modem, you can become part of the interactive media revolution for less than $50. This means you can access an enormous number of marketplaces known as on-line services or even networks such as Internet. You can advertise as well as do important market research to help your overall advertising program. Sounds to me like a way of improving your business.

A modem is like a water spigot, says Mr. Chase. Instead of water, it carries information. Fast modems even carry pictures. Once you've got a modem, you can connect with a growing collection of services.

Local electronic bulletin boards

There are over 50,000 *local electronic bulletin boards*, known as BBS's, right now. About 1,000 new ones are started each month. Special-interest groups, called *forums*, and membership organizations set up these services, which are free or require that you join the group for a nominal fee. You can start a forum or join one or tap into one simply by punching the right buttons on your computer and modem. You can be sure that some of these groups and organizations will be hot prospects for what you are selling. Members check into these services on their computer screen, tack up a message if they want, and read others.

Larry Chase joined his local Mac club and *started* an advertising forum simply by inquiring electronically if others would wish to join it. Many, probably guerrillas, were indeed interested. His foray into the forum put him in contact with art directors, account executives, and potential clients. He's used this self-promoting guerrilla tactic on a national scale in CompuServe forums. He's able to prospect for contacts in a wide-open playing field. He drops in on the Telecommunications Forum or the Entrepreneurs' Forum, two of the thousands of forums, and once made a valuable inroad to a *Fortune* 500 company. That company eventually turned into a client. Score one for on-line advertising.

Larry suggests that if you have a pet store or catalogue you can start a pet forum. Most BBS's don't allow out-and-out advertising in the forums, but if in the forum you started, someone asks for birthday suggestions for his dog, you can say, "I run Doggie Dreams pet store and will happily send you a catalogue. I'll even circle what I consider to be good dog gift ideas." This is customized guerrilla advertising at its purest.

Electronic mail, which by now you know is called e-mail, is a labor-saving way to send a letter: no envelopes, no stamps, no stationery. Send individually or to large numbers. E-mail isn't really an advertising medium because it is obtrusive in that guise, but it makes your company easier to do business with. And it's cheaper and faster than faxing.

On-line classifieds are offered by most BBS's and most of them are free. Even the large national networks offer classified ads at delightfully low rates. To see how you can advertise online, all you have to do is ask. Suppose you just started a company that manufactures exercise equipment. You'd probably be well-advised to start an exercise forum after first inquiring if any have already been started. Your forum ought to offer classified ads on its bulletin board since so many people's equipment ends up in their closet and is very much for sale. Sound like a forum for you to advertise the exercise equipment that you make?

On-line classified ads are usually free

National and international network services are similar to local BBS's, but are much larger, offer more forums, and even grant you access to AP, UPI, Reuters, and to many magazines and newspapers. As a guerrilla advertiser, you have access to an elite group of subscribers. The on-line service Prodigy currently has 2 million members, and its average household has two income earners who, combined, earn around $70,000 a year. CompuServe's 1.4 million subscribers earn about $93,000 annually per household. See a way to improve your business with that technology?

On-line ads now offered by Prodigy allow you to advertise nationally. Of course, right now your electronic ad will be only a stated message, somewhat like a classified ad. No visual opportunities yet, but be patient. Soon CD-ROM technology will let you transmit full-color images. The superhighway is under construction.

Part of the creative process in the nineties is to invent new channels for advertising messages. Starting a forum is one way your grandpa probably never considered. True guerrillas must investigate how new interactive technologies can best deliver their messages to a precisely targeted audience with zero waste. **Anyone can** *Almost any business can do it*. With fusion advertising, they **go on-line** can, and probably will, establish strategic alliances around the world. They'll learn ways to outsmart their competitors without outspending them. This is unquestionably an improvement on the horizon, if not here already, for countless guerrillas. It is the essence of guerrilla advertising. You can even have a phone consultation with Larry Chase himself by calling him at 212-876-1096. That's his phone number, not his modem number. Later he'll be glad to consult with you on-line.

Subscribe to the notion of location being all-important in business and you'll locate yourself right on your prospect's computer screen. Larry Chase reminds us that on-line shopping malls offer attractive prices because of reduced overhead, no salespeople, no rent, and no insurance. He suggests that you look into them. Example: CompuServe's mall has over 1,000 merchants, from a car dealer to a flower shop that delivers. A true guerrilla operation, it's open twenty-four hours a day and was patronized by over 4 million customers in 1992.

Interactive communication and on-line advertising will obviously change the whole way we do business in the twenty-first century. Just be sure you tap its opportunities only when it can mean an improvement to your business.

But new doesn't necessarily mean good. An example is MTV-type advertising — the advertising that looks like an MTV video. It's pretty to look at, but the emperor has no clothes. This is not advertising; it's public psychotherapy, mirroring the mind of the ad maker and the ad maker's impression of the prospects. Much of it seems to walk away from traditional advertising by eliminating copy, not mentioning the name of the company until the end, and then with subtlety. Much of it is minimalist art, created as a catharsis for an art director, writer, or TV producer. It is based upon esoteric psychological theories.

The emperor is a nudist

There is little question that MTV advertising is the right route if your market is young people, age fifteen to thirty-four, known these days as "Generation X." They relate to MTV-type entertainment, with its highly musical, highly visual imagery, a lot better than the far more affluent senior market. But many advertisers attempting to reach markets other than the Generation X-ers are smitten by the MTV approach. Why is the temptation so strong? Because of a driving force to change, not to improve. The counsel expressed by the word KISS — Keep It Simple, Stupid — is as valid today as it ever was. Even more valid. Change isn't nearly as important as improvement.

A KISS is still a KISS

Unless you do improve, you can be certain that competitors will pass you by, leaving you in the digital dust. Perhaps your improvements may come in stronger headlines, a better visual demonstration of your competitive advantages, the addition of television to your media mix, a powerfully worded on-line message on thousands of computer bulletin boards, or a gentle tweaking of your guerrilla advertising strategy. Just be sure you maintain your devotion to that strategy while you make improvements to keep up with the times.

41

Never a Need
to Compromise

Because guerrillas are never in a rush, being famed for their patience, they do not have to compromise in the creation of their advertising. The people who develop the strategy, those who come up with the creative idea, the writers, the art directors, the producers of the advertising, the media buyers — none are ever acting under emergency circumstances because guerrillas know how detrimental emergencies are to the advertising process, not to mention to the finished advertising and overall profitability.

An advertising strategy developed under pressure is less focused and wise than it could be. The idea is the best of five instead of the best of twenty, simply because the ad makers had to compromise with time. The writers, art directors, producers, and media buyers are bullied into compromising the quality they can offer in order to meet a deadline. The deadline is met. The advertiser loses out.

Meeting deadlines instead of standards

Former Secretary of the Interior James Watt was once quoted as saying he didn't care about the quality of a specific report from his department, just as long as it was finished on time. Hardly the attitude of a guerrilla.

Some advertisers think they must compromise on the style of their advertising to emphasize the substance. Not true. You can have it both ways. You can have advertising that makes you proud to run it, advertising that is fun to see, enjoyable to hear — and that same advertising can pull in the profits by the trainload.

Don't ever think that you have a choice between a hard-hitting advertisement and a great-looking one. You can and should have both. Nowhere is it written that a logical appeal must be ugly. Nowhere is it engraved in bronze that a gorgeous commercial must fail to motivate.

Some advertising pros will tell you that it is impossible to win advertising awards and handsome profits with the same advertising. False. The real truth is that most advertisers feel an unconscious need to *either* create or sell. Only guerrillas know the two are compatible. Starbucks Coffee, the gourmet coffee retailer, sells enough coffee to float an ocean liner while garnering armloads of advertising awards. Federal Express mastered the art of running award-winning commercials while building a huge company and amassing unthinkably high profits. Neither of these advertisers felt the need to compromise and neither must you.

What only guerrillas know

If you ever feel that you're making a compromise, step back and fix the situation. After all, it's your company, and your advertising is a reflection of it. Never show, say, or do anything that you'll regret. Don't get hooked on having constant promotions or you'll be forced to compromise their effectiveness.

According to advertising lore, a major oil company, scared silly of ever offending anyone with its advertising, would vote on five advertising campaigns presented by its agency. The company's marketing committee would assign one point to the fifth best, two points to the fourth, and so on, with five points going to the best campaign. The results would be tabulated. Then the oil company would run the campaign that *finished in the middle!* The third best campaign was always selected. This was because the oil company figured that anything that finished in first or last place ran the risk of turning some people off. The campaign in the middle would offend the fewest people.

No wonder it's called the ad game

This is compromise at its worst. This is folly. It is not guerrilla advertising. But if you knew the fear factor at large companies, you wouldn't be surprised at this annual compromise.

It even got to the point where committee members would vote for their favorite as third best — hoping it would get to see the light of national exposure!

Running advertising that is going to hit people between the eyes and right in the middle of their purchasing pattern requires some risk, a willingness to make a decision, and guts. It is no job for lilly-livered compromisers who fear offending.

Guerrillas realize that advertising is part of mass communications, and as such, has certain obligations. In this perspective, advertising may also be viewed as part of the evolutionary process because it elevates the information level of the population. Increasingly, advertisers are realizing this and promoting noble causes such as the environment, the economy, and eradicating diseases — along with selling their products and services.

This is not compromising, but instead is advertisers recognizing their power and their obligations. It is possible and highly advisable to create advertising that informs, enlightens, and sells the heck out of your offering — even though the advertising is highly enjoyable to read, watch, or hear. Guerrillas are known to compromise when they must, but the situations are rare.

Marriages are not compromises
A great, long-lasting marriage is not, contrary to what you have heard, one big compromise. Just the opposite is true. The best marriages have very little compromise, with each spouse getting their way about half the time. Sure beats never getting your way. As my wife and I near our fortieth year of marriage, we both feel that we hardly ever had to compromise.

Advertising should have at its helm a gutsy captain, willing to listen to all sides, but courageous enough to make a decision and take a stand. Such a captain would never dream of making a compromise, but instead would do the necessary studying of the charts and other navigational tools in order to make the best possible choice.

When I ran a forty-person creative department at a major ad agency, I realized, much to my liberal chagrin, that advertising decisions are not democratic ones. Somebody has to go out on a limb and pick a direction, a look, an approach. That's why when we voted, I had thirty-nine votes. I may have made some questionable decisions, but I never compromised, and neither have the entrepreneurs who studied all the options, then picked the ones they thought would help them achieve their goal. In that pursuit, unlike in politics, there is no compromise.

42

Always a Need
to Take Action

Some readers may complete this book, mull over the ideas, then return to their non-guerrilla ways. Others will actually take the action they now know they must take; some have already started.

The sad estimate of how many people take action based upon the information they are given at seminars is a lowly 15 percent. The other 85 percent gets the same information, but considers the data and the seminar as a mental exercise rather than a call to arms. Unless the soup of knowledge is stirred with the spoon of action, the soup becomes tasteless and useless.

A Chinese proverb for guerrillas A Chinese proverb adds clarity and vision:

I hear, and I forget.
I see, and I remember.
I do, and I understand.

By actively reading, you have gained even more than the benefits of passively hearing or seeing. There is little question that you'll remember what you have read. But you and I know that the fun is still to come — the fun of *doing what you set out to do*. Guerrilla advertising can get you to where you want to be. But guerrilla advertising requires a guerrilla to ignite it and keep it burning bright. There's work up ahead.

What you must do now 1. *You've got to do the research* to zero in precisely on the bull's-eyes of your product, your service, your benefits, your audience, your profit potential. This is time-consuming, but less so if you are on-line. Failing to research is committing business suicide.

2. *You've got to create a solid advertising strategy* that will state your goals and how you'll achieve them. Once you've done the research, this won't take a lot of time. Although it may take only one day, it can guide your efforts one decade. It's your road map through tough terrain.

3. *You've got to target your exact audience* — or your audiences, as is often the case. Sixty percent of direct mail success depends upon reaching the right audience; the figure for media advertising is very close to that. If you can't select your audience, you can't select your media.

4. *You've got to select your advertising media,* then do everything in your power to measure the effectiveness of each, not to mention the power of your advertising itself. The right message in the wrong media is an unfortunate waste of advertising that was already halfway home.

5. *You've got to plan your advertising schedule* and decide the role of promotions in that schedule. Planned schedules prevent emergencies, aid in decision-making, and serve as valuable tools when measuring the effectiveness of your advertising. They also let you get in on media discounts.

6. *You've got to climb into the minds of your prospects* to find out what's really in there. It's not always what they say. Sometimes they don't even have any idea and need you to help them. Your advertising can do that, but not unless you have a wealth of insight into your potential customers.

7. *You've got to come up with ideas that can generate profits* in the form of what is commonly called an ad or commercial. You've already been given six steps to get a crucial competitive edge. These will give you the ability to create advertising that is flexible, adaptable, and long-lived.

8. *You've got to test these ideas,* along with the media in which they ran. Doing the other seven things right but

skipping this step can undermine a bright future. Falling in love with a creative idea, ad, or commercial is fine, but only because it is an unceasing source of profits.

9. *You've got to produce your advertising* in a way that enhances your credibility, reinforces your identity, and doesn't murder your budget. As with the other steps, unless this one is taken properly, the others will crumble. Whatever you do, don't overspend on production.

10. *You've got to launch that advertising, then begin a constant quest to improve it.* You will maintain the identity, the theme, the visual format. But you can change the offers, the photos or drawings, and the headlines. All along, improve the media, the headlines, and the offers.

A secret called delegation

There. That's all there is to it. Is there any secret to succeeding at it and making it easy? Yes, there is. That secret is called *delegation.* If you don't practice what that word means, I predict dire results for your advertising. And I'd predict the same even if your name were John Caples, Leo Burnett, J. Walter Thompson, or David Ogilvy.

You may be able to do the research all by yourself, especially if you're already a techno-guerrilla with access to the right answers once you've come up with the right questions. If you can't do the research, delegate it.

Developing the strategy is another area that you can do all on your own, your brain nourished by all the important information you now have. I hope you don't have to delegate this function and can handle it yourself with a little help from chapter 1. Six sentences, that's not very long.

Defining your target audience is something you can also do by yourself. You certainly should be able to do it. But if you have even the palest shadow of a doubt, delegate this function to someone else — in market research.

Selecting your media is something you'd be well-advised to delegate. The same people who help you select it can help you define your audience, counsel you as to the best media for reaching them, and prepare a schedule that clicks comfortably with your budget and goals.

You can learn what makes your prospects tick without delegating that task to someone else. All it takes is talking with prospects, meeting with competitors from other areas, reading trade publications, sending out questionnaires, going to trade shows, and accessing on-line data banks and bulletin boards. On the other hand, maybe you have too little time to do it right. If that's the case, delegate it.

Unless you're SuperAdvertiser, I suggest that you delegate the complex tasks of coming up with persuasive ideas and powerful executions of your advertising strategy. Leave the task of the right words and pictures to professionals. You've got too much brainpower invested to go wrong now.

Testing the ideas is something you can do by yourself. You'll have to be able to gauge which ones are working and which ones aren't. And you know that working means pumping profits into your bank account. No need to delegate this.

By all means delegate the production of your advertising, and don't rely on your own skill with your home video camera or your school essays with A+'s on them. Get your jollies from your business, not from producing your advertising. If your name is George Lucas, disregard that last statement.

One thing you can't delegate is the patience after launching a campaign that must be in the soul of every guerrilla advertiser. To launch and maintain guerrilla advertising, there is always a need to take action, but sticking with a campaign is also a course of action to take.

You can't delegate patience

Please don't let your ego get in the way of your delegating. Half the steps you must take can be delegated. The other half should be handled by you. That's probably going to be true for you. But if it's not, delegate what you can't do in a gold-medal manner.

Don't let your ego get in the way of delegating, and don't try to do everything yourself because you want to save money. This is the primary symptom of a condition where an advertiser willfully saves dimes but wastes dollars. This is no place to save money. This is where you *must not waste money*. Guerrilla advertising sin number two is wasting money.

Guerrilla advertising sin number one is not taking action.

Epilogue

The Guerrilla's Advantage

The playing field is not equal. Everything in the vast arena of advertising favors the guerrilla players who are speedy, creative, and determined. These players are fully aware of the extra power they get from changes in media, communications technologies, information access, and our knowledge of what human nature is really all about.

Millions of other businesses, now from all over the world, are competing with these guerrillas for the *attention* and *money* of more consumers than ever. Most aren't going to get it. But you can — if you realize and act upon the benefits that come to the guerrilla advertiser.

Small-business owners everywhere are becoming more sophisticated. Many now engage in extensive research before embarking upon their advertising. More advertisers than ever, but still a minority, actually go to the trouble of creating an advertising strategy to guide their efforts. Congratulations to those of you who do. Consider all competitors without strategies to be blessings for your business. **Blessings for your business**

The successful companies of the nineties are a blend of old and new. Among the one hundred hottest marketers of 1993, selected by *Advertising Age*, are:

Listerine — with its new Cool Mint flavor **It's cool to be hot**
Kid's Room paint — by Sherwin-Williams
Zima — a clear malt liquor by Coors
Larry King Live — the TV show on CNN and the man himself

IBM PS/Valuepoint — the computer that helped turn IBM around

Kinko's — a 640-unit photo reproduction chain catering to small business

Duracell — with its Copper Top tester

The American Heritage Dictionary — by Houghton Mifflin

Ford Taurus — which ousted Honda's Accord as number one

Aqua-Fresh Flex — a toothbrush sired by a toothpaste

Starter — sports apparel licensed by pro sports teams

SnackWell's — fat-free cookies by Nabisco

Crayola — with dazzling new products and color names

Nissan Altima — positioned as an affordable luxury car

Sega's Sonic 2 — a hedgehog that's giving fits to Nintendo

Coca-Cola — with a new theme, "Always Coca-Cola"

President Clinton — with his electronic town hall meetings

Butterfinger — leaning on TV icon Bart Simpson

Barnes & Noble — their selection is keyed to the store's location

Tabasco — for encouraging consumers to use more of it

Nike — for the women's shoe division

EDLP — how Procter & Gamble says "everyday low prices"

Nature's Way — a line of homeopathic medicines

El Al — an Israeli airline flying Yanks from the Bible Belt

Big Bertha — a big-headed golf club from Callaway Golf

Publix — sixty-year-old supermarkets now focused on value

Other companies lauded by *Advertising Age* include Doritos/Lay's, Lee/Wrangler, *The Crying Game*, *The New Yorker*, Home Box Office, "Achy Breaky Heart," Sensor for Women, Target stores, Rembrandt toothpaste, Comedy Central cable TV network, the Club anti-theft auto device, Barney the Dinosaur, Sutter Home wines, VCR Plus, Snapple, Walgreens drugstores, Marvel Comics, the GM credit card, Ben & Jerry's, Jeep Grand Cherokee, Home Depot, Harley-Davidson, and Dannon yogurt. Keep your eye on these companies. See if they continue to deserve mention in the same breath as master advertisers and marketers such as Marlboro, Green Giant, United Airlines, and Energizer. Tell me your opinion in a decade or two.

The advertising agencies run by big names like John Caples, Leo Burnett, J. Walter Thompson, David Ogilvy, and Jay Chiat are being joined by new ones with names like:

Fallon McElligott of Minneapolis
Goodby Berlin & Silverstein of San Francisco
Hill, Holliday, Connors, Cosmopulos of Boston
The Martin Agency of Richmond
McKinney & Silver of Raleigh
Messner Vetere Berger Carey Schmetterer
    of New York
The Richards Group of Dallas
Temerlin McClain of Dallas
Weiden & Kennedy of Portland, Oregon

Keep your eye on these agencies

These in turn may soon have their ranks swelled even more by smaller, newer, guerrilla-like agencies with names such as Carmichael Lynch, Deutsch/Dworin, Cliff Freeman & Partners, Goldberg Moser O'Neill, Kishenbaum & Bond, Martin Williams, Merkley Newman Harty, Partners & Shevack, and Stein Robaire Helm. Time will eventually let us know if these are Hall-of-Famers in the Leo Burnett tradition. Perhaps one will become your agency and you'll know firsthand of its staying power, not to mention its advertising quality.

But for the moment, the ball is in your court and the future in your hands. I laud you if you've engaged in solid research and have a written advertising strategy. But even that's not enough to be sure that your advertising investment pays off handsomely and consistently. Guerrilla advertisers have a far greater chance for advertising success than non-guerrillas because they have a solid-gold advantage.

They are aware of the reality of advertising and know exactly what it takes to make advertising work. What it takes is commitment. *That commitment is the guerrilla's advantage.* All guerrilla marketers know that commitment is the first se-

The guerrilla's advantage

cret of success in marketing. And so it is in advertising. Naturally, many other factors such as quality and service must be part of the deal. Everybody knows that. Hardly anybody knows of the immense power of commitment.

Now that you do, you've got to know what you'll be committing to so that you can capitalize upon your advantage in a big way. *You'll be committing to your advertising identity, to your theme, to your look, to your sound if you're advertising on radio or TV, to your niche in the marketplace, to the media in which you should become a presence, and to your overall advertising strategy.* Failure to commit to those crucial elements of your advertising is an act of stacking the deck against yourself, of cheating yourself of the guerrilla's advantage.

Commitment takes time, which means that you aren't going to get that quick shot to the profit curve until you've been committing for several months. The true inner joy that accompanies the results of your commitment probably won't come for a year or more. But once it begins, it should keep getting better because, along with your advantage of commitment, you have seven other guerrilla advantages:

Seven other guerrilla advantages

1. *You have the insight of the guerrilla.* You know more than your competitors may ever know about focusing, targeting, planning, and creating. You're aware of the ways to reap bountiful profits from minimum budgets. You have information about advertising options that give you an unbeatable head start in the race toward your prospects. You know of the essential power you gain through delegation of advertising tasks. You know that your business depends not on making sales or even profits, but on making relationships. That kind of insight isn't in the advertising arsenal of most small businesses. Knowing it gives you another advantage.

2. *You can customize your advertising to your audience.* Because you've done your homework and know about the needs and wants of your prospects, your media selection can be more precise and your message can be tailored for your target people so that they feel as though you are

talking directly to them and not to a mass group. Your advertising can stand apart from your competitors' — and remember that *all other advertisers* are your competitors in competing for the attention of your prospects. The way you have customized your offer, benefits, competitive strong point, and copy to your prospects gives you another advantage.

3. *Your pace assures you of quality and economy.* The planning you have engaged in, along with your commitment, means you're not going to face many advertising emergencies. There will be no need to create your advertising in a rush, under pressure, or in any way that robs it of its potential. Speed, while very important in dealing with customers, is very dangerous when dealing with advertising. You have the advantage of never paying the high price for rush jobs.

4. *Your advertising has the flexibility to adapt to change.* Because you are so dedicated to the concept of commitment, your advertising will have a long life span. Because you created your campaign to maintain your identity — and still be compatible with promotions — while you changed your offers, headlines, and visuals, your advertising has the unbeatable combination of commitment, ideal timing, and a continuing freshness.

5. *Your advertising improves with time.* Your constant efforts to tighten up all the fittings with testing reward you with advertising that gets better all the time. You improve the programming times of your TV commercials. You shorten the length of your radio spots, gaining the same response with a smaller investment. You find a headline that outpulls any other you've ever used. You discover a consumer problem and you've got just the solution those folks want. Your budget works harder and harder, yet it grows smaller and smaller as fewer dollars do the work of many. Improving your advertising gives you the advantage of improving your bottom line.

6. *Your advertising takes quantum leaps as you learn more about advertising — and marketing.* You're not in busi-

ness to lose money. But most small business owners seem to be. They don't keep up with advertising options and technologies available to them, thereby losing their money and their shirts to eager competitors who know things they don't know. Some know about on-line advertising. Others know about cable TV. Others know of low-priced regional editions of national magazines. Still others know of point-of-purchase technologies that can win the hearts — and business — of your customers. As a guerrilla, you're aware of your obligation to continue learning about advertising. This advantage assures that you won't fall behind.

7. *You know that advertising doesn't work.* Unlike the bankruptcy-bound businesses that thought they were marketing when all they were doing was advertising, you know that there are at least a hundred weapons of marketing and that advertising is only one of them. It rarely, if ever, works on its own. It needs all the help it can get. You understand that many of the other weapons of marketing — such as direct mail, trade shows, public relations, special events, point-of-purchase signs, demonstrations, consultations — don't work very well on their own, either. But advertising helps them work better and they help advertising work better. Seeing the connection is a guerrilla advantage.

In the not-very-distant future, the entire idea of advertising agencies will disappear. The agency names I listed in this chapter will remain the same, but their services will expand. Count on it.

Keep that horse off auto row

Being an advertising agency in a world that requires a wide range of marketing vehicles is like being a horse and buggy store on automobile row. Advertising agencies, once necessary for capitalism to grow and prosper, are now outmoded and offer only 1 percent of the marketing small businesses need. The good ones will rise to the reality and offer 100 percent.

Some ad agencies have added PR departments, direct mail arms, sales training experts, toll-free phone services, even catalogue preparation. But none have added all of these guerrilla marketing weapons. Advertising agencies will have to evolve into marketing agencies, able to offer the full spectrum of what the small business owner needs. Or else.

But will they ever be able to offer the guerrilla advantage? I doubt it. That advantage of commitment to a tested campaign is going to have to come from deep within a single person, then be shared with those who aim at the same goal. You now have the spark that detonates guerrilla advertising. Others may create it, but it begins with you.

Glossary

Access. The ability to connect to a particular computer network, database, or bulletin board.

Account executive. The person in charge of running an advertiser's advertising at an agency; also called "a suit."

Ad agency. A team of account executives, copywriters, graphic designers, production managers, research executives, and media buyers who serve advertisers and are compensated by a fee, hourly charge, or commission.

Amortized cost. The cost over a long period of time; if a brochure costs you $1,200 to produce, its amortized cost over one year is $100 monthly.

Attitude. The nineties version of what once was called image, and what guerrillas call identity.

Bait and switch. Advertising a low-priced brand, then attempting to switch buyers over to a more costly brand.

Balance point. The ratio in a budget with ideal equilibrium between promotional and institutional advertising.

BPS. Bauds per second, the speed at which a modem can send and receive information.

Brainstorming. Working alone or with others to come up with ideas to solve an advertising problem or capitalize upon an opportunity; free-form, loose, and synergistic.

Brochure. A document with words and visuals about a product or service created to help sell the offering.

Bullets. Short, punchy lines of selling copy.

Camera-ready. A printed piece or advertisement with the type and graphics pasted in place ready for publication.

Catalogue. A booklet of from two to several hundred pages showing a selection of merchandise with descriptive copy and visuals; lets people order by phone, fax, or mail.

Classified ad. Words without pictures that appear in a special section of a publication, listing items for sale according to category of merchandise.

Claymation. An animation technique in which clay figures are bent many times and filmed or taped in each position, giving the impression of live action.

CompuServe. A database that can be accessed on-line with a computer and modem; offers forty-eight basic services plus special features; for more information call 1-800-848-8199.

Control ad. A tested ad with known results, used as a benchmark when testing other ads.

Copy. Words in advertising that generally are written to create a desire to buy by describing features and benefits.

Customer profile. Information about customers: income, age, sex, occupation, education, purchase patterns, media habits.

Demographics. Statistical data about customers and prospects, presented in a qualitative manner.

Designer. A person who decides where in an ad or brochure to place the main visual, headline, copy; also determines typeface, method of graphic presentation.

Direct response. Marketing that lets consumers consummate the sale; includes direct mail, telemarketing, catalogues, direct response radio and TV; asks for the order, aims for instant results, extremely easy to measure.

Direct mail. A form of direct response, usually involving an outgoing envelope, letter, brochure, response device, and return envelope; also utilizes postcards and postcard decks.

Display ad. A print ad that is not a classified ad and enables advertisers to show visuals.

Displays. In-store merchandising aids that have large graphic presentations and often bins holding the product.

Donut. A section, usually the middle, of a radio or TV spot left blank for special use; adds to the spot's flexibility.

Double-duty receipt. A receipt with standard numerical information plus an advertising message.

Download. When working on-line, to transfer an electronic file from a network to your own computer.

Down-sizing. Eliminating employees, often thousands at once, as a cost-cutting measure, also known as right-sizing.

Dumps. Display bins in which products are held in stores.

Electronic brochure. A video or audio brochure.

Electronic bulletin board. A system for on-line computer users to read and post messages and responses; also known as BBS for electronic bulletin board service.

Electronic mail. Messages that are sent and picked up by on-line computer users.

Flip chart. A stand-up book with pages that can be shown to viewers, then flipped up and over, exposing the next page; gives order and flow to presentations, has words and visuals.

Focus group. A research group of from ten to twelve people invited for a discussion that focuses on an offering and its advertising; often observed through one-way mirrors.

Font. A typeface that is usually specified by a designer to a typographer.

Forum. A term used by on-line services to indicate special-interest categories and discussions; also known as round tables, conferences, and SIGs (special interest groups).

Fusion advertising. Increasing ad exposure and reducing ad expenses by sharing costs with one or more businesses; formerly known as tie-ins and collaborative advertising.

Generation X. The people aged eighteen to thirty-four during the nineties; too young to be hippies, yuppies, or the beat generation.

Graphics. The visual presentation and details in any advertising; generally determined by a graphic designer.

Guerrilla. A person who employs unconventional and nontraditional techniques in business combined with common sense and a keen eye for the bottom line.

Headline. The largest and usually first line in an advertisement; tells the story or encourages further reading.

Illustrator. The person who draws or paints the picture that will be used in an advertisement.

Infomercial. A program-length interactive TV commercial that often appears to be a TV show; 55 percent of Americans have watched one; ratings are low, but responses by viewers are high.

Insertion schedule. A media plan that states when specific ads will run, where they will run, and what size they will be; also tells dates that ads must be at publications.

Institutional advertising. Nonpromotional advertising stressing features and benefits plus identity rather than offering specific merchandise on sale; the opposite of promotional advertising.

Internet. The world's largest on-line computer network providing access to data, forums, individual users; for free information call 1-800-695-4005.

Leads. Names and addresses of prospects.

Log on. The process of gaining access to an on-line network by giving one's ID and password.

Loss leaders. Products that are priced so low that retailers take a loss; sold to attract people who will purchase more products so that the net result is a profit.

Madison Avenue. The street in New York City where a multitude of advertising agencies are headquartered.

Mailer. A self-contained direct mail piece requiring no envelope; generally unfolds to reveal the entire message.

Mass media. Communications vehicles that reach many people at the same time — magazines, newspapers, TV, radio.

Media mix. The combination of media an advertiser has determined will be the most effective for its business.

Media rep. A salesperson representing one publication, one radio or TV station, one magazine.

Micro-marketing. Marketing to only a few key prospects instead of a mass market; allows customization and attention.

Modem. An electronic device that connects a computer to telephone lines, providing access to on-line services.

Narrowcasting. Aiming advertising at a small, well-defined target audience instead of a large number of people as in broadcasting.

On-line. Enabled by a computer and a modem to participate in activities and access databases by subscribing to services for conversation, recreation, and information; telephone company and service access charges accrue.

On-line classifieds. Advertising that appears on electronic bulletin boards allowing users to buy or sell; often these classifieds are free; they reach precise target audiences.

Organic advertising. Advertising centered around a theme and identity, yet capable of change and offering a high degree of flexibility; works in any media.

Package insert. An advertising message, frequently a small brochure, inserted into product packaging or retailers' bags.

Paste-up. The final form of an ad before it has been produced, with all words and pictures pasted in place; also known as a camera-ready mechanical.

Point-of-purchase. Signs and displays at the selling location; also known as P.O.P.

Positioning. The niche advertisers have selected as their own; determined by target audience, brand identity, what the product or service is to stand for in its advertising.

Pre-sell. To soften up the market, as in advertising's job to presell an offering so that the direct mail, telemarketing, and/or sales reps have an easier time selling.

Price point. The place on the cost spectrum where a product is positioned; may be low, high, or mid-range.

Prodigy. A large on-line service with a membership kit required; for free information call 1-800-776-3449.

Product insight. Knowing the details about one's offering, including its benefits, competitive advantages, weaknesses, competition, perception by the public.

Prospect insight. Knowing the details about one's prospects — their buying patterns, goals, dreams, personal details, family size, age, income, education, media habits.

Psychographics. A psychological description of an advertiser's target consumer; personality profiles.

Public relations. Gaining coverage in the form of positive publicity in the mass media; available at no cost, but must be focused on something of interest to readers or viewers.

Racks. Multi-purpose display pieces for retail environments; they hold quantities of the product and feature signs that merchandise it; some revolve; some fit on countertops.

Remote broadcast. A radio broadcast originating from a store or a special-event location; the show business element adds excitement, attracts store traffic.

Rights-free music. Prerecorded music of all kinds available at a nominal cost; used for radio and TV soundtracks.

Rushes. Film viewed to select "takes" for the final spot; not necessary when shooting tape because of instant playback; also called "dailies."

Satellite TV. Television beamed from earth to a satellite 23,500 miles away in space, then beamed down to satellite dishes owned by individuals and cable TV firms; in 1993, twenty-one satellites, each with twenty-four channels, were in space.

Side-panel copy. The words that appear on the side of a package, often containing promotional information, product benefits, and ingredients (in the case of food products).

Soft sell. Advertising that is gentle rather than strident, that attempts to convince people without pressuring them.

Sound bites. Snippets of sound taken from longer segments, used effectively for radio and television, especially by politicians running for office and by TV magazine shows.

Spiff. A special sales commission offered by a manufacturer or retailer to spur sales of a designated product.

Storyboard. A comic-strip type presentation of a TV spot, complete with pictures, dialogue, and words to describe the action.

Superimpose. To put written words over a visual scene in a television commercial.

Sweepstakes. Consumers enter these contests to win prizes, and advertisers gain their names for their prospect lists.

Synergy. A phenomenon where the sum of the parts is greater than the conventional total, such as two plus two equals five; synergy occurs when several advertising weapons are employed at the same time, each boosting the other.

Tag. The customized ending of a radio or TV commercial, written for a specific location or making a special announcement.

Theme line. The slogan or motto connected with a product or service and used in all its advertising materials.

Toll-free number. A 1-800 number, for which an advertiser pays the phone company a monthly fee, to let prospects phone or fax to the advertiser at no charge.

Track setter. A marketing consultant utilized at the start of a company's marketing to help set it in the right direction, and used later to be sure the firm stays on track.

Trade shows. Opportunities for advertisers to display, to sell, to intensify relationships, to get prospect names, to learn of new offerings, and to inspect the competition.

Typeface. The style of type chosen for an advertisement or brochure; can be used to further emblazon the identity of the advertiser; must be readable.

USP. The unique selling proposition that should underlie all advertising; coined by ad great Rooser Reeves, who said all products have a unique benefit that should be stressed.

Velox. A photo of a camera-ready mechanical furnished to newspaper and magazine publishers for faithful reproduction in their publications; also known as a Photostat.

Visual. The look and graphic content of any advertising.

Word of mouth. The positive recommendation of a product or service; very credible; cannot be bought; must be earned.

You can continue to be a guerrilla with
The Guerrilla Marketing Newsletter!

The Guerrilla Marketing Newsletter provides you with state-of-the-moment insights to maximize the profits you will obtain through marketing. The newsletter has been created to furnish you with the cream of the new guerrilla marketing information from around the world. It is filled with practical advice, the latest research, upcoming trends, and brand-new marketing techniques — all designed to pay off on your bottom line.

A yearly subscription costs $49 for six issues.

All subscribers to *The Guerrilla Marketing Newsletter* are given this unique and powerful guarantee: If you aren't convinced after examining your first issue for 30 days that the newsletter will raise your profits, your subscription fee will be refunded — along with $2 just for trying.

To subscribe, merely call or write:

> Guerrilla Marketing International
> 260 Cascade Drive, P.O. Box 1336
> Mill Valley, CA 94942, U.S.A.
> 1-800-748-6444
> In California, 415-381-8361

Get the Complete Guerrilla Arsenal!

Guerrilla Marketing: Secrets for Making Big Profits from Your Small Business   ISBN 0-395-64496-8 $11.95

The book that started the Guerrilla Marketing revolution, now completely revised and updated for the nineties. Full of the latest strategies, information on the latest technologies, new programs for targeted prospects, and management lessons for the twenty-first century.

Guerrilla Financing: Alternative Techniques to Finance Any Small Business   ISBN 0-395-52264-1 $10.95

The ultimate sourcebook for finance in the 1990s, and the first book to describe in detail all the traditional and alternative sources of funding for small and medium-size businesses.

Guerrilla Marketing Attack: New Strategies, Tactics, and Weapons for Winning Big Profits   ISBN 0-395-50220-9 $9.95

A companion to *Guerrilla Marketing*, this book arms small and medium-size businesses with vital information about direct marketing, customer relations, cable TV, desktop publishing, ZIP code inserts, TV shopping networks, and much more.

Guerrilla Marketing Excellence: The Fifty Golden Rules for Small-Business Success   ISBN 0-395-60844-9 $9.95

Jay Levinson delivers the 50 basic truths of guerrilla marketing which can make or break your company, including the crucial difference between profits and sales, marketing in a recession, and the latest uses of video and television to assure distribution.

Guerrilla Selling: Unconventional Weapons and Tactics for Increasing Your Sales   ISBN 0-395-57820-5 $9.95

Today's increasingly competitive business environment requires new skills and commitment from salespeople. *Guerrilla Selling* presents unconventional selling tactics that are essential for success.

These titles are available through bookstores, or you can order directly from Houghton Mifflin at 1-800-225-3362.

2